Sanctified Snake Oil

Sanctified Snake Oil

The Effect of Junk Science on Public Policy

SUSAN KISS SARNOFF

 PRAEGER

Westport, Connecticut
London

Library of Congress Cataloging-in-Publication Data

Sarnoff, Susan Kiss.
    Sanctified snake oil : the effect of junk science on public policy / Susan Kiss Sarnoff.
        p.   cm.
    Includes bibliographical references and index.
    ISBN 0–275–96845–6 (alk. paper)
        1. Political planning—United States.   2. Social scientists in government—United States.
    3. Waste in government spending—United States.   I. Title.
    JK468.P64 S37   2001
    001.4—dc21   00–042753

British Library Cataloguing in Publication Data is available.

Library of Congress Catalog Card Number: 00–042753
ISBN: 0–275–96845–6

First published in 2001

Praeger Publishers, 88 Post Road West, Westport, CT 06881
An imprint of Greenwood Publishing Group, Inc.
www.praeger.com

Printed in the United States of America

∞™

The paper used in this book complies with the
Permanent Paper Standard issued by the National
Information Standards Organization (Z39.48–1984).

10 9 8 7 6 5 4 3 2 1

Copyright Acknowledgment

The poems "Lies" and "Talk" by Yevgeny Yevtushenko that appear in this volume are from *Selected
Poems: Yevtushenko*, translated by Robin Milner-Gulland and Peter Levi (New York: Penguin Books,
1962), copyright © 1962 by Robin Milner-Gulland and Peter Levi. Reproduced by permission of
Penguin Books Ltd.

To all of the bureaucrats, politicians, researchers,
journalists, and service providers
who dare to call "snake oil" "snake oil."

LIES

Telling lies to the young is wrong.
Proving to them that lies are true is wrong.
Telling them that G-d's in his heaven
and all's well with the world is wrong.
The young know what you mean. The young are people.
Tell them the difficulties can't be counted,
and let them see not only what will be
but see with clarity these present times.
Say obstacles exist they must encounter
sorrow happens, hardship happens.
The hell with it. Who never knew
the price of happiness will not be happy.
Forgive no error you recognize,
it will repeat itself, increase,
and afterwards our pupils
will not forgive in us what we forgave.

—Yevgeny Yevtushenko

Contents

Preface

I first read of Kelly Michaels, accused of sexually assaulting dozens of children at the Wee Care Day Care Center in Maplewood, New Jersey, in the *New York Times*. The "paper of record," not only for New Yorkers, but for many other Americans, reported the case as if Michaels' guilt was an established fact. Even though I was, at the time, a victim advocate, I was also enough of a civil libertarian to be concerned whenever the media suggested that any accused person was guilty before trial. But there seemed to be so much evidence against Michaels, so many children reporting similar, horribly depraved abuse, and virtually no information suggesting otherwise, that even I concluded that Michaels was guilty. When Debbie Nathan's article "Victim or Victimizer: Was Kelly Michaels Unjustly Convicted?" appeared in the *Village Voice*,[1] it was the first to express doubt about Michaels' guilt. At that time I was so "sure" of her guilt that I assisted a colleague in composing a letter to that publication rebutting Nathan's claims.

As one of the developers of Services to Rape Victims in Nassau County, New York, I knew only too well how much child sexual abuse had been hidden and overlooked before mandated reporting and expanded funding for child abuse detection had led to greater recognition of this too-common crime. In fact, another colleague had coined the term "ghosts" to refer to the clients that mental health practitioners recalled, after training to work with sexual assault victims, having exhibited glaring signs of abuse that they hadn't recognized earlier. For instance, I once observed a graduate school class role play on alcoholism counseling, based on a real case, which was designed to teach how to break through denial. In it a mother, reluctant to enter inpatient treatment because her young daughter didn't want to be left alone with her father, was told that she was using this excuse to avoid dealing with her problem. When I suggested that the child might be experiencing abuse, the role players and my classmates told me that I too was "in denial"—although one of the role players admitted later that the girl's reason for wanting to keep her mother home was that she didn't like the way her father "tickled" her when they were alone. These "ghosts" caused practitioners considerable guilt and, I suspect now, caused some to so overreact that they later overidentified abuse as a means of righting the balance, subconscious—not to mention irrational—as this motivation might have been.

Although I was concerned about these issues, I also had no interest in the clinical side of social work, focusing instead on policy analysis, program administration, development, evaluation, and the other components of the "policy" side of my field. So while my colleagues counseled and studied sexual assault victims, continually complaining about the dearth of funding available to do so, I chose to analyze crime-victim compensation benefits and how they were allocated—an interest that carried through to my doctoral dissertation research.

What I learned surprised me: sexual assault victims received more funding than I had suspected—or had been led to believe. Sexual assault victims had long had programs designed just for them, on the premise that most fail to report their crimes to the police and are ineligible for direct compensation as a result. But these victims *were* receiving a healthy portion of compensation—as well as receiving services through programs funded not only by victim compensation agencies, but by the Department of Health and Human Services to prevent sexually transmitted diseases and child abuse. My study was conducted before the Violence Against Women Act added even more funds, once again targeted to a very narrow group of victims.

As I prepared my dissertation for publication in 1993, observing that 28% of compensation funds and 76% of combined compensation and program funds went to victims of sexual assault,[2] the National Association of Crime Victim Compensation Boards reported that counseling expenses had, very recently, risen to an average of 35% of all compensation agency outlays.[3] Not only was this increase staggering for its suddenness, but it could not be explained by any change in legislation, eligibility rules, or statistical increases in crime, all of which had stabilized after increasing over the prior two decades. Were victims "suddenly" feeling more comfortable about disclosing abuse? If they were, it was not being reflected in the rhetoric of victim assistance workers who claimed instead that a new "backlash" against victims, especially of rape and sexual abuse, was taking place.

When three years later I published a book, *Paying for Crime: The Policies and Possibilities of Crime Victim Reimbursement*, based in part on my dissertation, I had also begun to realize the extent to which some practitioners were purporting to "recover" memories of child abuse in adults who had not claimed to have been abused before the "memory recovery" process had been conducted. At the same time, the federal Department of Justice published a report, *Victim Costs and*

Consequences: A New Look, which noted that by then 50% of sexual assault victims were receiving counseling, as opposed to 3% of victims of crimes other than sexual abuse and homicide.[4,5] The report also observed that mental health care was "one of the least studied areas of crime costs" and that the rates at which victims sought counseling "reflect therapists' impressions about the reasons underlying treatment. Their impressions are obviously imperfect and may be confounded by patients' false memories and by other mental illness risk factors in patients' lives."[6]

As a result of a few lines that I had written in my dissertation, and a few more in my book, I was invited to a two-day meeting in Salem, Massachusetts, organized by groups that had seen through or were hurt by false or mistaken reports of sex crimes, and which commemorated the 300th Anniversary of the Day of Contrition. The original Day of Contrition had occurred when earlier Salem residents atoned for the witch-hunt. In Salem I met many of the formerly accused, and even some formerly convicted people. It was there that I first understood the experience of "subjective realities," because it was the first time that I had been in an entire roomful of people who also questioned some of these cases—people who could not understand how anyone could have ever believed them.

I learned from professionals at least as "expert" as those who had convinced me of the pervasiveness of child sexual abuse about how justice had been undermined in many of these cases. In some, the accused were actually convinced by their (most often court-appointed) attorneys to plead guilty—and were often rewarded for doing so with brief sentences. In other cases, accused people went to trial convinced that they could not be found guilty because no evidence against them could possibly exist. But evidence, usually in the form of "expert" testimony about the behaviors of children that was purported to prove abuse, was presented, and because it was unexpected, it was not effectively countered by the defense in those early trials.

In Salem I also met a handful of other mental health professionals who had tried to bring attention to this side of the issue. Some had been brought up on malpractice charges, some had been accused of sex crimes, and all had found themselves receiving fewer if any referrals, and receiving other "punishments" for trying to bring light into this dark area. That such attacks are neither imaginary nor warranted was demonstrated when the site of the second day's activities had to be changed—bomb threats had caused the owner of the original site to cancel with the group. At one point on that second day I found myself alone in an elevator but for a single other occupant: Margaret Kelly Michaels. I vowed to myself then to make up for the fact that I had believed the case against her by trying to explain, to myself and others, the social processes that permit such misperceptions.

However, it is important to note that ideologues exist on both sides of this issue—as they do on all issues. I mention the Michaels case because it was the one that forced me to see the side to which I had been blind—but I also found ideologues on that side who remain blind to the merits of many abuse cases for which clear evidence exists.

I had already begun thinking of the methods used by ideologically driven practitioners as "snake oil." As I began to look into the process of my own self-delusion, I recognized that a primary and constant contributing factor was that the "snake oil" that I was observing had been given the imprimatur of validity in some way—by confirmation of clergy and mental health professionals, media "investigation," government funding, or acceptance by a court. That was when I began to conceptualize this subgroup of "snake oil" as "sanctified." It is this "sanctification" that I find truly dangerous, because the public expects to trust professionals, media reports, and conclusions of government investigations, and losing this trust is dangerous to democracy. In fact, some observers have called the results of professional, government, and media endorsement of inadequate, unproven, or bogus methods "industries,"[7] following Elliot Currie's conceptualization of the original witch-hunt as an industry.[8] He based that idea on the fact that witch-hunters became invulnerable to external restraints, developed the power to suppress those who disagreed with them or their methods, and benefitted financially and otherwise from processing witches—the fact that witch-hunters benefitted from the sale of "witches'" property is one of the reasons recognized by historians for why the witch-hunt lasted so long, and did so much damage.

As a victim advocate, I take particular pride in the increased attention that victims have received from policymakers and the media. In this, though, I am unlike those victim advocates who seem so intent on bringing attention to victims' plights that they ignore any successes that have occurred in this area. This strikes me as truly perverse, because it seems that victim advocates can hardly demand to be considered "experts" when they claim no success in past efforts to help victims.

Yet my study of compensation and other benefits based on victim status has made me skeptical of the excessive amounts of counseling being provided to "victims" of sexual and domestic assault, particularly when so much of it seems not only unwarranted, but harmful to victims, wasteful of compensation funds, and threatening to the integrity and viability of these programs. I base my conclusion on three factors:

- the likelihood that increased victim compensation, and reduced oversight of its provision, inevitably leads to an increase in false as well as appropriate claims for funds;
- that victim compensation programs encourage and even fund "case finding" efforts, which can be construed as "case creating" in extreme circumstances; and
- that these programs also spawn their own "experts," who are then funded to train others in their "methods" and to offer expert testimony in court based on them (which "trained" prosecutors are particularly likely to promote, and "trained" judges particularly likely to accept).

Increasingly, other researchers are reaching similar conclusions.

I once believed too that my training and experience made me particularly aware of child sexual abuse. What I realized, however, was that my very awareness blinded me to equally serious sexual abuse hoaxes occurring around me. While I still berate myself for taking so long to recognize the bogus nature of "recovered memory therapy" and the coerced testimony of children, I am even more astounded that many others, including policymakers and mental health professionals, have yet to see what is by now obvious to anyone with open eyes and an open mind. And what is even more troubling to me is that this is not an individual problem of self-delusion and denial, but a process that distorts public perceptions of crime and risk, skews public funds toward particular victims and victim services (and therefore away from other victims and alternative public needs), and corrupts the criminal justice system.

The public must have a clear picture of the crime problem so that funds can be allocated where they will be most effective, and they must be able to trust that criminal convictions are based on fair evidence and due process. As my small contribution to this effort, I have written this book. In it I explore how government support and funding of "junk social science" creates an implied approval of these bogus methods that is unwarranted and wasteful of tax dollars. I hope that this book will explain how people could be taken in by sanctified snake oil; but more importantly, I hope that it makes it harder for junk science to pass for legitimate social policy.

In considering this process, I have analyzed policy to find parallels to these activities and to trace their histories. Frankly, what began to take shape surprised even me. As I traced the roots of satanic ritual abuse (SRA) and recovered memory therapy (RMT), I began to see parallel methods used in other policy arenas—and across political spectra—to justify the continuation of ineffective programs, thereby blocking the way for better alternatives. These methods all serve to confuse the public, the media, and the government into believing that they are supporting a universally appealing goal, such as preventing child abuse, by supporting a government-supported program that espouses that goal. Similarly, analysts describe alcoholism and drug treatment and efforts to address sexual harassment, prisons, and much of the field of psychology as industries that, while they have a clear place in society, have exceeded their natural boundaries to address false and exaggerated cases. These cases drain public resources and attention away from real, serious cases and distort public perceptions of the magnitude of these crimes.

As this book documents, "meaning well" does not always equate with "doing good." Ineffectiveness, incompetence, lack of technology, incorrect methods, ideology masquerading as policy—and even outright fraud—contribute to this discrepancy. But it is the bureaucratic need to "cover asses" by not admitting to past mistakes, however innocently made, that ultimately results in "snake oil" methods being given the imprimatur of the government and relevant professionals, who should be able to judge these things but often submit to political pressure instead. Today the proliferation of media (some of it almost completely unfiltered—even for accuracy or truth—some of it presented in sound bites too short to be meaningful, and none of it as carefully explained or understood as a more self-critical media and a better-educated public could manage) spreads this questionable information until its sheer repetition confuses the public about its accuracy—and feeds "industries" based upon these inaccuracies. This is the concern of this book—not merely the existence of "snake oil," but the fact that some of it is taken seriously by government, which then bestows on it not only the appearance of approval by sanctioning it, but the money of taxpayers by perpetuating it. These actions result in intended and unintended consequences that combine to close off alternative solutions and even information that might alert the public to the inadequacies of these services.

For the purposes of this book the term "snake oil" is used to refer to any purported "explanation" or "solution" to a social problem (such as treatment and prevention programs for mental illness, "trauma," or substance abuse) that:

- is unscientific (proven ineffective after rigorous testing);
- has not been adequately tested;
- is incompletely or inadequately defined;
- is confused with its *use*;
- is used inappropriately, such as for a longer time than necessary or for any significant length of time when no positive change results or when negative change results; or
- is used with a client who is not mentally ill (or traumatized or an abuser of substances) or whose problem could be better treated by an alternative method.

"Sanctified" snake oil refers to any such treatment that is funded, mandated, or otherwise endorsed or accepted by a government entity. Throughout this book the term "government" is used to refer to any or all levels (local, state, or federal) or entities (agency or department) of government relevant to the specific issue under discussion.

In considering this analysis of "snake oil" and its "sanctification," I have developed paradigms of the characteristics of snake oil and its media and government sanctification. These paradigms are presented in Table 1. A "Rogue's Gallery" of programs and issues that exemplify "sanctified snake oil" appears in Table 2 to demonstrate how the various characteristics of snake oil and its sanctification are exemplified in each. Chapter 1 will introduce the discrete aspects of the "snake oil" paradigm; the issues introduced here will then be explored further throughout the book as they relate to the topic areas. Chapter 2 will explore the history of snake oil and how ideology and advocacy perpetuate it. The third chapter will analyze the characteristics of media and government sanctification, and why they exist.

Table 1

The Snake Oil Paradigm

1. Frame the subject so that it cannot be opposed.
2. Once the issue is defined, stretch the concept as broadly as possible in order to:
   a. increase the size of the "target" group;
   b. make the problem appear to be universal;
   c. make the problem appear to be of crisis proportions.
3. Consider anyone who resists identification with the target group to be "in denial" in order to:
   a. define all "sufferers" as in need of "treatment";
   b. make treatment seem more effective because many of the treated will not suffer from the problem or will have a mild, easily treatable degree of the problem, and nonimprovement can be blamed on denial.
4. Identify "poster children" who "suffer" from the problem but are appealing to the public (e.g., completely innocent and in no way responsible for their circumstances).
5. Use anecdotal evidence (preferably about "poster children") and single, dramatic cases to publicize the problem.
6. Use biased or "cooked" data—if forced to present any statistical proof of the problem.
7. Confuse goals and processes.
8. Confuse satisfaction with effectiveness.
9. Ignore unintended consequences and never admit that they might emanate from the "solution."
10. If criticized for any of the above, attack the opponents instead of their positions.

The Sanctification Paradigm

Media

1. Write "human interest" stories on single, extreme cases, suggesting that they are "typical" of the problem.
2. Publish statistics without consulting source data or confirming accuracy.
3. Oversimplify complex issues and policies.
4. Publish the results of research studies without discussing the methodology of the research (e.g., samples, controls).
5. "Bury" corrections and retractions in back pages and small print.

Government

1. Accept "expertise" at face value.
2. Fund training that presents ideology or "junk" science as fact.
3. Mandate treatment and fund services because of the importance of their goals, without regard to their effectiveness.
4. Provide third-party payments for services so that consumers won't care (and often won't know) how much they use the services.
5. Once services designed to meet a goal are funded, continue funding more of the same rather than insisting on continual evaluation, improvement, and innovation. Never consider alternative means of attaining the same goal.

Chapter 4 will explore why people believe in sanctified snake oil and how it can be identified. Chapter 5 will analyze how sanctified snake oil has affected our perceptions of mental health, trauma, and drug treatment and prevention. Chapter 6 will explore its worst effects, particularly on the criminal justice system. And the final chapter will consider means of eliminating the sanctification of snake oil as well as alternative means of meeting the same goals that current forms of "sanctified snake oil" purport to address.

I have struggled with the writing of this book for many reasons. Any book is a challenge to conceptualize, research, and write, but this book forced me to wrestle with my own preconceived notions; that is, those ideas I had accepted for reasons other than that facts demonstrated them to be accurate. I also struggled because I originally wanted to write on the broad policy level, rather than that of examples that may reflect those policies incompletely or distortedly. I have tried to integrate both, realizing that many readers require examples not only to understand the policies they reflect but to have proof of how they are implemented. Furthermore, I have been frustrated by the fact that, due to the very problem I address in this text, all sources are open to question. Therefore, I note at the outset that I have tried to present both accurate and balanced information, but particularly in regard to sources that reflect unpopular ideas, some references are less scholarly or more

Table 2
A "Rogue's Gallery" of Sanctified Snake Oil

- Abstinence Training
- All Involuntary or Mandated Treatment
- Biblical Creation Theory
- Chemical and Surgical Castration as Rape Prevention Mechanisms
- Child Abuse Accommodation Syndrome
- Chiropractic (for other than low-back pain)
- The Domino Theory
- Drug Abuse Resistance Education (DARE)
- Eye Movement Desensitization and Reprocessing (EMDR)
- The Illegality of *Cannabis Vulgaris*
- Marijuana Scheduling (as a narcotic with no medicinal value)
- McCarthyism
- Pornography as a Cause of Sexual Violence
- Prohibition
- Psychiatric Predictions of Future Behavior
- Recovered Memory Therapy (RMT)
- Satanic Ritual Abuse (SRA)
- All 12-Step and Anonymous Programs that Deviate from Their Original Principles
- The Violence Against Women Act (VAWA)

anecdotal than I would prefer. However, these only demonstrate the difficulty of identifying sources that meet the standards of scholars along all ideological continua. My purpose in writing this book is to encourage readers to begin their own quest for truth, because it will take a mobilized mass to demand the degree of irreproachable accuracy that this book notes does not currently exist.

I have primarily used examples from the criminal justice and mental health systems (particularly where the two intersect). This is not to suggest that these are the only areas in which these problems exist (although these may be the areas where the most damage can be done). Frankly, however, I have chosen these examples because they are the ones with which I am most familiar.

In regard to references, I have included page numbers only for journal articles. Having conducted most of my research online, I find that page numbers of newspaper and popular magazine articles have little importance when retrieving archival material. (This is not yet true of journal articles, which are often proprietary when they are online.)

I have omitted page numbers of book references for a very different reason. Researching this book has convinced me that one of the many reasons that so much information is misinterpreted is that many people read only snippets of information out of context. I hope that my failure to refer to specific passages encourages readers to read the referenced texts, if not in their entirety, then at least substantially.

My discomfort with examples goes further. I am uncomfortable "naming names," because I am interested in *how* policy is distorted, not in identifying those who do no more than take advantage of poor policy. More important, I do not want to suggest to readers that by "outing" particularly egregious policy manipulators, policy will change. Instead, new manipulators will replace the old, and policy will continue as ever. So I reluctantly but necessarily identify some of the individuals who "sanctify" snake oil, as well as those who merely "use" or "push" it, because I feel that it is necessary to convince readers of its existence. I urge you, however, not to focus on who the sanctifiers are, because they are legion, but to focus on why they have been able to do what they have done. For it is only when our attention is drawn to rectifying the problem of sanctified snake oil at the policy level that a solution can be effected.

NOTES

1. Debbie Nathan, "Victim or Victimizer: Was Kelly Michaels Unjustly Convicted?" *Village Voice* (August 2, 1988). [referenced online]

2. Susan K. Sarnoff, *A National Survey of State Crime Victim Compensation Programs: Policies and Administrative Methods* (Ann Arbor, MI: University Microfilms International, December 1993), pp. 172–178.

3. Susan Kiss Sarnoff, *Paying for Crime: The Policies and Possibilities of Crime Victim Reimbursement* (Westport, CT: Praeger Publishers, 1996).

4. Ted R. Miller, Mark A. Cohen, and Brian Wiersema, *Victim Costs and Consequences: A New Look* (Washington, DC: National Institute of Justice, February 1996).

5. (These figures contrast with the 25% upper limit of estimates determining the proportion of victims whose symptoms *warrant* counseling.) Daniel Goleman, "A Key to Post-Traumatic Stress Lies in Brain Chemistry, Scientists Find," *New York Times* (June 12, 1990).

6. Ted R. Miller, Mark A. Cohen, and Brian Wiersema, op. cit.

7. See, for example, Tana Dineen, *Manufacturing Victims,* 2nd ed. (Montreal: Robert Davies Publishing, 1998); Kenneth Lanning, "The 'Witch Hunt,' the 'Backlash,' and Professionalism," *The APSAC Advisor* 9, no. 4 (Winter 1996); Daphne Patai, *Heterophobia* (New York: Rowman & Littlefield, 1998); Eric Schlosser, "The Prison-Industrial Complex," *Atlantic Monthly* (December 1998).

8. Elliott Currie, "Crimes without Criminals," *Law and Society Review* 3 (August 7, 1968).

Acknowledgments

I am grateful to so many people for their help in enabling me to research and write this book, and to have it published. First, as ever, I am indebted to my husband, Jerry Sarnoff, who has always assisted me in locating source material, but who took on extra burdens for this book because of my temporary disability. Then, I am indebted to Dr. Robert Duarte, director of the Pain Clinic at the Long Island Jewish Medical Center, for curing my sciatic pain so that I could return to my computer, and my writing. And I am indebted to Heather Ruland Staines, my editor at Praeger, who helped me to shape this text to appeal to the broadest possible audience.

Then, despite the extensive criticism I give to many social work practitioners and professional societies, I am indebted to the many social workers who contributed to my knowledge of social policy and social program evaluation. These include my professors, mentors, and colleagues, especially Susan Robbins, Tom Oellerich, Carolyn Tice, Trudy Goldberg, Risha Levinson, Bob Mason, and Ralph Dolgoff.

I also want to thank Kenneth Lanning of the FBI; Alan M. Rubinstein, District Attorney of Bucks County, Pennsylvania; and Nassau County, New York, District Attorney Denis Dillon for their kind assistance in sharing information with me, and for being the kind of public servants who serve all of the public. I also want to thank attorney Dominick Barbara for sharing his extensive research on Eileen Treacy, and Richard Leo for sharing his research on miscarriages of justice that result in false convictions. I also want to thank, for their inspiration, Cathy Tijerina, who is working for her husband's release on false—and recanted—charges, and Frank Zepezauer, secretary of the Men's Defense Association, whose mental challenges inspired this book. And last but not at all least, I want to thank Betty Duffey, who introduced me to many of the people fighting to expose false allegations of sex crimes and who is herself one of their strongest—but also fairest—voices.

Finally, I wish to thank my editorial team from Praeger/Greenwood: Aquisitions Editor Heather Staines, Permissions Editor Marcia Goldstein, Production Editors Andrew Hudak and Betty Pessagno, and Copy Editor Gloria Lewis. All have shown incredible skill as well as extraordinary patience with me, and deserve no criticism but any credit for this book's readability.

Chapter 1

What Is Sanctified Snake Oil?

We should stop demanding that we all become instant saints and be more tolerant of our comrades, especially if they are active. The cultism of the left often appears as three people, two of whom plot to kick the third out. It's always because of another ism. Sexism, racism, elitism, deviationalism. I'd rather see people kicked out because they don't follow through on their commitment. . . . But deviate from the manners or the vocabulary of the party line and out you go. That's sick to me and self-defeating.

—Abbie Hoffman

We have seen the technique of the "Big Lie" utilized here for the first time on a sustained basis in our history. We have seen how, through repetition and shifting untruths, it is possible to delude great numbers of people. We have seen the character of private citizens and government employees virtually destroyed by public condemnation on the basis of gossip, distortion, hearsay, and deliberate untruths. . . . We have seen an effort to inflame the American people with a wave of hysteria and fear on an unbelievable scale. We are constrained fearlessly and frankly to call the charges, and the methods employed to give them ostensible validity, what they truly are: A fraud and a hoax perpetrated on the Senate of the United States and the American people.

—Report of the Subcommittee of the Senate Foreign Relations Committee Investigating Communist Infiltration of the State Department

Throughout history there have been all too many con artists, incompetents, and true believers who have offered ineffective "cures" for every type of physical, mental or spiritual ailment. As early as 1841, Charles Mackay wrote *Extraordinary*

Popular Delusions and the Madness of Crowds, which chronicled "the most remarkable instances of . . . moral epidemics . . . and . . . show[ed] how easily the masses have been led astray, and how imitative and gregarious men are, even in their infatuations and crimes." Mackay used such examples as alchemy, fortune-tellers, witch-hunts, and "tulipomania" to exemplify the phenomenon of mass hysteria throughout history.[1]

Mass hysteria has not diminished with time or universal education. In fact, the only thing that has changed today is that our government funds, sanctions, and even mandates, some of these bogus "cures." This suggests to the public that they are effective, even though government requires no proof of effectiveness when it funds or mandates treatment—nor does it require proof of effectiveness of the orientations or methods of expert witnesses who are used to determine the guilt of criminal defendants, the removal of children from their parents, and a host of other critical decisions that profoundly affect people's lives and have the potential to affect all of society. This may occur less because government believes in these things than because government wants to appear competent—and does so by echoing popular public opinions and making the solutions to social problems seem simple.

For instance, William Bennett, former drug and education czars (and now co-director of the Partnership for a Drug-Free America), was not effective at reducing drug use or improving education, "but he has an unerring sense of the yearning many adults have for simple definitions of right and wrong to preach to their kids." Due to his former and current positions, he is taken seriously.[2] This desire for simple solutions also translates into an acceptance of simplistic, global "solutions"—regardless of their chance of success. Consider the attacks at Columbine High School and the subsequent efforts to blame the entire incident on the media, access to guns, absence of school prayer, drugs, the Internet, and any number of factors that at most contributed slightly to a very complex, multifaceted problem. It is not the isolated efforts of a deluded few, but government's response—backed by self-serving "studies" offered by advocates not because of their methodological rigor but because they support favored solutions—that undermines careful analyses of causes and thoughtful comparison of alternative solutions. Following is a brief overview of the methods used to sanctify snake oil.

ISSUE FRAMING

Definitions determine our perceptions of issues, as well as perceptions of their magnitude and frequency. Advocacy groups vie to define issues, because "whoever controls the formulation of an issue eventually determines its outcome."[3] Advocates often do this by using "atrocity tales," which are purported to be typical examples, but instead are always extreme ones. As a result the public, along with policymakers and the media, comes to equate many issues with their most extreme forms.[4] When an advocacy group's definition becomes recognized as the primary or only definition of an issue, and when representatives of that advocacy group are recognized as authorities regarding it, they shape social policy regarding the issue and are said to "own" the issue.[5]

Issues can be framed in a number of ways. For one, they can be framed as positional issues, which may be contested, or as valence issues, which are perceived as incontestable. Prior to 1985, child sexual abuse was widely perceived as a valence issue. After 1985, as more people became aware that some children's testimony was being coerced, sometimes by parents in custody disputes, often by therapists who did not recognize that their methods constituted "coaching," and who had been indoctrinated with the truism "Children Don't Lie," child sexual abuse became a positional issue, about which many opinions could be reached.[6]

Another way to frame issues, which is similar but not parallel to the ways described above, is *condensationally*, that is, at an abstract and ambiguous level that is prone to encourage projected emotions and personal associations; or *referentially*, focusing in a specific or concrete way on objective elements and limiting the emotion they can invoke.[7] Ideologues frame their positions condensationally, allowing no alternative views of their issues. Thus, for example, "child advocates" often assert that all reports of child abuse must be believed, regardless of how implausible they might be or whether innocent people might be harmed in the process. All-or-nothing reasoning is another aspect of the condensational mode, which asserts that everyone is really a victim of every problem, victimhood differing only by degree, and degree makes little difference. Radical feminists who assert that all sex is rape and all women are victims of domestic violence are examples of this. Contrary arguments made referentially tend to be more accurate but are less anecdotal, sensational, and all-encompassing, attracting less media interest.[8]

It has been noted that despite the impressive gains made by the victims' movement in the past decade or so, it reflects a very narrow ideological bias. This bias has in turn largely reflected a conservative criminal justice agenda, and has benefitted a limited number and type of victims.[9] As the *Boston Globe* observed, "The basic questions of who is a victim and which victims qualify for compensation have led to long and costly legal battles, several of which have run all the way to the Supreme Judicial Court."[10] The result is that there has been little open dialogue about various aspects of crime, victimization, punishment, and their overall effects on society, limiting not only alternative views, but alternative solutions. "The vehicle for this bargain is the mechanism for funding victim services around the country . . . victims program are [federally] supported entirely from fines levied against those convicted of federal crimes . . . [which] locks victim advocates into a dangerous dependence on the country's law-and-order climate."[11]

It has also been observed that victims' issues are particularly prone to this type of distortion, because victims themselves rarely organize politically. Those who advocate on their behalf, in turn, are often professionals who see not a cross section of victims, but those victims of extreme violence or trauma who are hospitalized medically or psychologically, or who otherwise seek extended treatment, so their perceptions of victims' experiences become skewed toward the extremes.

It is in this way that discussions of policy are often framed as debates between two extremes, which in turn define the public's and policymakers' perceptions.[12] When such extremes are assumed, policymakers and the media "may end up scouring the margins of science and the fringes of lunacy to find it,"[13] whether out of a desire for fairness or to create the excitement of contentiousness. Either way, there is a danger that the extremes will be perceived as constituting the issue, and that it will appear that many people share these extreme opinions (rather than leaning toward that side), with the extremes diverting attention from more commonplace, but more common, problems.

CONCEPT STRETCHING

In 1993, Charles Krauthammer wrote an article for the *New Republic* titled "Defining Deviancy Up." This was a response to Senator Daniel Patrick Moynihan's article for the *American Scholar*, "What is Normal? Defining Deviancy Down,"[14] which lamented the devolution of standards of behavior that, more and more, was resulting in behavior previously thought of as deviant being considered mainstream; Krauthammer's article similarly lamented that formerly mainstream behavior is being redefined as deviant. For example, Krauthammer noted that "Entirely new areas of deviance—such as date rape and politically incorrect speech—have been discovered. And old areas—such as child abuse—have been amplified."[15] These examples are far from extreme when radical feminists such as Andrea Dworkin suggest that "Romance . . . is rape embellished with meaningful looks."[16] To overcome the common problem of redefining deviance both up and down, we need to identify a common understanding of what constitutes serious crime of any type, as opposed to significant, substantial, or minor crime, before we can discuss their effects.

Concept stretching, instead, defines issues to the point of ridiculousness, as when little boys are charged with sexual harassment for kissing little girls. But concept stretching is not mere hyperbole—it serves an important (if nefarious) purpose in social policy. Defining every woman who has ever had a shouting match with a loved one as a "victim of domestic violence," or defining anyone who has ever tried an illicit drug as a "drug abuser," enables ideologues to claim huge numbers of "afflicted." This also makes "their" issue seem to be of crisis proportions and sometimes even allows ideologues to claim "universalization" of the problem, or that everyone "suffers" from it to some degree. "One of the dangers of the habitual use of adversarial rhetoric is a kind of verbal inflation . . . legitimate, necessary denunciation is muted, even lost, in the general cacophony of oppositional shouting."[17]

This exaggeration not only justifies attention to the problem, but justifies higher funding than if the problem were defined more realistically. But the most significant advantage to concept stretching is this: if everyone whom ideologues define as suffering from a problem is included in the "target group" for treatment or other services, because some of those people fit the definition *only* in the minds of ideologues, some "sufferers" will later be evaluated as "cured" (or "recovered")—*only because they didn't manifest the problem in the first place.*

Examples of concept stretching abound. It has been suggested that the term date rape no longer has much literal or objective meaning. It tends to be used figuratively as a metaphor signifying that all heterosexual encounters are inherently abusive to women, a popularized form of the Dworkin-MacKinnon dogma that in a male-dominated culture that has "normalized" rape, yes can never really mean yes."[18] In response to Catherine MacKinnon's assertion in her book *Only Words* that pornographic pictures and words *are* sex, Wendy Kaminer remarked, "[I]f pornography is sex discrimination, then an editorial criticizing the President is treason."[19]

Radical feminists frequently, but not exclusively, exemplify this aspect of sanctified snake oil. (In fact, the very inclusion of women in the group "minorities" may be the single most absurd, and is certainly the most common, example of concept stretching in use today.) By this "verbal inflation . . . the ordinary vicissitudes of life become 'traumas.' Any situation which they wish to change becomes a 'crisis,' regardless of whether it is any worse than usual or is already getting better on its own."[20] Similarly, "The word 'victim' has a new, diluted meaning . . . frequently refer[ring] to someone who is momentarily upset or generally less satisfied, less happy, less successful or less fulfilled than they believe that they should be and who attributes that feeling to an event which was done to them, supposedly done to them, or merely witnessed or worried about."[21] It can also convey unskeptical acceptance of people whose claims of ritual abuse, alien abduction, or monitoring by the CIA may reflect psychosis or coercive suggestion by others.

Kenneth Lanning, the FBI agent who led the seven-year, $8 million investigation that debunked the satanic ritual abuse myth, noted that concept stretching is used by both sides in ideological battles. He observed that the child sexual abuse "witch-hunt" is characterized by the tendency to exaggerate child sexual abuse, to emphasize believing the children, and to criticize the criminal justice system only for the lack of investigation or for acquittals. When child sexual abuse is alleged, ideologues assume it has happened and try to prove it.

[In contrast,] the backlash is characterized by a tendency to minimize child sexual abuse, to emphasize false allegations, and to criticize the criminal justice system only for aggressive investigation or for convictions. When child sexual abuse is alleged, they assume it has not happened and try to disprove it. Each side conveniently fails to define its terminology or inconsistently uses the terms it does not define. When volume is needed, a child is anyone under 18 years old. When impact is needed, a child is under 12 years old."[22]

Lanning's description explains how concept stretching can result in the statistical distortion so common in advocacy statistics. Consider Table 3, which is a diagram developed to depict Lanning's explanation. Note, however, that it is not specific to child abuse, but can be applied to any advocacy statistics. The point of the diagram is to explain that statistical distortions do not prove anything, because they are based on widely disparate premises. Ideologues make it easy to "prove" their contentions by accepting self-reports as "truth" and defining concepts as broadly as possible. Contrary "evidence," however, is subjected to extreme standards of proof and narrow definitions.

Consider another example of concept stretching: statistics have been identified that "prove" that each American has roughly two physical or mental disorders![23] One reason for this is "The fading distinction between normal and abnormal that these newly defined diseases suggest [has been stretched into] so-called 'shadow syndromes.' Proposed by John Ratey, a psychiatrist at Harvard Medical School whose book takes the term for its title, the syndromes represent 'hidden psychological disorders.' People who are 'a little bit' depressed or anxious or display bad tempers suffer from them.[24] Although Ratey concedes that the manifestations are too mild to fit what he calls 'the DSM's [Diagnostic and Statistical Manual] concrete blocks,' he nevertheless argues that feelings of this sort pose genuine risks: 'People's lives can and do crash . . . because of small problems.'"[25] This is not a fringe idea—in fact, the *New York Times* ran a front page story in which it reported that Surgeon General David Satcher called for mental illness to become destigmatized so that the half of Americans who need mental health treatment will not hesitate to seek it.[26]

Many experts have observed that the DSM is wholly unscientific. In fact, some observers have argued that it is not only unreliable and diagnostically imprecise, but that its primary purpose is to provide consistent terms for billing to simplify mental health providers' receipt of reimbursement from insurance carriers.[27] Furthermore, my own training in DSM diagnoses, as was typical of such training prior to this decade, specified that there were "acceptable levels" of each problem, for which no form of treatment would be necessary. In fact, because people learn to cope with major problems by gaining experience with smaller ones, problems that fall "within normal limits" actually help people to develop coping skills. Today, however, while research has not changed these perspectives, the "business" of treatment targets people without regard to the severity of their troubles—or whether helpful interventions even exist. Robert Grossmark, a clinical psychologist who wrote a tongue-in-cheek reply to the *New York Times* in response to a

Table 3
Advocacy Statistics

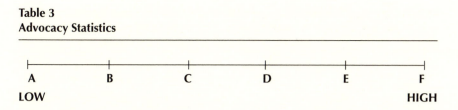

The points are defined as follows:

Point A depicts the extreme low point which reflects the number of cases that the most extreme opponents concede reflect the problem—that is, these cases both fit opponents' narrowest definition of the problem and withstand opponents' strictest demands for proof.

Point B depicts the number of cases that opponents concede reflect their narrow definition of the problem, but do not meet their standards of proof.

Point C depicts the low number of cases that most people with knowledge of the issue, but no ideological bias regarding its definition or standards of proof, would accept as reflective of the problem.

Point D depicts the high number of cases that most people with knowledge of the issue, but no ideological bias regarding its definition or standards of proof, would accept as reflective of the problem.

Point E depicts the number of cases that proponents assert reflect their broad definition of the problem and withstand their looser standard of proof.

Point F depicts the extreme high point which reflects the number of cases that the most extreme proponents assert reflect the problem—that is, these cases fit proponents' broad definition of the problem, for which no further "proof" is required.

Note: This depiction is not intended to suggest specific measures of or distances between points, but only to suggest the relationships among the points.

Times article on the expansion of the DSM, identified "DSM disorder . . . characterized by a compulsive need to construe all facets of human functioning as distinct psychiatric disorders."[28] In another letter responding to the same article, the author noted that the addition of minor disorders formerly defined as "bad behavior" to the DSM not only serves to increase the incomes of mental health providers, but encourages such behavior by removing social stigma from it. Such removal reduces the sense of personal responsibility not only by bypassing blame, but by making insurance companies rather than individuals responsible for paying for efforts to address it.[29] Clearly, too, these are not benign misperceptions, but calculated distortions made for ideological purposes, career advancement, and financial gain.

Another example of concept stretching is the use of war analogies to describe efforts to address drug abuse, for example. War analogies make moderate solutions or compromises appear to be failures—and also make anything but total "victory" (a near impossibility in any form of social policy) appear to be a devastating defeat.[30]

DENIAL

The obverse of concept stretching, which serves the same purpose, is to suggest that anyone who rejects being categorized according to these extreme definitions is "in denial." We are most familiar with the term in relation to addiction. "Of all the ideas presented by the alcoholism movement, that of denial—which means that the drinker doesn't agree with what the alcoholism movement or treatment personnel tell him or her—has the most malicious potential."[31] Ironically, however, when alcoholism treatment programs, and the range of programs modeled on AA, discourage critical thinking and objective analyses that separate methods from goals, and disregard emerging research and program changes that radically affect program performance, they exhibit the very denial of which they accuse skeptics and nonparticipants. And if particular methods fail to be as successful with some individuals, the problem is not attributed to the method, but to the individual (contrary to evidence that treatments must be matched to various aspects of personality and behavior patterns). This form of denial can prevent a person in need of treatment from finding a more appropriate treatment, or even recognizing that an alternative is possible.[32]

However, denial extends to many other areas. For instance, while not using the term denial, Dr. Mary Koss' assertion that her research detected rapes that *she* says occurred—even though the "victims" did not consider themselves to have been raped—is another example.[33] And Dr. Roland Summit theorized Child Abuse Accommodation Syndrome, which conjectured that many victims deny victimization to protect their abusers. Proponents took this speculation to the illogical extreme of claiming that denial of sexual abuse by children is so characteristic that it should be considered a symptom that supports a finding of abuse.[34] In regard to child abuse investigations, "Among social workers and therapists . . . the word *denial* . . . took on a new meaning, one lifted from the lexicon of therapy. . . . [Therefore] the father who denied the charges was especially despicable."[35]

But denial too has purposes beyond the obvious. Not only does denial allow ideologues to overcount sufferers, as well as to count "sufferers" who do not self-identify with a problem; denial enables service providers to argue that because so many people *they* define as sufferers fail to seek help, those people should be coerced into treatment. Mandated treatment is so pervasive today, particularly for DWI, substance (ab)use, domestic violence, and sexual assault, that it is clear that without such mandates, a great many service providers would be unemployed.

Mandating also pulls nonsufferers into treatment, who improve recovery records, as noted earlier. But it is doubtful that mandating people into counseling situations (which require motivation to be successful) is ever effective. Moreover, it can be particularly dangerous if the treatment is mandated in lieu of more effective controls, like incarceration.

Mandating treatment is popular for several reasons, however. Some misguided liberals believe that mandated treatment is an effective alternative to imprisonment. Mandating also makes it unnecessary to "sell" treatment to its recipients or compete in the marketplace of alternatives. As a result, mandating ensures a caseload and income for service providers regardless of its effectiveness or even the satisfaction of its clients.

POSTER CHILDREN

The media are particularly effective at identifying "ideal types" of sufferers, who then become so synonymous with the problem they are purported to represent that we cannot think about the problem without imagining them. While they do not actually have to be children, it helps if "poster children" are young, absolutely innocent, and unusually attractive. Consider Alexander Cockburn's description of "the beatification of Ryan White by *People* in prose passages unrivaled in mawkishness by anything since Dickens finished off Little Nell."[36]

The poster child is the star of what was earlier defined as the "atrocity tale." What ideologues never state, but hope we will assume, is that these poster children and the anecdotes and atrocity tales told about them are typical examples, rather than examples handpicked because their extreme characteristics and tear-jerking "stars" tug at heartstrings. But ideologues present a very skewed picture of "sufferers": people who have contracted AIDS from blood transfusions, people later exonerated of crimes of which they had been accused (as opposed to people who were charged with excessive crimes), and any victims of severe violence.

"Sufferers" often differ considerably from "poster children." Ralph Nunez, CEO of Homes for the Homeless, observed that people defined as homeless have deeper problems, which are ignored if they are only provided with housing. As a result, these people often find themselves back in shelters, because the problems that originally caused them to become homeless were not addressed.[37] Poster children also suggest one of the dirty secrets of ideologues: that they privately despise those they represent who are not poster children; unlike poster children, these people never quite fit their theories or reflect the "innocent victimhood" they want to project onto their causes.

Poster children, because they are themselves victims, are also impervious to attack simply because victim sensitivity has become such a sacred cow. And because poster children are individuals, their presence reduces policy issues to personal concerns, so that funding priorities cannot be weighed rationally but instead are considered solely in terms of whether further pain to the poster child will be countenanced.

UNINTENDED CONSEQUENCES

Some of the most effective social policies produce negative, unintended consequences; so the possibility of unintended consequences alone should not thwart policy or program development. Negative consequences, however, should be identified, so that policies can be modified to reduce them, or policies can at least develop means to address these consequences. Too often, instead, ideologues fear that the unintended consequences militate against the policy's perpetuation, and either deny their existence altogether or deny that they are causally related to the policy that produced them. There is also the danger that rushing to solve problems as they are defined by advocates will create other problems or costs because of the perceived urgency and intensity of the problems, when what might really be needed is time to gather data, plan, and develop multiple solutions.[38]

Examples of unintended consequences proliferate. People are more likely to divorce if divorce is easy and financial support is available. (Of course, making divorces and support more difficult to obtain would also produce unintended consequences.) Once children are designated with the label "special needs" or "learning disabled, "[t]hey are magnets for federal funds, so that the school has a fiscal incentive to maintain the classification of the child as handicapped, quite contrary to the nominal purpose of the program, namely, to render these children unhandicapped."[39] The movement to "protect" patients by credentialing mental health professionals "spawn[ed] a number of 'diploma-by-mail' and 'pay-me-and-I'll-say-you're-good' schemes."[40] The incentives created by increased government benefits and insurance coverage for a range of issues that are vaguely defined cannot help but encourage professionals seeking clients and people looking for vindicating causes for behavior to take advantage and become increasingly dependent on these mechanisms.

The criminalization of drug use results in increased crime and a greater likelihood of infection through shared needles and overdoses due to unreliable supplies. As economist Milton Friedman wrote in an Open Letter to the then drug czar William Bennett, "Illegality creates obscene profits . . . leads to the corruption of law enforcement officials . . . [and] converts that tragedy into a disaster for society, for users and non-users alike."[41] And continual payments for drug treatment, with endless acceptance of relapse, keeps service recipients and service providers dependent on each other's dysfunction. Demanding results from both would not only reduce costs but improve outcomes.[42]

"[T]he current war on drugs is a perfect illustration of the *balloon principle*: Push on one part of the balloon and it simply spreads out in another direction."[43] During the Nixon years, for example, money poured into anything that could be defined as anti-drug, while many other government programs were being cut back. As a result, many kinds of programs became defined as promoting drug prevention, and they proliferated because they were not only poorly monitored, but because the government wanted to tout its spending for this issue.[44]

This is not to suggest that drug prevention programs are never worthwhile—only that their worth is likely to be diminished if they are poorly monitored and not required to produce results. Similarly, worthy efforts to help crime victims, who were virtually ignored before the 1970s, became so well funded and loosely defined that they encouraged people to embrace a "victimhood-based identity."[45] Consider that the Menendez brothers and Jesse Timendequas (the murderer of Megan Kanka) both used "abuse excuses" as their criminal defenses.

Universal definitions are fraught with similar problems. For instance, it has been found that orders of protection are useful for women who are victims of minor domestic violence but dangerous to women who have been severely abused. Yet the prevailing notion that "abuse is abuse" does not allow for such distinctions—endangering the very women who most need protection.[46] Some have defined the victims' movement as a "cranky, special interest lobby." Embracing the victim label too strongly has allowed the movement to be portrayed as a "bunch of weaklings, complainers or even psychological dysfunctionals in the 'recovery' movement."[47]

And, while challenges to Megan's Law failed to overturn the legislation, they did manage to require due-process hearings for any sex offenders who challenge their classification or listing in the program. This unintended consequence has added considerable untolled—and unanticipated—costs to the legislation.[48] Furthermore, Megan's Law places many kinds of convicted sex offenders into a single category—"a classic example of legislation by anecdote and legislation by high-profile case. . . . It's the hatchet versus the scalpel."[49]

Child abuse, particularly due to the phenomenal number of child sexual-abuse cases reported, has had its own share of unintended consequences. The most dangerous is no doubt that "between 1979 and 1983 . . . reported cases of child abuse increased almost 50 percent. But over the same period, the number of substantiated cases actually declined. In other words, the 22,000 increase of reported cases yielded no net increase of real cases."[50] What this suggests is that efforts to encourage reporting also encouraged false reporting or overreactions, which diverted resources from the investigation of truly serious cases.

The detection of child abuse itself has had unintended consequences due "to the fact that Child Protective Services (CPS), state agencies established by federal law, receive a federal bounty for breaking apart families and putting children in foster care."[51] As a result of wrongful prosecutions, many of those accused are now suing the community civilly.[52] Sadly, it seems that only the threat of lawsuits mitigates against the wholesale focus on "case finding" encouraged by these federal funds.

Perhaps the most sweeping unintended consequence I came across while researching this book is the one reported by Richard Morin in the *Washington Post*: "Many Americans simply don't believe government economic statistics. . . . Many also suspect that the government numbers aren't merely wrong, they're manipulated to hide the truth from the American people.[53] If this is the effect of sanctified snake oil, then it suggests better than anything else why it is imperative that we stop it.

VILIFICATION OF OPPONENTS

The final characteristic of snake oil is that it vilifies opponents and otherwise relies on polemical arguments, because what makes snake oil snake oil is that it is not defensible on rational grounds. And what makes "true believers" is that their investment in their belief system is so great that they cannot tolerate criticism of it, nor can they alter their beliefs in light of contradictory evidence.

One of the most unfortunate effects of the triumph of ideological rhetoric over logical analysis is that challenges to faulty methodology are often met with personal attacks against those who dare to make the challenges. This does lessen their frequency, but also suggests that no reasoned response could be made.

Consider that when Catherine MacKinnon and Andrea Dworkin attempted to pass a sweeping antipornography ordinance in Indianapolis, MacKinnon reportedly called her opponents, who filed a court brief opposing the legislation, "House niggers who sided with the masters." Those "house niggers" included such feminist luminaries as Judy Blume, Karen DeCrow, Nora Efron, Barbara Ehrenreich, Susan Estrich, Nancy Friday, Betty Friedan, Susan Isaacs, Molly Ivins, Erica Jong, Jamaica Kincaid, Kate Millett, Katha Pollitt, Anne Rice, Adrienne Rich, Alix Kates Shulman, and Wendy Wasserstein.[54]

In a similar vein, proponents of recovered memory therapy accused their critics of being "perpetrators," and Marian Wright Edelman called those who disagreed with her on how taxes should be spent "Herods."[55] Several psychologists have learned that questioning the practice of colleagues who recover memories or routinely make rare or even disputed diagnoses can result in accusations as strange as belonging to satanic cults or as threatening as practicing unethically.[56] McNeely, Cook, and Torres documented that McNeely himself, as well as noted domestic violence researcher Suzanne Steinmetz, and Erin Pizzey, the founder of battered women's shelters, has numbered among the practitioners and researchers who have received attacks against their professionalism and livelihoods as well as their lives for results of research that, while methodologically sound, ran counter to the beliefs of domestic violence orthodoxy.[57]

Similarly, "researchers and counselors who have championed—or even tried to investigate—moderation as a treatment strategy [for alcoholism] have been threatened and sometimes fired. We've been accused of murder. That we're all in denial. That we're enablers."[58]

These types of attacks—even attacks by those that have been and still are oppressed by the groups they attack—cannot be tolerated by any group against any other group. Such hyperbole not only dissuades people who are undecided about the issue; it also puts at risk the support among those who agree with the ideology but also believe in justice.[59]

Hyperbole, too, serves a purpose beyond the obvious. Those who are unfairly attacked must spend time, effort, and money defending themselves—actions that take away from their ability to contribute to their fields and promote their careers, even as their work is often marginalized or ignored. This, in turn, serves to dissuade others who might otherwise produce valid but politically unpopular research.

Consider the words of two former Supreme Court justices on free speech. Justice Louis Brandeis opined that

It is the function of speech to free men from the bondage of irrational fears. . . . If there be time to expose through discussion the falsehood and fallacies to avert the evil by processes of education, the remedy to be applied is more speech, not enforced silence.[60]

Justice William O. Douglas similarly observed that "[A] function of free speech under our system of government is to invite dispute. It may indeed best serve its high purpose when it induces a condition of unrest, creates dissatisfaction with conditions as they are, or even stirs people to anger."[61]

NOTES

1. Charles Mackay, *Extraordinary Popular Delusions and the Madness of Crowds* (New York: Harmony Books, 1980). (Originally published London: Richard Bentley, 1841.)

2. Jon Katz, *Virtuous Reality* (New York: Random House, 1997).

3. Susan J. Tolchin, *The Angry American: How Voter Rage Is Changing the Nation* (New York: Westview Press, 1996).

4. Joel Best, *Threatened Children* (Chicago, IL: University of Chicago Press, 1990). Quoted in Daphne Patai, "Sexual Harassment on Campus," *Sexuality and Culture* 1 (1997).

5. Ibid.

6. Kathleen Beckett, "Culture and the Politics of Signification: The Case of Child Sexual Abuse," *Social Problems* 43, no. 1 (February 1996): 57–76.

7. Murray Edelman, *Political Language: Words that Succeed and Politics that Fail* (New York: Academic Press, 1977). Also see Lance Bennett, *Public Opinion in American Politics* (New York: Harcourt Brace Jovanovich, 1980).

8. Marjorie Randon Hershey and Darryl M. West, "Single-Issue Politics: Prolife Groups and the 1980 Senate Campaign," in *Interest Group Politics*, edited by Allan J. Cigler and Burdett A. Loomis (Washington, DC: CQ Press, 1983), 31–59.

9. Robert Elias, *Victims Still* (Beverly Hills, CA: Sage Publications, 1993).

10. Nick King, "Victims Victimized," *Boston Globe* (May 10, 1981), A22.

11. Bruce Shapiro, "Victims and Vengeance," *The Nation* (February 10, 1997), 11–19.

12. Celeste Michelle Condit, "Two Sides to Every Question: The Impact of New Formulas on Abortion Policy Options," *Argumentation* 8, no. 4, (1994), quoted in Deborah Tannen, *The Argument Culture* (New York: Random House, 1998).

13. Deborah Tannen, *The Argument Culture* (New York: Random House, 1998).

14. Daniel Patrick Moynihan, "What Is Normal? Defining Deviancy Down," *Current* (September 1993), 12–19.

15. Charles Krauthammer, "Defining Deviancy Up," *New Republic* (November 22, 1993).

16. Andrea Dworkin, quoted in Charles Krauthammer, Ibid.

17. Deborah Tannen, op. cit.

18. Wendy Kaminer, "Feminism's Identity Crisis," *Atlantic Monthly* (October 1993), quoted in Reinder Van Til, *Lost Daughters* (Grand Rapids, MI: William B. Eerdmans Publishing Co., 1997).

19. Wendy Kaminer, quoted in Nadine Strossen, *Defending Pornography* (New York: Anchor Books, 1996).

20. Thomas Sowell, *The Vision of the Anointed* (New York: Basic Books, 1995).

21. Tana Dineen, *Manufacturing Victims*, 2d ed. (Montreal: Robert Davies Publishing, 1998).

22. Kenneth Lanning, "The 'Witch Hunt,' the 'Backlash,' and Professionalism," *The APSAC Advisor* 9, no. 4 (winter 1996).

23. Bob Garfield, "Maladies by the Millions?" *USA Today* (December 16, 1996).

24. John Ratey and Catherine Johnson, *Shadow Syndromes* (New York: Pantheon Books, 1997).

25. Sheila M. Rothman, "There's a Name for What Ails You," *Washington Post National Weekly* (April 21, 1997).

26. Robert Pear, "Few People Seek to Treat Mental Illnesses, Study Finds," *New York Times* (December 13, 1999).

27. Tana Dineen, op. cit.

28. Robert Grossmark, Letter to the *New York Times*, *New York Times* (September 30, 1997).

29. Pierre E. Biscayne, Letter to the *New York Times*, *New York Times* (September 30, 1997).

30. Joel Best, *Random Violence* (Berkeley: University of California Press, 1999).

31. Stanton Peele, *The Diseasing of America* (New York: Lexington Books, 1995).

32. Michael J. Lemanski, "The Tenacity of Error in the Treatment of Addiction," *The Humanist* (May/June 1997), 18–23.

33. Christina Hoff Sommers, *Who Stole Feminism?* (New York: Simon & Schuster, 1994).

34. Roland Summit, "The Child Abuse Accommodation Syndrome," *Child Abuse and Neglect* 7, no. 2 (1983) and Roland Summit, "Abuse of the Child Abuse Accommodation Syndrome," *Journal of Child Sexual Abuse* 1, no. 4 (1992), 153–163.

35. Debbie Nathan and Michael Snedeker, *Satan's Silence* (New York: Basic Books, 1995).

36. Daniel Harris, "The Kitschification of AIDS," *The Rise and Fall of Gay Culture* (New York: Hyperion, 1997), cited in Alexander Cockburn, "AIDS, Kitsch and Charity," *New York Press* (June 18–24, 1997).

37. Fred Siegel, *The Future Once Happened Here* (New York: Free Press, 1997).

38. Thomas Sowell, op. cit.

39. Deborah A. Stone, "Clinical Authority in the Construction of Citizenship," in *Public Policy for Democracy*, edited by Helen Ingram and Steven Rathgeb Smith (Washington, DC: The Brookings Institution, 1993), 45–67.

40. Tana Dineen, *Manufacturing Victims*, 2d ed. (Montreal: Robert Davies Publishing, 1998).

41. Milton Friedman, "An Open Letter to Bill Bennett," *Wall Street Journal* (September 7, 1989).

42. Charles Murray, *What It Means to Be a Libertarian* (New York: Broadway Books, 1997).

43. Daniel K. Benjamin and Roger Leroy Miller, *Undoing Drugs* (New York: Basic Books, 1991).

44. Eva Bertram, Morris Blachman, Kenneth Sharpe, and Peter Andreas, *Drug War Politics* (Los Angeles: University of California Press, 1996).

45. Cathy Young, *Ceasefire: Beyond the Gender Wars* (New York: Free Press, 1999).

46. Ibid.

47. Robert Elias, op. cit.

48. "Megan's Law," *Wall Street Journal* (August 22, 1997).

49. Todd S. Purdum, "Registry Laws Tar Sex-Crime Convicts with Broad Brush," *New York Times* (July 1, 1997).

50. Quoted in Charles Krauthammer, op. cit.

51. Ibid. Also see San Diego County Grand Jury, *Analysis of Child Molestation Issues. Report No. 7* (San Diego , CA: San Diego County Grand Jury, June 1, 1994).

52. Paul Craig Roberts, "Benching the Witch Hunters." *Washington Times* (September 13, 1996).

53. Richard Morin, "You Figure It Out: The People Can Do the Arithmetic, But They Have a Hard Time Believing the Numbers," *Washington Post National Weekly Edition* (January 6, 1997).

54. See, for example, Lynne V. Cheney, *Telling the Truth* (New York: Touchstone, 1995); and Nadine Strossen, op. cit.

55. Reinder Van Til, op. cit.

56. Ibid.

57. R. L. McNeely, Philip W. Cook, and Jose B. Torres, "Is Domestic a Human Issue?" *Journal of Human Behavior in the Social Environment* (fall 1999).

58. Nancy Shute, "The Drinking Dilemma," *U. S. News and World Report* (September 8, 1997), 54–65.

59. Daphne Patai, "The Feminist Turn Against Men," *Partisan Review* (fall 1996), 580–594.

60. Supreme Court Justice Louis Brandeis, *Whitney v. California* (1927).

61. Supreme Court Justice William O. Douglas, *Terminiello v. Chicago*.

Chapter 2

The History of Sanctified Snake Oil

The truth which makes men free is for the most part the truth which men prefer not to hear.

—Herbert Agar

A little learning is a dangerous thing;
Drink deep, or taste not the Pierian spring;
There shallow draughts intoxicate the brain,
And drinking largely sobers us again.

—Alexander Pope

While various forms of "snake oil" have been with us throughout recorded history, its "sanctification" is a relatively recent phenomenon. This is true because the kinds of "cures," "treatments," and other "solutions" that constitute it were not sanctioned—or supported—by government on a large scale until the beginning of this century. Only then did government begin to mandate that states provide insurance benefits for people injured at work. Over time, government expanded the venues through which it approved and supported questionable interventions. Since the 1960s, Medicare, Medicaid, and a host of other benefits, including crime-victim and workers' compensation and public disability insurance, have been the primary mechanisms through which government has done this. While these benefits do not in themselves constitute snake oil, the fact that they were created enables patients to obtain (without out-of-pocket payments) a wider range of services that they had formerly done without—including services that they do not need, if they can be convinced that they *do* need them. This has led to a vast expansion of services, and justifications for these services, which receives little attention from the public because the services are created by internal agency "tinkering," rather than by more visible policy development.

Policies are developed incrementally, so when they are introduced they tend to be narrowly drawn and poorly funded—addressing only the needs of "poster child" recipients. Over time, however, as their very existence creates constituencies of recipients and service providers who come to depend upon them, they are gradually expanded to meet new definitions and to obtain expanded funding, which is done outside the public arena.

History suggests another reason that sanctified snake oil has gained ground during this century. Beginning in the mid-1800s, there was a focus on "civilizing" the population to prepare for the vast increase in industrial jobs that were being created. In fact, as late as the turn of the present century, roughly 90% of Americans were still self-employed, most on family farms or in small, family-owned businesses. Alcoholism, gambling, and other vices were then truly personal problems, because they had little effect on society. But this was changing rapidly. By 1992, only 4% of workers were self-employed.[1]

The connection is clear. While America emphasized individualism and self-government, it presumed self-control. It would be impossible to end vice, but it was vital to create an ethos that "encouraged self-control, enthroned models of right behavior, and punished *extreme* deviance." This would not eradicate vice, but would force it into hiding—a contradiction, hypocritical though it was, which became the Victorian Compromise. Its purpose was to simultaneously laud self-respect as the ultimate virtue and scapegoat vice as the ultimate social ill.[2]

The Victorian Compromise created a dichotomy between how people behaved and the behavior and attitudes to which people admitted. This was effective as long as the United States remained a nation of like-minded citizens who agreed to these hypocritical social rules; but it began to disintegrate as "strangers" from Eastern Europe and farther away began to challenge its most basic premises. The Victorian Compromise had another, less obvious effect: it created a justification for government to enter realms of personal behavior that had formerly been regulated by families and communities.

By the beginning of this century, Americans of English ancestry, who had formerly made up most of the population, had been reluctantly forced to share "their" country with people of different languages, customs, and beliefs. This led to an outgrowth of the Victorian Compromise: the Temperance Movement, which had begun as an attempt to reduce alcohol use, but had given way to fanatical calls to ban all liquor, or Prohibition. Prohibition resulted from alliances between Temperance extremists and xenophobic Know-Nothings. Their perceived loss of power and status due to the influx of immigrants who challenged their ways of life made those who were different—and the differences themselves—targets for legal enforcement of what society could no longer ensure by social pressure alone.[3]

Prohibition died amid the Great Depression with hardly a murmur. In fact, it had hardly been enforced, constituting instead what has been described as a "symbolic crusade."[4] But the idea that government could intervene in social behavior—even when that behavior conformed with the norms of some segments of society—had been established.

Snake oil tactics were taken up once again when publisher William Randolph Hearst and Bureau of Narcotics chief Harry Anslinger set out to demonize hemp, a common weed indigenous to North America that has long been used in cloth- and rope-making. (Proponents of relegalization point out that Betsy Ross sewed her flag from hemp cloth, and hemp was a major crop on many American farms, including Monticello and Mount Vernon—production of hemp having been mandated in Virginia in 1619.) And I began this book in the township of *Hemp*stead, so named by its Dutch settlers because stands ("steads" in Dutch") of hemp grew wild, as in their homeland, assuring them a familiar climate and soil.[5]

Following Prohibition Anslinger, with considerable help from the Hearst newspaper chain, began to spread rumors about people being driven violently insane by a "new" drug with a foreign-sounding name: marijuana. Keying into the tone of the times, Anslinger suggested that Mexicans and Negroes were particularly prone to the "horrifying" effects of marijuana. Although he never documented a single case, Anslinger's fear tactics, and his powerful position, enabled him to convince Congress, over a span of only ten weeks, to pass a bill that made the production of marijuana prohibitively expensive and provided prison terms for noncompliance.[6]

Congress did not realize, as it outlawed the demonized marijuana, that it was actually outlawing hemp. This confusion stemmed from the fact that the plant with the botanical name *Cannabis* produces several strains, including *Cannabis sativa*, which has mild hallucinogenic properties, and *Cannabis vulgaris*, or hemp. There is no doubt, however, that Hearst and Anslinger intended to demonize both. Hearst, after all, owned the timberland used to produce his newspapers, but recent advances had so improved hemp paper that if research and development had proceeded unchecked, it would likely have devalued his forests. And Anslinger had gotten his job through the powerful connections of his uncle, Andrew Mellon, whose oil wells stood poised to fuel the new automobile industry. However, the Ford Motor Company was then developing cars that could run on plant matter, as could the alternative engine recently developed by Rudolph Diesel; and it is no coincidence that hemp seed, hemp seed oil, and the hemp plant are the most efficient plant-based engine fuels.[7]

World War II changed America's priorities. Due to fear that the Navy would lose its major source of rope if the Philippines were captured by Japan, American

farmers were encouraged to grow hemp during the war, but rather than amend-
ing the Marijuana Tax Act to prohibit only the growing of *Cannabis sativa*, the
law was simply overlooked. After the war, all hemp production was prohibited
once again.[8]

During the war "snake oiling" became unnecessary, because unpleasant facts
could be withheld from the public for "security" reasons. After the war, the threat
of communism perpetuated the rationalization, if not the reason, for keeping
many government activities secret. This did not, however, prevent the single most
dramatic instance of sanctified snake oil from being played out on America's new
stage: television. Senator Joseph McCarthy led a witch-hunt without evidence—
and with only his senatorial seat to lend credence to the lie—that he had lists of
(the numbers changed with each telling) communists who had infiltrated the federal government. Once they were exposed, of course, McCarthy's tactics were de-
plored. Perhaps more significant, politicians realized that the new medium of
television had played a major role in exposing McCarthy's tactics to a public eager
to see its government in action.[9]

This appeared to result in a brief reduction in the sanctification of snake oil.
But when it reappeared, it was with improved methods, including "disinformation," which were better-adapted to television news. While disinformation was by
no means an innovative method, it would reach new dimensions during the
Vietnam War.[10]

That war created great rifts in American society: between pro-war "hawks" and
anti-war "doves"; between a generation that had fought "the Good War" and a
generation that had hidden under school desks in fear of nuclear annihilation, for
which no war could be considered a good war; and between students for whom
college meant not only an education but a deferment and blue-collar workers
whose children would replace the deferred in the jungles of Vietnam. Family
members, neighbors, and coworkers disagreed about the war, and as it continued
to escalate, the number of sides one could take on it escalated as well. Some
Americans supported the use of nuclear weapons just to bring the war to a quick
end, some preferred an endless ground war to any use of nuclear weapons, and still
others would countenance nothing but an all-out attempt to win, regardless of the
costs. Some opponents supported gradual de-escalation while others wanted the
war to end immediately. Some opposed the war only because it had never been declared a war by Congress. Some supported the war for the jobs it created at home
and in the military. Others were most disturbed by the war's classism—forcing a
draft lottery that eliminated many types of deferments for the unlucky who drew
low numbers.[11]

It has been observed that the first casualty when war comes is truth.[12] This was
never more true than during the Vietnam War. As the war escalated, the government underreported wounded and dead American soldiers and overreported the

damage, in lives and property, to the enemy. The government also lied about its offensive tactics, its expansion into Laos and Cambodia, and its support of puppet governments in Southeast Asia that were supportive of the American presence in Vietnam.[13]

Those opposed to the war were vilified in the press and set upon by the government, experiencing everything from IRS audits to wiretaps to campaigns to discredit them professionally. Efforts to oppose the war became more focused on college campuses, where students had the greatest stake in ending it before their graduations, and more underground as opponents sought to avoid government retribution.[14]

By the mid-1960s, a new source of information for war protesters was those veterans who had joined the anti-war movement—some while they were still in Vietnam. Returning veterans told not only of falsified body counts, but of an enemy more adept at jungle fighting than American soldiers, of insufficient and inappropriate weapons and other resources, of atrocities committed against women and children, and of widespread drug use among American servicemen.[15]

Ironically, it was these soldiers' stories of massive use of marijuana, hashish, and heroin by American soldiers (who, to everyone's surprise, were easily able to overcome their habits, even of heroin use, when they returned)[16] that gave the lie to the government's "drug prevention" propaganda, which, following Harry Anslinger's approach, had consisted solely of scare tactics that wildly exaggerated the effects of even onetime use of *any* illicit drug.[17] Anslinger's methods may not have worked on soldiers, but they had been very effective in scaring government workers, including J. Edgar Hoover, who reportedly had ruled that even undercover FBI agents were forbidden to engage in the use of marijuana. Whether or not this was true, it became a tenet of the anti-war movement that groups should always, "Pass joints to 'smoke out' the feds." In this climate, *not* to smoke was to be suspected of spying.[18]

In today's health-conscious atmosphere this may seem like a foolish rationalization. But with the possibility of going to war all too real for most young men, and the possibility of all-out nuclear war all too real for all Americans, long-term thinking seemed like a luxury to many. In fact, some young men purposely became addicted to drugs because addiction, and the effects of many drugs, could qualify the user for a draft deferment.[19]

Shortly after the end of the war, the Watergate scandal brought down the Nixon presidency. In its wake, reporters scrambled to conduct exposés, if only because they all wanted to be like Bob Woodward and Carl Bernstein, the *Washington Post* reporters who had broken the story.[20] Anti-war activists, once accused of paranoia, learned that the government cover-ups, disinformation campaigns, and attacks against opponents had been more blatant and better organized than even they had suspected.

Some policymakers saw this as an opportunity, or even a mandate, to create a more open government. "Sunshine" laws gave citizens access to many classes of government documents that had formerly been withheld, strengthening the Freedom of Information Act, which had been passed in 1966 but had not been well enforced before passage of the "Sunshine" laws;[21] and a reexamination of the assassinations of John and Robert Kennedy and Martin Luther King soon followed.[22]

But the lessons taken from this period varied. Some became cynical about government while others believed that government had been "cleansed." Some were drawn to government to change its nature, others in order to "infiltrate" a corrupt system and expose or sabotage it. Some saw the effects of government suppression and vowed to make the government more open, while others learned the tactics of coercive government and applied them to their own interests.

Nowhere was this last lesson more clearly exemplified than in the academic departments devoted to minority and gender studies, known collectively as "oppression studies" because they focus on the causes and effects of oppression on these groups. These were new departments staffed primarily by young faculty who had cut their teeth on anti-war activism and were eager to incorporate their "real-world knowledge" into academic theories. This was particularly easy to do because the theoretical bases for these programs were just being developed (and perhaps, as a result, have been slow in developing to any level of sophistication).

Therefore, while subjective and a priori beliefs had long been relied upon by ideologues who had no factual basis for their policies, some devotees of minority and gender studies *justified* them as a "methodology," arguing that objectivity and science are artificial constructs that can be ignored. The logic of this argument is clearly flawed, but proponents refuse to debate it—asserting that debate is a tool of the powerful that is inferior to "intuiting truth." They further argued "that women have effectively been 'silenced' by patriarchal institutions; hence . . . [there should be] an emphasis in women's studies programs on nurturing women's lost 'voice' in a nonhierarchical setting."[23] This embraces the theory that when people from the bottom of a stratification ladder embrace an ideology, they also endorse an instrument of their oppression, which leads to "false consciousness," that is, consciousness that undermines their struggles for freedom.[24] "The problem of false consciousness has long bedeviled the left, especially in its Marxist varieties. The assumption that large groups of people are blinded by a false consciousness has often been a handmaiden to repressive antidemocratic policies and regimes. The idea of false consciousness offers a convenient justification for discounting, dismissing, or even suppressing the preferences and beliefs of others."[25]

Ironically, when similarly repressive methods were used during the Vietnam War to withhold truths from the American people, it was the liberal tradition taught in American schools, especially schools of higher education, that allowed students to see through them. More recently, however, it has been in American colleges, especially in "oppression studies" courses, that these antiliberal ideas have been nurtured. Radical feminism has defined excellence, objectivity, abstract principles, intellect, rationality, and logical thinking as male constructs to be rejected. These ideas, in part because they were subjects of popular books, have become widespread and influential.[26] Similarly, some African-American studies programs teach Afrocentrism, "disinformation" which claims that Africans and Africa were responsible for virtually *all* major contributions to civilization.[27]

Let me be clear that there was indeed a time when the experiences and perceptions of most people, especially minorities, women, and the poor were overlooked in history and policy making. There is no doubt that attention to them is long overdue and adds important dimensions to our understanding of the world and of human needs. But philosophizing without factual basis that women and minorities think differently, learn differently, and "know" differently, and arguing that these ideas do not have to be supported by empirical evidence of any kind, weakens rather than strengthens the argument for addressing them.

As a result of the links between academic departments and their government counterparts, however, these groups of ideologues have been able to perpetuate their ideas by obtaining government funding to study them, teach them, develop programs based upon them, have those programs mandated, and eventually, present them as courtroom "evidence." They have been so successful, in fact, that ideological groups on the political right, which had at first attacked and attempted to expose them, quickly realized that they were better off copying them instead. This is a clue to why, while both sides attack each other's "facts," they less often attack the methodologies by which those "facts" were obtained. This is also a clue to why, in this generation in particular, so many ideologies have become "industries." Not only are their ideas pervasive, but these ideas generate funding for services that create numerous and varied stakeholders with vested interests in perpetuating these ideologies. Frankly, too, ideas do not have to be convincing to be pervasive — it is enough that legislators feel that they must throw bones to each of their voting constituencies, which is why most legislators support a few issues popular with women, minorities, the Religious Right, victims, and so forth.

However, allowing ideas into the marketplace of ideas requires vigilance. Permitting ideas to simply be regarded as "false consciousness," or nurturing the "lost voices" of women and minorities and to be dismissed by not subjecting them to the same challenges to which other ideas are subject, both infantilizes the idea-generators and creates the appearance that these ideas are unchallengeable rather than simply unchallenged. The ideas espoused in oppression studies are not universally accepted even by members of the groups they purport to represent, and the degree to which oppression studies courses focus on ideology and disinformation rather than appropriate academic content varies according to the school. This has been the subject of many books, represented in this text by extensive quotes from the writings of Christina Hoff Sommers, Cathy Young, Lynne Cheney, Thomas Sowell, Daphne Patai, and Noretta Koertge. The bibliography cites many of these works.

Some of these theorists posit that affirmative action has pushed some minority members into academic programs in which they are less capable than their white male counterparts, not because they are inferior, but because affirmative action has created inequitable "matches" between groups of white and minority students at the same colleges and universities. In geographic areas known to be particularly "politically correct," such as Washington, DC, New York City, and California, what began as a legitimate desire for diversity devolved into programs that accepted ever-increasing numbers of poor students, but failed to adequately assist those with deficient early educations, and accepted rationales endemic to oppression studies programs, which created disincentives to learn in lieu of providing adequate remedial assistance to those students who required it. (This may be a clue to why California was the first state to reject affirmative action, which may be less of a reflection of dissatisfaction with affirmative action than an extreme reaction to extreme overimplementation.)

Other theorists suggest that weaker and emotionally fragile students are drawn to oppression studies, where their concerns are easily translated into an us-them mentality. Whatever the cause, these issues have caused breaches within formerly cohesive groups, but none more than within feminism. These perceptions are echoed by Margaret Hagen in her 1997 book, *Whores of the Court*, which deals with psychologists who testify as "expert" witnesses to all types of unproven theories. Hagen describes the women who enter the field of psychology as reflecting two types: *fully developed feminists*, whom she describes as "women . . . who recognized the inequities in traditional roles and strove . . . to equalize the power and the responsibilities; and *arrested feminists* who embrace the idea of women-as-exploited-and-dependent." According to Hagen, these clinicians encourage their clients to distrust men, in part because they themselves may have been hurt, and in part because it increases the market for female therapists.[28] Tana Dineen, another psychologist critical of trends in her profession, refers to the latter group as, "the patriarchy in drag."[29] As she sees it,

Many female therapists have found that they can create a niche for themselves in the field by supporting the messages "women are safe" and "men are dangerous." This may be one of the reasons that the "don't trust men" message is so much a part of current practice and why it is so popular to portray men as villains and the cause of most of women's problems . . . perpetuating the same old arrogant know-it-all attitude.

Dineen notes too that this perpetuates the perception of women as needy and incompetent, a sexist attitude regardless of the sex that imparts it, but one that perpetuates the "clientizing" of women.[30]

Yet another trend that contributed to this was alluded to in the Dineen quote (and discussed more specifically in the book from which the citation was derived). That is, that as government "privatized" many services, mental health providers in particular were encouraged to become "entrepreneurial." Entrepreneurialism can quickly descend from client-oriented services to services focused more on marketing and client satisfaction than professional standards and client needs. Furthermore, entrepreneurialism tends to result in a proliferation of services targeted to those who can pay, or in today's third-party payment environment, targeted to maximize payment from available sources. Service commodification also compromises the role of client advocates, who often take on the unseemly role of advocating for their own self-interest as service providers and legislative advisors.[31] Universities, too, increasingly view students as "clients" whose "customer satisfaction" outweighs external standards such as grades or career success.

Of course, most women and minority students take traditional courses, graduate, and have successful, nonexploitive careers. But those who are poor students or who are emotionally fragile (cannot take criticism, deal with the stress of tests, and so forth) often gravitate to oppression studies, where they do not so much gain useful knowledge as learn justifications for their feelings of victimization, because the "nurturing of their lost voices" fails to challenge these perceptions. This is not to deny the existence of racism or sexism, but to recognize that some people seek excuses that externalize blame and exaggerate and even misperceive situations to their advantage. Such people are likely to adopt any currently popular excuse, especially if it is a "sacred cow" unlikely to be held up to logical scrutiny. These programs in turn funnel many of their graduates into the "helping" professions, which may be the only place that they are comfortable once they have focused so much on their own "damage" as well as that which they perceive as pervasive in society.

As in any movement, once certain common goals are achieved, those who have reaped the most, or needed the least, move on. The disgruntled stay, however, and instead of building on past successes, differentiate into separate interests and often develop a "philosophy" to explain why they are less successful. This is a clue to why the most visible strain of "feminism" today is the inverse of the original: focusing on why women are disempowered instead of how they can be empowered, focusing on protection *from* instead of rights *to*, and focusing on compensatory, and even special, treatment instead of equality.

This split within feminism began in 1982 at a Barnard College Feminist and Scholar conference called "Toward a Politics of Sexuality."[32] The editor of the anthology that emerged from the conference observed that "On the day of the conference, members of Women Against Pornography leafleted attendees with a flyer that not only decried and mischaracterized the conference but made allegations about the sexual practices of some of the speakers, calling them by name. This action caused lasting damage to those defamed." The final split came when Andrea

Dworkin and Catherine A. MacKinnon attempted to pass an ordinance in Minneapolis that would have banned pornography as a civil rights issue—an activity opposed by many feminist civil libertarians.[33]

Thereafter, the word "feminist" ceased to describe adequately the many women who support various legislation that they see as helpful to women. Instead, they were sorted into two categories by those aware of the split: those whom Christina Hoff Sommers has described as "equity feminists," who sought equal rights for women, and "gender feminists," who sought, instead, special protection for women.[34] However, this split has been largely ignored by the media and the public, who continue to paint feminists with the broadest possible brush and, as a result, blame all feminists for the excesses of the most extreme gender feminists.

"Anti-pornography feminists played into the hands of the right, which updated its morals campaign with feminist rhetoric and succeeded in demonizing sex itself—not [just] the harm done by sexual aggression."[35] In exchange, gender feminists obtained government sanctioning, along with government funding, to falsify statistics and stretch concepts in order to exaggerate the causes and degree of their oppression. Then their task became to perpetuate these ideologies so that they become equated with the mainstream issues to which they relate. This suggests why antipornography and antirape efforts have found greater success than other "feminist" issues—these are the areas that find coalitions of gender feminists, victim advocates, and the Religious Right, groups which agree on few other issues.

Perpetuating these issues is a difficult task, however. It requires not only spreading ideology, but denying alternative explanations. This requires not only an indoctrination to the ideology, but a "groupthink" that cuts off or dismisses conflicting data or debate, until people "own" the ideology. One way that this is facilitated is by focusing on the need for such a high degree of sensitivity that "every action and statement is painstakingly examined to see if it could somehow offend someone. Those who don't like that conformist practice risk being despised, even ostrasized."[36] These actions are at least as insensitive as the behaviors that engendered them, although this contradiction, too, seems to escape ideologues. "The purpose of all propaganda, and indoctrination, is not to force a man to *do* that which others will, but rather, through manipulation of his emotions, to force him to *will* that which others will."[37] Or, as Andrea Dworkin commented regarding her extreme view that all forms of what *she* defines as pornography should be banned, "The time has ended for dealing with materials that subordinate women in the way that a 'liberal political culture' usually does: that is, through reason and persuasion. We're not trying to convince them. We're trying to move society around so that they have to change or die."[38]

The ironic result of this split was that feminism was no longer perceived as a movement that loosened roles and stereotypes of all kinds, but one that demanded rigid conformity. Where it had once advocated sexual freedom, it now called for "policing"; and where it had once represented self-actualization and nonstigma-tized identity, it now pressured women to conform and, further, to reject those mechanisms that had led to male success, such as science, logic, and reason, for fe-male modes based on sentiment and identity politics.[39]

In her 1990 book, *A Fearful Freedom,* Wendy Kaminer offers a clue to this reac-tionary response to the original goals of feminism in the observation that "Equality doesn't presume sameness, but it does promise choice and the unsettling search for identity that goes with it."[40] *A Fearful Freedom* explores the ways that proponents of gender feminism have reacted to the fears engendered by the free-dom that equity feminists created, by attempting to renarrow "women's sphere." Such narrowing and oversimplification are not only characteristic of sanctified snake oil; they suggest *why* snake oil is so seductive to so many ideologues.

IDEOLOGY AND SNAKE OIL

Issues or problems are never in themselves "snake oil." Snake oil consists of in-effective proposed "solutions" to those problems that stand in the way of the im-plementation of better solutions. Often these solutions involve substituting the spread of propaganda under the rubric of "education"—and to add insult to injury, paying for it from funds earmarked for such concrete services as food and shelter. However, one aspect of "snake oiling" is to confuse the genuine problems with the bogus solutions proposed to address them. For example, women's status improved markedly after the beginning of the Women's Movement. This occurred not only because the early movement was successful, but because many of its priorities dovetailed with such factors as the economic need for dual-earner households and the lessening of infant and adult mortality that gave women more years to devote to work outside the home. In fact, feminism became somewhat superfluous there-after, except to some few extreme feminists who, dissatisfied with this degree of success, used "exaggeration, scare tactics, concept stretching, and raging rhetoric" to maintain interest in their issue. As a result, recent focus on sexual harassment and sexual and domestic violence, which all have a legitimate core, have been in-flated to "intensify the needs for . . . services, discredit opponents, assume male guilt, and ignore . . . inconsistencies."[41]

Alcoholics Anonymous (AA) is another example of an ideology that is effective because it is treated by adherents like a religion, which helps it to deflect criticism. In fact, detractors from Thomas Szasz to George Vaillant to Stanton Peele, who have all written carefully documented exposés of the ineffectiveness of AA, have seen their critiques virtually ignored by government policymakers who set drug treatment standards and, as a result, by the mainstream press as well.

This obfuscation of the line between scientifically proved methods and ideol-ogy is symptomatic of all sanctified snake oil. As Karl Popper explained in his seminal 1962 philosophical work on differentiating science from ideology, *Conjectures and Refutations: The Growth of Scientific Knowledge*, the essential difference between science and metaphysics is refutability. Claims not subject to refutability are then, by definition, ideologies.[42] And as Eric Hoffer observed in his 1951 classic, *The True Believer,*

It is the true believer's ability to "shut his eyes and stop his ears" to facts that do not deserve to be either seen or heard which is the source of his unequaled fortitude and constancy. He cannot be frightened by danger nor disheartened by obstacles nor baffled by contradictions because he denies their existence. . . . Thus the effectiveness of a doctrine should not be judged by its profundity, sublimity or the validity of the truths it embodies, but by how thoroughly it insulates the individual from his self and the world as it is. . . . If a doctrine is not unintelligible, it must be vague; and if neither unintelligible nor vague, it has to be unverifiable.[43]

In fact, recovered memory therapy, which purports to "retrieve," with complete accuracy, forgotten memories of abuse that "victims" have forgotten for years or even decades, is not only contrary to all that is scientifically known about memory, it is actually the translation of a principle of the "religion" of Scientology. Scientology is a copyrighted religion that science fiction writer L. Ron Hubbard based on the discredited pseudoscience of psychologist Karl Lashley. Lashley spent a quarter of a century trying to find the "storage site" for memories.[44] Ironically, RMT has been adopted by both "feminist" counselors (to support their contention that sexual assault is "pandemic") and by Christian counselors, because many "recovered memories" recall satanic rituals, which Christian ideologues promote as pandemic."[45]

Hubbard claimed that people are "immortal spirits who have lived through many lifetimes and accumulated traumatic memories that are obstacles to achieving their full potential." Scientology denounces psychiatry as a hoax (as have others)—but Scientology replaces psychiatry with its own form of "counseling," known as "auditing," which is both coercive and costly to members. (It is the financial pressure that Scientology places on its members, as well as its cultlike behavior, that the German government uses as a reason for refusing to recognize Scientology as a religion. In fact, the IRS did not recognize Scientology as a religion for twenty-five years and reversed its decision only after extreme pressure, including investigations of government officials by the "Church.")[46]

The parallel between religion and ideology does not end there. For instance, the real threat that evolution poses to "creation scientists" is not that it will shake belief in G-d, but that it will shake belief in the human beings who claim to speak for or interpret G-d to the masses. Yet the recent vote by the Kansas School Board to require creation "science" to be taught with evolution proves how even hard science is subject to ideology in the United States. Similarly, ideologues are threatened by heresy not because it threatens the ideals they espouse, but because it threatens the methods they use, the credentials and experience they have, and the spokespeople who claim to explain the ideology (i.e., patriarchy causes rape) the heresy rebukes. "Moral sermons easily seem priggish and unsophisticated, which is one reason the literary intelligentsia have usually despised the prevailing morality of their times . . . [but] combining race, gender and class criticism with the language of deconstruction [enables] . . . politicized criticism [to] give . . . deconstruction an apparent seriousness of purpose . . . mak[ing] a rigidly moralistic position seem avant-garde and sophisticated."[47] Wendy Kaminer has even suggested that religion causes people to develop habits of faith that then discourage them from thinking critically about scientific realities.[48] On the other hand, "unlike a true religion, the new dogma makes almost no demands on its followers. . . . Adherents need not demonstrate any spirituality or improvement in their own lives, or show any greater kindness to individuals. They don't have to examine their true thoughts and ingrained prejudices and hypocrisies."[49]

This confusion between ideology and religion is a common factor in the perpetuation of beliefs that have no validity. Yet ideology is more pervasive in government than is religion, presumably because the incorporation of religion into government (or vice versa) is clearly prohibited by the First Amendment. It is important to recognize, however, that laws prohibiting discrimination based on religion or the preference for one religion over another liken religion to ethnicity, race, and gender and also prohibit such discrimination or preference based upon *creed*— a synonym for *ideology*.

Many critics would go further, claiming that the ideological groups which support the use of bogus "treatment methods" are not only religions, they are cults. However, the definition of "cult" is itself too vague to be scientific[50]—people never define groups that they themselves belong to as cults, but they often charge that groups they disapprove of are (especially if those groups' beliefs have been adopted by their loved ones). The community commitment-building process in communes has been described as incorporating: sacrifice (abstinence from food, drink, sex, "worldly" adornments, books), investment (time, money, belief, renunciation of family), communion (regularized group contact, ritual), and mortification (sign of group trust, confession, mutual criticism, sanctions against deviance, de-individuating mechanisms).[51] Similarly, charismatic groups have been described as having a shared belief system, a high level of social cohesiveness, group behavioral norms, and imputed power to the group or its leader.[52] But degree of commitment to such groups varies, as does the degree to which conversion changes identity and beliefs.[53] Perhaps even more significant is the degree to which a group permits free thought and a climate for free thought: whether members are permitted time alone and time with others who do not belong to the group, and whether there are restrictions on what or how much they read. Extreme control clearly reinforces group beliefs, or what Irving Janis characterized as groupthink. "Groupthink-dominated groups [are] characterized by strong pressures toward uniformity, which incline their members to avoid raising controversial issues, questioning weak arguments, or calling a halt to soft-headed thinking."[54]

Such methods are also characteristic of witch-hunts. "Medieval witch crazes existed because the internal and external components of a feedback loop periodically occurred together, with deadly results. Internal components include the social control of one group of people by another, more powerful group, a prevalent feeling of loss of personal control and responsibility, and the need to place blame for misfortune elsewhere; external conditions include socioeconomic stresses, cultural and political crises, religious strife and moral upheavals."[55] Scapegoating was an important element of the craze, and ordinary people often use scapegoating as a means of resolving grievances.[56] These characteristics exemplify many current women's studies programs, which "also too often exhibit an anti-intellectualism and, more specifically, an anti-science animus."[57] In this way the recovered memory movement and feminism as it has come to be practiced on college campuses bear many similarities. Emphasizing subjective experience and solidarity leads to an ethos in which the objective truth of an accusation takes on secondary importance.[58]

In a similar way, the development of drug laws and the increase in enforcement have been characterized by "hysteria, demagoguery, racial bias, political opportunism, disregard for the weight of scientific evidence, and ignorance of the unintended consequences of the policies." Legal and social sanctions do not correspond with the actual harm caused by various types of drugs. Drug laws are not questioned by the majority of Americans; therefore, they are largely misunderstood, if understood at all. The drug war so violates American principles that Justice Thurgood Marshall referred to it as the "drug exception to the Constitution."[59]

One reason that drug-related snake oil is sanctified is exemplified by J. Edgar Hoover, whose attitude toward marijuana has already been discussed: "Since the use of marijuana *and other narcotics* is widespread among members of the New Left, you should be alert to opportunities to have them arrested by local authorities on drug charges [italics mine]." This statement is snake oil not only because drug laws were being used to target a particular ideological group rather than to control drug use, but because marijuana is *not* a narcotic.[60]

In a completely libertarian society, in which citizens would be free to do whatever they chose, as long as it had no negative consequences on others, but could not expect involuntary or automatic financial or other assistance from their fellow citizens, snake oil would be a personal, rather than a social, problem. Of course, in such a society (which has never existed in reality, although the early days of the United States represented its closest realization in economic, if not in moral, terms) there would be no entitlement to public income maintenance or other so-cial service, and no more than "the justice one could afford." Court-appointed at-torneys or government-paid expert witnesses would be impossible to imagine.

But ours is far from a libertarian society. Nor is it a truly egalitarian society, in which income would be redistributed directly to the needy, as in a negative income tax program. Instead, ours is defined as a "brokered" society in which government funnels money to (often ideologically driven) voluntary organizations, which then provide the services that they perceive the needy to require—to those of the needy they define, by their own subjective standards, to be "worthy" or otherwise eligi-ble for them.[61] As a result, snake oil poses a social problem for any taxpayers who prefer not to see their money misspent.

In fact, ideology is used to justify social welfare programs launched by the state. The reasons for the development of social welfare are inherent in the process of industrialization, and ideology is used by interest groups after that development to justify or oppose welfare programs.[62] Social welfare supports "the legitimation and preservation of the dominant classes."[63] Furthermore, the presence of ideology is most visible in the realm of personal social services. Therefore, how a problem should be solved, or even what constitutes a problem worthy of community atten-tion, becomes a matter for ideologues to define.[64] In one study that compares the alcohol-producing and alcohol-treatment industries, both industries cited scien-tific studies and quoted ideological positions to support their arguments, but both behaved according to other interests, keeping the sale of alcohol legitimate and keeping the disease concept of alcoholism in the forefront and treatment centers open.[65] Similarly, a study of educational policy making noted how ideology af-fected interpretations of the effectiveness of the Head Start program.[66]

It is clear that both political parties, and positions along the ideological spec-trum from far right to far left, support that snake oil which confirms their beliefs. It is belief, unadulterated by scientific proof of effectiveness, that most basically characterizes all forms of snake oil. For instance, "several leading feminist causes, such as Gloria Steinem's New Age spirituality, the eager promotion of repressed memory syndrome, twelve-step groups, transformative philosophy, and the insis-tence that incest and child abuse underlie alcoholism and eating disorders in women (but not men), were adopted straight from inner-directed self-help move-ments of the eighties."[67]

What is more, partisan politicians on all sides, whether due to their own igno-rance or their presumption of the ignorance of their constituents, endorse budget increases and cuts along ideological lines, rather than according to program effec-tiveness. So, for instance, politicians either support increases to Medicare or Medicare cuts, rather than increasing or excising discrete aspects of Medicare cov-erage according to the effectiveness of each specific service. This is because in our society, as this book demonstrates, government resources tend to go to "issues" that have broad, theoretical support, regardless of whether the methods used to solve problems are effective, or whether superior alternative methods or alternative problem analyses exist.

Add this to the idea of "oppression studies" and we see an insidious result: perpetuation of the belief that certain people, due exclusively to their gender, race, ethnicity or sexual orientation, are "victims" of discrimination. While there is more than a grain of truth to this belief, it overshadows the much larger issue of class discrimination, and conversely, gives some an excuse for personal limitations that they might otherwise be motivated to overcome. The result of the former is that rich women and minorities, due to their greater political power and access to the media, disproportionately benefit from taxpayer-funded services supported by the public to help poor women and minorities. The result of the latter is that some are so demoralized by the belief that no amount of effort will overcome systemic discrimination that they fail to take steps that could improve their chances for career success.

It does not have to be this way. The American public is intelligent enough to recognize snake oil, but it has been confused by government and media sanctification. Recognizing and eliminating sanctification of snake oil would eliminate this confusion, which would in turn enable the elimination of massive, wasteful government spending based on beliefs so close to religion that they would be found unconstitutional if challenged on First Amendment grounds. This would not only save untold tax dollars, and make America a freer country, but it would pave the way and free the resources to fund concrete services, innovative pilot programs, and the perpetuation of truly effective services.

Consider that the school system of the District of Columbia paid Abena Walker $164,739 to create an Afrocentric program as well as a teacher training program in "African-centered methodology." Mrs. Walker founded and ran the Pan-African University, an unaccredited and unlicenced school that had awarded exactly one degree—a master's degree to Abena Walker.[68] Sadly, some might conclude from this that DC residents, who are overwhelmingly black, are less intelligent than others, rather than seeing that DC's students are being poorly educated and miseducated and that this poor education translates into poor services to residents, as well. Keep in mind too that DC is not self-governed, but is overseen by the federal government. This speaks volumes about community decision making, and the lack thereof, as well as Congress's inability to see beyond ideology. In a pseudofeminist take on this attitude, Representative Carolyn Maloney of New York argued that the Intermodal Surface Transportation Efficiency Act was a "woman's issue"—because women make 10% more trips (on *all* modes of transportation) than do men.[69]

Ideological definitions can also distort service eligibility, skewing funds toward or away from those supposedly ideologically targeted for assistance. The $5.3 billion 8 (a) program of the Small Business Admininstration (SBA) directs a portion of federal procurement to "socially and economically disadvantaged business concerns," while defining its targets as racial, ethnic, and cultural minorities. As a result, it denied the application of a wheelchair-bound, formerly battered white woman because she failed to fit SBA's definition of disadvantaged.[70] However, the same program has provided assistance to black millionaires, including Colin Powell, O. J. Simpson, Patrick Ewing, Bill Cosby, and Vernon Jordon.[71]

There have been many reports about battered women's programs placing more emphasis on ideology than on services to victims. One of the reasons that there is an inadequate supply of shelter for battered women is that so much domestic violence funding goes to ideological "educators" who harangue audiences, ranging from high school students to police officers and judges, with inflated statistics about the prevalence of domestic violence. In fact, a "1988 nationwide survey of over 100 shelters found that about half stressed feminist activism over assisting battered women."[72] And an article on how feminists who started a battered women's refuge in Austin, Texas, lost leadership of it complained that

The new leadership [separated] the issue of feminism and sexism from that of battered women . . . [choosing] to look at battered women as a "family violence problem." It is [instead, according to Ahrens] essential that women who organize shelters have an identifiable feminist analysis, which encompasses an understanding of the ways in which that analysis affects services to battered women. . . . This policy is necessary in order to make all who come in contact with the shelter understand that feminist ideology is not a tangential issue, but basic and essential. It will serve the dual purpose of informing possible shelter participants of the ideological basis of the program, as well as continually place the issue of battered women in a feminist cultural and political context.[73]

Sociologist Claire Renzetti's survey of 100 battered lesbians found that 4 of them failed to go to their local domestic violence shelter because their abusers worked there. Other lesbians "are turned away from shelters,"[74] because shelter workers, "are unable to help women whose circumstances defy their 'understanding' of violence as a male-initiated problem."[75] This is also exemplified by the debate within the battered women's movement over disclosing the location of shelters. Proponents feel that visible shelters make the public more aware of domestic violence, make it easier for women to reach shelters, help shelters raise funds, and reduce the stigma of battering. Yet such publicity has endangered battered women and shelter workers.[76]

Battered women vary, as do their needs. No one shelter model will meet the needs of all women—nor will *any* model based upon the ideologies of its operators rather than the needs of its residents. A choice of models, reflecting various ideologies and providing specialized services would be ideal—but value-free shelters would at least be an improvement over the current system, which is itself responsible for making many women dissatisfied with shelter services. Ironically, no lesser feminist than the founder of the shelter movement in England, Erin Pizzey, has recently spoken out against the distorted ideology that assumes that women never contribute to domestic violence, an assumption that she fears has endangered the children left with violent mothers.

These misrepresentations make it appear as if the feminist gains of the 1970s and 1980s have had little effect, that reforms of rape and domestic violence laws, along with advances made by the victims' rights movement, sea changes in societal attitudes about victims, and pressure on law enforcement to enforce the new laws have had little effect. Failure to recognize these gains are now more likely to be the reason that victims still hesitate to report crimes and the public still feels that little work has been accomplished in these areas.

But that is clearly the hope of the pushers of "advocacy statistics." After all, if victims and society realized how much things have changed, the advocates might have to look elsewhere for employment. Instead, they redefine crimes so that circumstances previously undefined as crimes are now counted in crime statistics, and victims still seem underserved. Then they find new supporters for their distortions who want to be labeled as victims—who benefit from advocates' insistence that "victims" be treated so "sensitively" that they have to "prove" abuse only to the advocates!

Who would want to be falsely labeled as a victim? Divorcing women who can gain sole custody and even limit paternal visitation by such claims; poor women who are being cut from public assistance rolls unless they claim that they were victims of domestic violence; and homeless women who know that domestic violence shelters offer better accommodations than do homeless shelters, among others.[77] Hate crimes and stalking were shown to have gained attention because several diverse victim constituencies were able to stretch definitions of these crimes to redefine crimes common to their constituencies so that they would gain renewed attention.[78]

When I operated a program for rape victim counselors, I contacted the local Planned Parenthood chapter, recognizing that some of their clients seek their services as a result of rapes, including incestuous rapes. I was shocked to learn that it was Planned Parenthood's philosophy not to question their clients about the sexual activities that brought them there—out of respect for their "confidentiality." My work with victims of assault had taught me that most sought an opportunity to disclose their experiences, and that such disclosures enabled helpers to refer victims to other services they might need, including the criminal justice system. It is also important to understand that this perception of "respect" was not inspired by their clients, but by what Planned Parenthood workers *thought* (incorrectly, I believe) their clients wanted. It also, of course, shielded workers from hearing about assault—or from potentially having to testify in court. And it not only violated mandatory reporting laws, but also, ironically, limited the reporting of the very sex crimes that produced the most proof of having occurred—a pregnancy or sexually transmitted disease. Similarly, the San Diego County Grand Jury has observed, "confidentiality in the juvenile system can be used, not for the best interest of the child, but as both sword and shield against the families and the public."[79]

Another factor that distorts thinking is so-called political correctness. Historians have noted political correctness was originally developed by the Nazis and the Stalinists. In its wake were book burnings and purges of "liberal" professors from universities, and publishing was limited to authors who espoused politically correct ideals.[80] It is significant in this regard that the noted opponent of political correctness Daphne Patai lived and taught under the military dictatorship that ruled Brazil in the late 1960s[81] and that another opponent, journalist Cathy Young, was raised in the Soviet Union.[82]

Today we see attempts by so-called liberals to restrict speech on college campuses and elsewhere and to ban art as "pornographic." An outgrowth of political correctness is the subjective analysis of damage, so that anything that hurts anyone's feelings can be prohibited as politically incorrect. A comical example of this is that in 1996, People for the Ethical Treatment of Animals (PETA), observing that politically sensitive legislators had changed words in public place-names that were offensive to members of Indian tribes and other groups, petitioned New York State to remove the appellation "kill" from several locations that linked it with animals, such as Fishkill and Beaverkill. It had to be pointed out to PETA members that they were being ethnocentrically insensitive, since "kill" is the Dutch word for "stream," and that the many descendants of the Dutch settlers of New York State would find it equally offensive to change these place-names.

The most illogical extreme of this is the "self-esteem movement," which sees self-esteem as a means rather than an end. That is to say, self-esteem is, in reality, the result of effective performance or other positive qualities or efforts; but the self-esteem movement seeks to raise self-esteem by removing means that might lower self-esteem—including grades in school, punishment for bad behavior, and nearly anything else that might make nearly anyone "feel bad."

ADVOCACY AND SNAKE OIL

The Reagan administration strengthened laws prohibiting the use of federal funds for political purposes. Since then, however, advocacy organizations have not stopped their work; they have simply recharacterized it as helping the needy or advancing the "public interest" by "protecting" the consumer, the environment, or minorities. "This partly explains why the billions of dollars ostensibly spent each year to alleviate the plight of the poor, the hungry, the elderly, and the unemployed have had so little effect."[83] For example, the "National Endowment for the Humanities . . . authorized for public funding on the basis that scholars would search for truth, seek objectivity, and strive for excellence . . . [found that] these scholars were not only seeking financial support for projects that advanced their agendas, but sitting on NEH [National Education for the Humanities] panels recommending that taxpayer dollars go to politicized projects."[84]

Battered women's shelter directors have violated funding rules by resisting accountability, using funded resources for political lobbying, and "making up fictitious ratings for each other's proposals after divvying up the money." Not all programs are politicized, but some, such as the National Coalition Against Domestic Violence and its member coalitions, the National Resource Center on Domestic Violence and the Family Violence Prevention Fund, are "thoroughly ideological."[85] For example, a weak report devoid of references published by the American Psychological Association (APA) was incorporated into the proposed VAWA II legislation by these groups. The APA report recommends against custody or unsupervised visitation for men accused of abusing their wives, while claiming without any verification that women rarely lie about abuse to gain custody, and focuses only on the danger that fathers might present to their children.[86]

These forms of advocacy are most damaging when they are adopted by the criminal justice system. "Child protection workers are not expected to be impartial investigators searching for evidence of wrongdoing. Instead, they are advocates for children and commonly act on the presumption that children have been victimized in some way whenever allegations have been made."[87] This belief fails to protect children from overzealous workers, incompetent therapists, and parents who would use their children as pawns in custody battles.

Academia has not only been a party to such advocacy; it has also developed its own form, advocacy scholarship, which openly or covertly abandons the traditional obligation to deal with significant contrary evidence or arguments. In fact, advocacy scholarship is not scholarship at all, "for its research is not conducted with an open mind and its results are not presented with a view toward advancing knowledge about the subject treated. . . . What is novel in recent years is the degree to which one-sided advocacy in the guise of scholarship has gained respectability."[88]

Kenneth Lanning, who led the FBI's investigation into allegations of ritual sexual abuse and, after an investment of millions of dollars and years of effort, concluded that they were untrue, observed that "Abused children need more people addressing their needs from the professional perspective and fewer from the personal and political perspectives. This raises the complex and difficult question of whether individuals with strong political or personal agendas can even be professionals. While many can rise above their direct or indirect victimization and their individual or practical needs, some are deluding themselves in claiming to have done so."[89] In a comparison of satanic abuse in the United States and Britain, a British author noted that in the United States, concern centered on fears of family breakdown being caused by women going out to work, and child-care workers were accused of ritual abuse of children in their care, while in her own country, concern focused on the need for professional intervention to strengthen families, and families were accused of abusing their own children. "In both . . . societ[ies], there is not a profound sense that things are out of control. The fear and insecurity which results often concentrates first on worries about family breakdown and the vulnerability of children. The Satanic abuse panic crystallizes the fear that people feel about a loss of stability in society."[90]

Child abuse advocates are not unique in using these tactics, nor are gender feminists. In fact, "Feminist groups are no bigger (or smaller) users of advocacy information than any other special interest group." Public policy studies rank second only to advertising research in their disregard for truth and objectivity. In other areas researchers would be embarrassed to admit that their research was partisan, while this is a badge of honor in public policy.

Exaggeration, hyperbole, creative projections, wild assumptions and hand-waving are the building blocks of public policy research, where people fight for the ear of the people and the good of the world. . . . Most public policy wars are fought on huge plains, where people are counted in the millions, economic impacts in the billions and the very survival of mankind and the earth may be at stake—the very places it is most tempting to justify means with ends. Public policy studies are seldom challenged by either the press or public because they address mammoth and complex questions about which most people have little if any experience or knowledge. . . . In public policy debates and deliberations, words like decency, right and wrong, peace, fairness, trust and hope have lost their force. Numbers, which can offer so much illumination and guidance if used professionally and ethically, have become tools for advocacy.[91]

The *Boston Globe*'s environmental reporter, Diane Dumanoski, admitted that "There is no such thing as objective reporting. I've become ever more crafty about finding the voices to say the things I think are true. That's my subversive mission."[92] In another example, the last thing that former National Institute on Drug Abuse (NIDA) director Bob DuPont did before leaving that position was to give Nosy Parents' Association founder Keith Schuchard a contract to write a handbook on the parents' movement and the medical dangers of marijuana.

That Schuchard had no scientific qualifications to write a government drug-abuse booklet was, to DuPont, refreshing. The "experts" had let the country down, he thought, and it was time to put power in the hands of those with a real stake in the future of public policy.[93]

Or, it might be argued, it was time to give power to like-minded ideologues. Similarly, when a Research Triangle Institute study on the effectiveness of DARE (Drug Abuse Resistance Education), funded by the National Institute of Justice (NIJ), found DARE to be ineffective, an NIJ official reportedly admitted to "working with DARE to voice their concerns" about the study—hardly an impartial method of dealing with critics.[94]

In a similar vein,

President Bush proclaimed the war on drugs in September 1989 with the drums and flourishes of a rhetoric that was as cynical as it was dishonest. It was a genuinely awful speech, rooted at the beginning in a lie, directed at an imaginary enemy sustained by a false argument, proposing a policy that already had failed, playing to the galleries of prejudice and fear. The first several sentences established its credentials as a fraud. "Drugs," said Bush, "are sapping our strength as a nation. The gravest domestic threat facing our nation," said Bush, "is cocaine." None of the statements met the standards of either minimal analysis or casual observation. The government's own figures at the time showed that the addiction to illegal drugs troubled a relatively small number of Americans and that the current generation of American youth was the strongest and healthiest in the nation's history.[95]

An article in *Consumer Reports* observed that chiropractic "is a belief system that credits the spine with a major role in health and disease."[96] Although a July 1991 RAND study "concluded that [some] people with low-back pain might benefit from spinal manipulation,"[97] the field of chiropractic, developed by "magnetic healer" Daniel David Palmer, claims that it can be effective for such illnesses as irritable bowel syndrome, dysfunctional gallbladder, asthma, angina, prostate problems, impotence, and epilepsy—assertions which have never been proved.[98] Despite these facts, however,

Under pressure from a relentless lobbying campaign, the New York State Legislature pass[ed] a highly contested bill . . . that for the first time would require health insurance companies to pay for most chiropractors' services. Both chiropractors and their critics expect the measure not only to be a boon to chiropractors' businesses but also to bestow a new level of legitimacy upon a profession that has resentfully viewed itself as a stepchild of the medical establishment . . . in a testimony to the tenacious and methodical lobbying by many of the state's 4,500 licensed chiropractors and their patients, the Legislature turned a deaf ear to the critics' appeals . . . New York [is] the third state to require virtually unbridled access to chiropractors, though more than 40 states make insurers pay for at least some chiropractic care . . . physicians contend that there is little empirical evidence to bolster . . . claims [of chiropractic effectiveness]. Doctors who oppose the bill say that it confers official cachet on an unproven and potentially unsound profession.[99]

It is significant to note that the legislation does not limit chiropractors to lower-back treatment.

One of the problems with medical care in general, and mental health care in particular, is that it is impossible to quantify people's needs for them either individually or collectively. Despite the existence of hypochondriasis, however, most people avoid excessive medical care unless they are terminally ill and desperate. Not so with mental health care, which some people use as a form of self-actualization or even as a status symbol. More and more often, too, people are using the purported need for mental health treatment as justification to avoid responsibility for crimes and other bad behaviors.[100]

Ideologues are convinced that their issues are important and often believe that they are the only ones who really understand that importance. So it is not surprising that they use extreme measures and hyperbole to alert the public to their concerns, but, ignoring objectivity, they even go so far as to ignore factual evidence that contradicts their beliefs. It is vitally important that policymakers learn to differentiate between ideology and fact, to recognize the distortions in advocacy that parallel those in commercial advertising. It is only with this insight that policymakers can be alert to the difference between useful treatments and treatments that are well intentioned but ineffective or inappropriately used—especially when they are to be taxpayer funded, government mandated, or used in lieu of criminal sanctions.

NOTES

1. Lewis H. Lapham, *The Wish for Kings: Democracy at Bay* (New York: Grove Press, 1993).

2. Lawrence M. Friedman, *Crime and Punishment in American History* (New York: Basic Books, 1993).

3. Joseph R. Gusfield, *Symbolic Crusade* (Urbana: University of Illinois Press, 1970).

4. Ibid.

5. *High Times Encyclopedia of Recreational Drugs* (New York: Stonehill Publishing, 1978).

6. House Ways and Means Committee, April 27–30, 1937, Senate Hearing, July 12, 1937.

7. Carl Solberg, *Oil Power: The Rise and Imminent Fall of the American Empire* (New York: New American Library, 1976).

8. Sackett and Hobbs, *Hemp: A War Crop* (New York: Mason & Hanger Co., 1942); and *Hemp for Victory*, USDA film (Washington, DC: 1942); for a fuller discussion of these issues, see Jack Herer, *Hemp and the Marijuana Conspiracy: The Emperor Wears No Clothes* (Van Nuys, CA: Hemp Publishing, 1991); and Chris Conrad, *Hemp: Lifeline to the Future* (Los Angeles, CA: Creative Xpressions, 1993).

9. William Bragg Ewald, Sr., *Who Killed Joe McCarthy?* (New York: Simon & Schuster, 1984).

10. Marvin E. Gettleman, Jane Franklin, Marilyn Young, and H. Bruce Franklin, "General Introduction," in *Vietnam and America: A Documented History*, edited by Marvin E. Gettleman et al. (New York: Grove Press, 1985); John Kerry, "Vietnam Veterans Against the War: Testimony to the U.S. Senate Foreign Relations Committee" (April 22, 1971), in *Vietnam and America: A Documented History*, edited by Marvin E. Gettleman et al. (New York: Grove Press, 1985); and *The Pentagon Papers* (Boston, MA: Beacon Press, 1971).

11. Marvin E. Gettleman, Jane Franklin, Marilyn Young, and H. Bruce Franklin, "A Call to Resist Illegitimate Authority," in *Vietnam and America: A Documented History*, edited by Marvin E. Gettleman, Jane Franklin, Marilyn Young, and H. Bruce Franklin (New York: Grove Press, 1985); Rev. Martin Luther King, Jr., "Declaration of Independence from the

War in Vietnam" (1967), in *Vietnam and America: A Documented History*, edited by Marvin E. Gettleman et al. (New York: Grove Press, 1985); Colonel Robert D. Heinl, Jr., "The Collapse of the Armed Forces" (1971), in *Vietnam and America: A Documented History*, edited by Marvin E. Gettleman et al. (New York: Grove Press, 1985).

12. Senator Herman Johnson, U. S. Senate Speech, in *Home Book of Quotations*, 10th ed., edited by Burton Stevenson (New York: Dodd, Mead, 1967).

13. Marvin E. Gettleman, Jane Franklin, Marilyn Young, and H. Bruce Franklin, "General Introduction," in op. cit.; *The Pentagon Papers*, op. cit.

14. Marvin E. Gettleman, Jane Franklin, Marilyn Young, and H. Bruce Franklin, "Editors' Introduction to 'Vietnamization 1969–1975,' " in *Vietnam and America: A Documented History*, edited by Marvin E. Gettleman et al. (New York: Grove Press, 1985).

15. Ibid. Also see Colonel Robert D. Heinl, Jr., op. cit.; John Kerry, op. cit.

16. Ronald K. Siegel, *Intoxication* (New York: E. P. Dutton, 1989); and Norman E. Zinberg, "The Use and Misuse of Intoxicants," in *Dealing with Drugs* (Lexington, MA: D. C. Heath and Company, 1987).

17. Richard J. Bonnie and Charles H. Whitebread II, *The Marihuana Conviction: A History of Marihuana Prohibition in the United States* (Charlottesville, VA: University Press of Virginia, 1974); Chris Conrad, *Hemp: Lifeline to the Future* (Los Angeles, CA: Creative Xpressions, 1993); Ronald Hamowy, "Introduction: Illicit Drugs and Government Control," in *Dealing with Drugs*, edited by Ronald Hamowy (Lexington, MA: D. C. Heath and Company, 1987); Larry Sloman, *Reefer Madness: The History of Marijuana in America* (Indianapolis, IN: Bobbs-Merrill, 1979).

18. David F. Musto, "The History of Legislative Control Over Opium, Cocaine, and Their Derivatives," in *Dealing with Drugs*, edited by Ronald Hamowy (Lexington, MA: D. C. Heath and Company, 1987).

19. Colonel Robert D. Heinl, Jr., "The Collapse of the Armed Forces" (1971), in *Vietnam and America: A Documented History*, edited by Marvin E. Gettleman, Jane Franklin, Marilyn Young, and H. Bruce Franklin (New York: Grove Press, 1985).

20. Carl Bernstein and Bob Woodward, *All the President's Men* (New York: Simon and Schuster, 1974); also see Deborah Tannen, *The Argument Culture* (New York: Random House, 1998).

21. John B. Harer, *Intellectual Freedom* (Santa Barbara, CA: ABC-CLIO, 1992).

22. Gaeton Fonzi, *The Last Investigation* (New York: Thunder's Mouth Press, 1993).

23. Richard J. Ellis, *The Dark Side of the Left* (Topeka: University of Kansas Press, 1998).

24. J. Israel, *Alienation: From Marx to Modern Sociology* (Boston: Allyn & Bacon, 1971).

25. Richard J. Ellis, op. cit.

26. Lynne V. Cheney, *Telling the Truth* (New York: Touchstone, 1995).

27. Stephen Thernstrom and Abigail Thernstrom, *America in Black and White* (New York: Simon and Schuster, 1997).

28. Margaret A. Hagen, *Whores of the Court* (New York: ReganBooks, 1997).

29. Tana Dineen, *Manufacturing Victims*, 2d ed. (Montreal: Robert Davies Publishing, 1998).

30. Susan Sarnoff, "Interview with Tana Dineen," unpublished telephone interview (March 1998).

31. Pranab Chatterjee, *Approaches to the Welfare State* (Washington, DC: National Association of Social Workers Press, 1996).

32. Adele M. Stan, "Introduction: Feminism and the Culture of Sexuality," in *Debating Sexual Correctness* (New York: Bantam Doubleday Dell, 1995).

33. Adele M. Stan, *Debating Sexual Correctness* (New York: Bantam Doubleday Dell, 1995).

34. Christina Hoff Sommers, *Who Stole Feminism?* (New York: Simon and Schuster, 1994).

35. Ibid.

36. Martin L. Gross, *The End of Sanity* (New York: Avon Books, 1997).

37. Willard Gaylin and Bruce Jennings, *The Perversion of Autonomy* (New York: Free Press, 1996).

38. Quoted in Lynne V. Cheney, op. cit.

39. Daphne Patai and Noretta Koertge, *Professing Feminism* (New York: Basic Books, 1994).

40. Wendy Kaminer, *A Fearful Freedom* (Reading, MA: Addison-Wesley, 1990).

41. Daphne Patai, "The Making of a Social Problem: Sexual Harassment on Campus," *Sexuality and Culture* 1 (1997), 219–256.

42. Karl Popper, *Conjectures and Refutations: The Growth of Scientific Knowledge* (New York: Basic Books, 1962).

43. Eric Hoffer, *The True Believers* (New York: Harper & Row, 1951).

44. Susan Smith, *Survivor Psychology: The Dark Side of the Mental Health Mission* (Boca Raton, FL: Upton Books, 1995).

45. Ibid.

46. Douglas Frantz, "Death of a Scientologist Heightens Suspicions in a Florida Town." *New York Times* (December 1, 1997).

47. John M. Ellis, *Literature Lost* (New Haven, CT: Yale University Press, 1997).

48. Wendy Kaminer, *Sleeping with Extraterrestrials* (New York: Pantheon Books, 1999).

49. Martin L. Gross, *The End of Sanity* (New York: Avon Books, 1997).

50. Susan P. Robbins, "Cults," *Social Work Encyclopedia* (Washington, DC: National Association of Social Workers Press, 1995), 667–677.

51. Rosabeth Moss Kanter, *Commitment and Community* (Cambridge, MA: Harvard University Press, 1972).

52. Marc Galanter, *Cults: Faith, Healing and Coercion* (New York: Oxford University Press, 1989).

53. T. Robbins, *Cults, Converts and Charisma* (Newbury Park, CA: Sage Publications, 1992).

54. Irving Janis and Leon Mann, "Admiral Kimmel at Pearl Harbor: A Victim of Groupthink?" in *Public Administration: Politics and People*, edited by Dean L. Yarrow (New York: Longman, 1987), 251–260.

55. Michael Shermer, *Why People Believe Weird Things* (New York: W. H. Freeman and Company, 1997).

56. Quoted in Ibid.

57. Daphne Patai and Noretta Koertge, *Professing Feminism* (New York: Basic Books, 1994).

58. Lynne V. Cheney, *Telling the Truth* (New York: Touchstone, 1995).

59. Arnold S. Trebach in Arnold S. Trebach and James A. Inciardi, *Legalize It? Debating American Drug Policy* (Washington, DC: American University Press, 1993).

60. Hoover quotation from Dan Baum, *Smoke and Mirrors* (New York: Little, Brown & Co., 1996); Steven B. Duke and Albert C. Gross in *America's Longest War* (New York: Putnam, 1993) define narcotics as a form of depressant that inhibits the perception of pain by the central nervous system.

61. Pranab Chatterjee, op. cit.

62. Gaston Rimlinger, *The Welfare State and Industrial Relation in Europe, America and Russia* (New York: John Wiley & Sons, 1971).

63. I. Choi, E. Martin, P. Chatterjee, and T. Holland, "Ideology and Social Welfare," *Indian Journal of Social Work* 39, no. 2 (1978): 139–160.

64. Pranab Chatterjee, *Approaches to the Welfare State* (Washington, DC: National Association of Social Workers Press, 1996).

65. M. Chapin, "Functional Conflict Theory, the Alcohol Beverage Industry, and the Alcohol Treatment Industry," *Journal of Applied Social Sciences* 18 (1994): 169–182.

66. Maris A. Vinoskis, *History of Educational Policymaking* (New Haven, CT: Yale University Press, 1999).

67. Rene Denfield, *The New Victorians* (New York: Warner Books, 1995).

68. Stephen Thernstrom and Abigail Thernstrom, op. cit.

69. New York Post, "Taken for a Feminist Ride," *New York Post* (August 3, 1997).

70. Lawrence B. Lindsay, "Why Whites Are Never 'Disadvantaged,' " *Wall Street Journal* (October 8, 1997).

71. Stephen Thernstrom and Abigail Thernstrom, *America in Black and White* (New York: Simon and Schuster, 1997).

72. Cathy Young, *Ceasefire: Beyond the Gender Wars* (New York: Free Press, 1999).

73. Lois Ahrens, "Battered Women's Refuges: Feminist Cooperatives vs. Social Service Institutions," in *Community Organizers*, 2d ed., edited by Joan Ecklein (New York: John Wiley & Sons, 1984), 194–201.

74. Quoted in Patricia Pearson, *When She Was Bad: Violent Women and the Myth of Innocence* (New York: Viking, 1997).

75. Ibid.

76. Pam Belluck, "Shelters for Women Disclosing Their Locations, in Spite of Risk," *New York Times* (August 10, 1997).

77. Ibid.

78. Joel Best, *Random Violence* (Berkeley: University of California Press, 1999).

79. San Diego County Grand Jury, *Families in Crisis, Report No. 2* (San Diego, CA: San Diego County Grand Jury, February 6, 1992).

80. Martin L. Gross, *The End of Sanity* (New York: Avon Books, 1997).

81. Daphne Patai, "There Ought to Be a Law," *William Mitchell Law Review* 22, no. 2 (1996).

82. Personal conversation between Cathy Young and author, August 1997.

83. James T. Bennett and Thomas J. Lorenzo, *Destroying Democracy* (Washington, DC: Cato Institute, 1985).

84. Lynne V. Cheney, op. cit.

85. Cathy Young, op. cit in note 72.

86. Susan K. Sarnoff, "The Institutionalization of Misinformation: VAWA II," *Women's Freedom Network Newsletter* (August 1998).

87. Jeffrey S. Victor, *Satanic Panic* (Chicago, IL: Open Court Press, 1993).

88. Maryanne Glendon, *A Nation Under Lawyers* (New York: Farrar, Straus and Giroux, 1994).

89. Kenneth Lanning, "The 'Witch Hunt,' the 'Backlash,' and Professionalism," *The APSAC Advisor* 9, no. 4 (winter 1996).

90. Sara Hinchliffe, "Are Satanic Cults Stalking Our Children?" *Living Marxism* 75 (January 1995).

91. Cynthia Crosson, *Tainted Truth* (New York: Touchstone Books, 1994).

92. Quoted in Richard Berman, "Junk Research Distorts Public Policy," *The Oregonian* (January 4, 1998).

93. Dan Baum, op. cit.

94. Dennis Cauchon, "Yet High-Level Supporters Argue, 'It's Better to Have It Than Not to Have It,'" *USA Today* (October 11, 1993).

95. Lewis H. Lapham, *The Wish for Kings: Democracy at Bay* (New York: Grove Press, 1993).

96. "Chiropractors," *Consumer Reports* (June 1994).

97. Cited in Ibid.

98. Ibid.

99. James Dao, "Albany Is Poised to Require Insurance Coverage of Chiropractic Care," *New York Times* (July 27, 1997).

100. Alan M. Dershowitz, *The Abuse Excuse* (New York: Little, Brown & Co., 1994).

Chapter 3

The Sanctification Paradigms

The most important kind of tolerance is tolerance of the individual by society and the state. . . . When the state becomes the main thing and the individual its weak-willed tool, then all finer values are lost.

—Albert Einstein

Right . . . is the child of law: from real laws come real rights; but from imaginary laws, from laws of nature, fancied and invented by poets, rhetoricians, and dealers in moral and intellectual poisons, come imaginary rights, a bastard brood of monsters.

—Jeremy Bentham

Thus it comes about that all armed prophets have conquered and unarmed ones failed; for . . . the character of people varies, and it is easy to persuade them of a thing, but difficult to keep them in that persuasion. And so it is necessary to order things so that when they no longer believe, they can be made to believe by force.

—Machiavelli

To compel a man to furnish contributions of money for the propagation of opinions he disbelieves is sinful and tyrannical.

—Thomas Jefferson,
Virginia Statute of Religious Liberty

Having explored the characteristics of snake oil, its history, ideology, and the advocates that perpetuate it, this chapter will now analyze the ways that media and government increase belief in it through their own acts (and omissions), which I refer to collectively as "sanctification." It is this "sanctification" process, and not the mere existence of "snake oil," that leads the public to believe that "sanctified snake oil" is both effective and worthy of public expenditure.

MEDIA SANCTIFICATION

The media play a role second only to government in "sanctifying" snake oil. Consider the following statement by Nat Hentoff (which was written with no prompting from me):

Whatever his sanctified line, the true believer is wholly convinced he or she is acting in the very best interests of both the proximate and ultimate truth. And if he is on a newspaper, it is his responsibility to see to it that the readers are told what to think; that they are not distracted by ambivalences and ambiguities; and that no language can be used that could possibly offend any group whose side the paper should be on.[1]

Media coverage and the rhetorical strategies of advocates construct society's perception of the existence and gravity of a problem. Not only does this distort our image of problems of which we are aware, but it may keep us in the dark about problems with insufficient or ineffective constituencies.[2]

Bias contributes to sanctified snake oil, but it does not create it. "Bias entails a value-directed departure from accuracy, objectivity, and balance—not just a distorted presentation of facts. . . . Charges of bias are . . . frequently leveled incorrectly in response to superficial presentation of facts."[3] Echoing these sentiments, another reporter noted that reports of "junk science" are the result of "shabby research, superficial journalism, or a triumph of motivated public relations."[4]

Much of what is called political bias in the media is more often traceable to the fact that journalists are outsiders whose lack of in-depth understanding of issues as well as their deadline demands, cannot help but result in superficiality. "Bias also may or may not be ideological. . . . Bias may derive from various sources, including irrationality, illusion, prejudice, greed, ambition, and religious fervor. And the distortions introduced may be intentional or unintentional."[5] This suggests that although bias exists, it is often blamed for things for which it is not responsible, because it is easier to acknowledge bias than to acknowledge incompetence, laziness, insensitivity, and other causes of poor decision making and poor implementation of program goals.

Simply choosing which stories to pursue is a massive act of interpretation. . . . And taking an aggressive stance in wording and tone drenches news stories in interpretation. It is the very opposite of objectivity. . . . Appearance in print or on television has a way of lending legitimacy, so baseless claims take on a mantle of responsibility. . . . A scale will balance only when the items placed on both sides are of equal weight. When journalists showcase marginal, extreme, or even thoroughly discredited views and people in order to provide balance, they give them more weight than they deserve and bestow upon them the credibility of the press.[6]

A recent survey of public perceptions of the media, conducted by and published in *Parade* magazine, reported that the public perceives, and resents, media bias. The article reported that "the media need to eradicate bias in reporting . . . eliminate their editorial comments and limit news reporting to the facts. . . . Newspeople should keep their personal observations to themselves, whether they personally agree with them or not, and make every effort to be fair and just to all parties. . . . unless labeled as commentary, the news media should strive for objectivity in their reporting and keep their personal slant out of the reports." The survey found that respondents "think it is time that the news media start acting as if they are reporting the news to relatively intelligent and informed individuals. . . . [They want] more 'hard' news . . . in-depth reporting with enough solid information to give me some real understanding of the issues. . . . News persons should get better informed. . . . They often read reports with obviously flawed information and are totally unaware of the inaccuracies."[7] The media are not unaware of these criticisms. In fact, a group of journalists recently organized to develop a blueprint of core values, minimum standards, and better training and to create a greater connection to readers and viewers.[8]

Lack of historical perspective makes intelligent, dedicated reporters vulnerable to manipulation by people who wish to magnify one particular set of factoids that continuously streak across our information horizon. . . . In consequence, passing blips on the historical radar screen are all too often mistaken for major vehicles of social change.[9] Norman Mailer coined the term "factoid," which he defined as, "a piece of information that becomes widely accepted simply because it has been asserted and repeated, sometimes through the media, often by an individual with some culturally valued signs of credibility.[10]

Scientist Richard Dawkins described such "factoids" as *memes,* which he defined as "unit[s] of cultural transmission, or . . . unit[s] of imitation . . . just as genes propagate themselves . . . so memes . . . leap . . . from brain to brain."[11] (While there is debate in the hard sciences on the existence of memes, I use the term metaphorically here to suggest transmitted ideas.) Memes are easily manufactured and spread by those advocates whose government funding allows them to fill the mail with press releases that, even if inaccurate or vague, simplify the job of the journalist, who can quote them wholesale, and blame the sources if the information is later proven false.

Memes also have a cumulative effect. As a case in point, although crime rates actually dropped between 1991 and 1995, "the proportion of *media depictions of crime* quadrupled from 1991 to 1995 [italics mine]."[12] This is simply a manifestation of the age-old news strategy, "If it bleeds, it leads."[13] But this so-called electronic crime wave perpetuates the contradiction between the public's perception of the crime problem and the reality of crime.[14] Ironically, much coverage of crime is not editorially driven. "It's the easiest, cheapest, laziest news to cover, because crime reporters only need to listen to the police radio, send out a mobile camera unit, spend a brief time covering it and put it on the air." One study of early evening news in eight cities, conducted by NBC News, found that criminal justice stories took up 29% of the average newscast.[15] Other recent studies have found that around one-third of local newscasts consist of crime stories, even though the stations that were using the least amount of crime news were getting the highest ratings.[16]

It is interesting to note that many so-called crime waves coincide with election years and demands for higher budgets by law enforcement.[17] This exaggeration of crime is not new, however. Consider that

Lincoln Steffens and Jacob A. Riis, as New York newspapermen, once created a crime wave. Crime cases in the papers reached such proportions, both in numbers and in space and big type given to them, that the public demanded action. Theodore Roosevelt, as president of the reform Police Board, was seriously embarrassed. He put an end to the crime wave simply by asking Steffens and Riis to lay off. [Throughout this time], the official police record showed no increase at all.[18]

So we might conclude that, in addition to "media bias" sanctifying snake oil that fits the ideologies of members of the press, the media also sanctify snake oil for other reasons. By its focus on human interest stories, for example, the media presents single, extreme cases to the public—who often erroneously conclude that such cases are typical or at least representative, when they are more often atypical and extreme. And oversimplification—to fit a sound bite or to discuss a complex policy decision within the confines of a 500-word column—further distorts the public's perception of social issues. It is a primary rule of journalism to "get the human angle." However, with a complex, technical story, the concerns and fears of ordinary people always carry more weight than the cautions and quarrels of experts. Sloppiness and deadlines also cannot be overlooked as factors resulting in media misinformation. Accuracy is in conflict with both generating interest and meeting deadlines—it requires background work and waiting for confirmations, sometimes unsuccessfully. Furthermore, misquotes, or even errors of fact, are often buried in a correction box.[19] Accuracy in Media echoed this observation, noting that "TV has been quick to air the scare stories based on junk science and slow to report the hard science that refutes them."[20]

Media can assist in unfair vilification unknowingly, as when Senator Daniel P. Moynihan and former Secretary of State Henry Kissinger were both victims of

Lyndon LaRouche's libels, but, because the media discounted him as a "kook," little was done to clarify the facts. Even worse, a LaRouchian smear of Michael Dukakis (false claims that he had been psychiatrically treated for depression) was cleverly given credence by the then President Ronald Reagan when he refused to respond to questions about Dukakis' "condition" by saying that he wouldn't "pick on an invalid."[21] Media polls often distort, mischaracterize, or misstate policy issues.[22]

Distortion is at its most extreme when media report on statistical studies and scientific research. A cursory reading of almost any popular media report on research, by any but a handful of science editors who display a modicum of scientific knowledge, demonstrates that most reporters and commentators are woefully ignorant about the mathematics and the politics of research. Most will copy statistics from press releases without confirming their accuracy or seeking alternative interpretations of the findings. Pitifully few understand research methodology well enough to describe it, let alone to recognize methodological errors or omissions, such as lack of control groups, insufficient sample sizes, or nonrandom samples that nullify results.

These latter issues are often due to poor journalism. "The news media play a crucial role in misinforming people about studies, surveys and polls. Journalists rarely try to pull apart the inner workings of a study." The media also tend to limit data because many journalists consider it boring, perhaps because they do not comprehend its importance.[23]

The media perpetuate these distortions not only by failing to print corrections or retractions, but by burying them in small print on back pages. Few popular newspapers and magazines devote sufficient space to reader letters so that readers can become aware of the extent to which statements and statistics are contested after publication. Similarly, only a handful of talk radio and television call-in shows entertain real public debate about the topics they present, a factor that may be a clue to their popularity. For example, Spokane television newsman Tom Grant concluded that one reason the Wenatchee child sexual abuse witch-hunt was able to continue for as long as it did was that "most journalists just didn't do their job. They blindly reported assertions of people in authority. . . . As one man . . . said, 'The watchdogs turned out to be lapdogs.' "[24] A rare exception in another child abuse hoax occurred when

The Los Angeles Times published a detailed analysis of the media's coverage of the [McMartin] case, including its own reporting. [It noted that m]ore than most big stories, McMartin at times exposed basic flaws in the way contemporary news organizations function. Pack journalism. Laziness. Superficiality. Cozy relationships with prosecutors. . . . In the early months of the case in particular, reporters and editors often abandoned two of their most cherished and widely trumpeted traditions—fairness and skepticism.

As most reporters now sheepishly admit—and as the record clearly shows—the media frequently plunged into hysteria, sensationalism and what one editor calls "a lynch mob syndrome."[25]

GOVERNMENT SANCTIFICATION

Government sanctification takes many forms, which can be formal or informal, explicit or implicit, and recognized by government or not. This confusion stems from the fact that government oversight and government approval have limits and degrees, but the public is rarely aware of these parameters unless they are specifically challenged in court or in legislatures.

For example, governments set standards for professionals who are licensed in their jurisdictions, but licensing only guarantees that the licensee has met minimum standards set by the profession and the state to perform certain work. There is no guarantee that agencies in the state will limit their payments to those who are licensed. Some states have multiyear backlogs in investigating reports of malpractice and even unlicensed practice. Often investigations are not even conducted unless a complaint is filed, suggesting that much poor and illegitimate practice goes undetected. Professional standards are often lowered, or even ignored, when there is a particular need for professionals that cannot be met by the existing supply (or when nonprofessionals charge lower fees). Standards tend to be extremely low in states that have difficulty attracting sufficient numbers of professionals; many professional schools even hire teachers that lack teaching credentials or have not been trained to teach the courses that they do. Nothing about credentialing ensures that practitioners or even the field credentialed have any degree of effectiveness. One of the reasons social workers get such bad press is that, while "professional" social workers have at least a master's-level education, many government agencies give the title "social worker" to people with no more than a high school education. Most child protection workers fit the latter definition; and because their job is among the most difficult, dangerous, and thankless, some have other agendas for doing that type of work (if not ideology then the desire to earn referral kickbacks).

Debbie Nathan and Michael Snedeker reported that social worker Kee MacFarlane presented herself to the Los Angeles District Attorneys' Office as an "expert" in child abuse and offered to "interview" the children who had attended the McMartin PreSchool after allegations of sexual abuse by an employee of that school were reported. However, MacFarlane's experience was not in interviewing children for court testimony (a role traditionally—and legally—assigned to the criminal justice system in any case) or in determining whether children had been abused—MacFarlane's experience was with treating children who had already been determined to be abused. That is to say, MacFarlane had no experience with children who had *not* been abused and simplistically believed that any child brought to her had been. In fact, her faulty methods of questioning the children were later determined to have coerced them to lie (after they all had initially denied being abused at the PreSchool). But none of these facts prevented MacFarlane's agency from receiving both federal and (California) state funds to interview more McMartin children—and to train others in her methods of interviewing children! (Most funders know very little about the topic they are funding—and especially in government this is seen as a good thing, because it is perceived as avoiding conflicts of interest. Instead, funders look for grantees who will reliably spend their grant funds as they promise, because failure to do so carries the greatest sanctions to bureaucrats.) Nathan and Snedeker observed too that

The budget for the National Center for Child Abuse and Neglect is another example of the ritual-abuse panic's coattail effect on funding. In 1983, the agency had only $1.8 million to spend on all types of abuse research and demonstration projects (of that, only $237,000 went to sex-abuse studies). Following the McMartin scandal the next year, NCCAN's budget more than quadrupled, and included $146,000 to Kee MacFarlane to interview and examine more McMartin children. In addition, CII [Childrens' Institute International, MacFarlane's agency] received $350,000 in 1985 from California funds, making the institute that state's first publicly funded training center for child-abuse diagnosis and treatment.[26]

MacFarlane was not the only self-styled "expert," many of them clergy, who lectured and trained professionals around the country about what they claimed were huge, international conspiracies of Satanists who torture and murder young children. These reports led the FBI to conduct a seven-year, multimillion-dollar investigation which concluded that *no such cases had ever been corroborated.*[27] Nathan and Snedeker demonstrated similar career ladders for Joseph and Laurie Braga, who with the then Dade County prosecutor Janet Reno railroaded a series of cases in Miami, all of which have since been overturned because of the methods used to question the children. This exemplifies another way that snake oil becomes "sanctified"—government acceptance that leads to further perpetuation of the misinformation on which the "experts" have based their own practice.

How could a group of "experts" spring from nowhere? Ideological and religious groups offer "educational" programs as public relations tools to gain community acceptance and to interest likely converts. The link of Satan with child abuse and child caregivers enabled religious organizations to obtain government funds and then invite government employees to "trainings" on child protection that made themselves appear to be experts in an area long controlled (and funded) by government. The decreasing funds for social services at the time had decimated the training budgets of government agencies, which had also been lowering the educational requirements of staff for budgetary reasons. Government agencies were, as a result, happy to send staff to any training programs that did not charge fees to their agencies. Government funding for religious-based training appealed to the Religious Right who promoted these programs for their own sake and because they offered "modern" reasons to preach against working mothers and all kinds of sins, recast as "dangers to children." It also created a truly unholy alliance with so-called victim feminists, who also saw little difference between sexuality and sexual victimization and cast all women and children in the victim role.[28]

But the core of almost all of these cases was the "expert" testimony of a handful of self-proclaimed "evaluators" with special "expertise" in interviewing children and eliciting their reports of abuse. Some evaluators *do* have particular skill in developing rapport with children and encouraging them to express themselves; but, as the child sexual abuse witch-hunts demonstrated, too many of those who called themselves evaluation "experts" were really ideologically driven "validators" who assumed that abuse had occurred and then used spurious methods to convince others of what they had already convinced themselves. While such ideologues cannot alone turn false allegations into false convictions, when validators are used as "hired guns" by prosecutors, and when defense attorneys and judges fail to challenge their assertions, false allegations can lead to false convictions.[29]

In the Kelly Michaels case, for instance, "expert" Eileen Treacy constructed a thirty-two-point checklist of "symptoms" of sexual abuse, culled from various studies of children who were known to have been abused, and asked the parents of the children suspected of having been abused to record their children's behaviors on the list. By failing to train the parents in the use of the checklist and by not defining its terms, Treacy could count on their overreactions to any behaviors that remotely resembled those on the list, causing them to identify factors that "indicated" abuse. And indeed, she testified that nearly all of the children demonstrated signs of abuse. Jurors admitted later that they had been skeptical of Treacy's testimony, especially when she had claimed to believe the children's wildest allegations, including that Michaels had inserted knives in the children's rectums and made them do the same to her. (None of the children nor Michaels had any scarring suggestive of such abuse.) They were convinced, however, when the mother of one of the children stated on the witness stand that Michaels had told her that she was seeing a doctor for rectal bleeding. The jurors never learned that the mother had been investigated in a child pornography case, or that the charges against her had been dropped around the time that she had agreed to testify against Michaels, and Michaels' attorneys had been forbidden to question her about that case.[30]

Although Treacy called herself a psychologist (which she no longer does since being sanctioned by the New York State Office of Professional Discipline), her training had been in early childhood education, and she had no experience in counseling any patients other than sexual assault victims, nor did she have any experience with children traumatized by factors other than sexual abuse. She also had no experience in *evaluating* children for signs of abuse, other than having attended a handful of training seminars from true experts, which required no proof of having comprehended the material presented.[31] Treacy and a few other ideologues who, like herself, believed that child sexual abuse, including satanic ritual abuse, was far more widespread than others recognized, then began to declare themselves "experts." Since few experts existed, prosecutors desperate to address what appeared to be a sudden "epidemic" of child sexual abuse never asked them to provide credentials. In fact, Treacy has stated that "God gave [her] a special blessing" that enables her to help children disclose abuse.[32] Treacy's bias is also suggested by the fact that Michaels was acquitted on appeal, in large part due to a deposition from researcher Dr. Suzanne Sgroi, who was cited by Treacy as one of the experts under whom she had trained. Sgroi stated that her research had been misinterpreted and misstated by Treacy, who had made "indicators" of abuse appear to "prove" abuse.[33]

Treacy also testified in the fourteen Bronx Day Care Center (PRACA) cases. In those cases, Mario Merola, then district attorney of Bronx County, had staked his professional reputation, and his hope to run for mayor, on the prosecution of what appeared at first to be the largest case of child sexual abuse in the history of the country. When it became clear that the children's testimony was so bizarre and inconsistent that it would not withstand cross-examination, Merola ordered that the children be videotaped and that the videotapes take their place at trial. Information that might have exonerated at least two of the defendants was also withheld from the defense. All the defendants were convicted, and all of their convictions were later overturned due to the methods used to elicit the children's testimony.[34] Even today, few people are aware that these cases were overturned, and even fewer recognize that they were not overturned because of esoteric technicalities, but because no evidence existed against those accused other than Treacy's "interpretations" of the children's behaviors in the Michaels case, and their coerced statements in the Bronx/PRACA cases. Treacy has gone on to parlay her early "successes" into a lucrative career not only as an expert witness, but as a trainer who imparts her "expertise" to others.[35]

The pendulum appears to be swinging away from "recovered memories" and the most coercive forms of child interrogation now that so many of these cases have failed and so many malpractice lawsuits against therapists who have "uncovered" memories have been won[36]—the largest to date for $10.6 million.[37] But ideologues consign these efforts to the "backlash" that purportedly opposes all victim compensation and other victim-targeted services. Such a backlash does exist. Some of its most strident supporters purport that nearly all sexual assault allegations are false, and that such allegations are railroaded through the criminal justice system by radical feminist ideologues intent upon implying that *all* men are potential rapists, and obsessed government workers steal children from their parents to perpetuate the billion-dollar child protection, foster care, and adoption industries.

Not all of those who recognize—and question—the inequitable nature of victim benefits and services and their effects on criminal-case outcomes are extremists, however. Some have become aware of how far the child protection and criminal justice systems have become skewed away from due process—and toward rubber-stamping all allegations of abuse as founded—because they or their loved ones were falsely accused. Increasingly, too, professionals and concerned citizens are becoming aware of these problems. This last group, of which I consider myself a member, is also concerned that the very real systemic problems that the "back-lashers" have identified will eventually be addressed, as are so many social problems, by a pendulum swing away from all forms of victim assistance, instead of a simple rooting out of abuses.

The preponderance of cases that reflect sexual assault, used by ideologues to "prove" how frequent and serious these crimes are, glut agencies, cause processing delays, and ensure that the bulk of funding for victim services goes to a narrow group of victims (and others who claim to be victims). This suggests that other victims groups may be less than adequately compensated by the 3% of counseling that they receive,[38] which is woefully below the acknowledged need for it among victims of nonfatal, nonsexual violent crimes. In fact, "victim compensation" and "victim rights" are so skewed toward sexual assault victims, and more recently to adult female victims of domestic violence, that I would suggest that the current manner in which victim funds are distributed violates the "equal protection" rights of victims of nonsexual, nondomestic violent crimes.

In addition to making direct grants to service providers, government provides third-party payments by direct funding, mandates services and service levels that private insurers must cover, and perpetuates the funding of particular service models—such as Alcoholics Anonymous (AA) and DARE—when alternative models might more effectively meet the same goals that these programs purport to meet. Governments pay for ineffective treatments in the name of "client choice." Ironically, client choice is based on the faulty assumption that clients are capable of determining the type of treatment that best meets their needs. (HMOs justify requiring primary care physicians to assess clients' needs for referrals to specialists precisely because they know this to be untrue.) Furthermore, the very fact that government sanctions payments for certain types of "snake oil" implies (erroneously, as this book demonstrates) that these services are effective.

The role of government in regard to ideology, as with religion, is not to mediate among competing factions, but to make rules to ensure that the scales cannot be tipped in the favor of any one, few, or many.[39] As Charles Murray observed,

Government is the one entity in society that must be absolutely forbidden to discriminate. Whereas citizens and private institutions have the freedom to follow their tastes and beliefs, the government is permitted neither tastes nor beliefs. Government has only carefully stipulated arenas of action, and within those arenas the only thing that counts is whether the law, stated to the utmost limits of objectivity, has been violated . . . [because t]he government can back up its tastes and beliefs with police power.[40]

Murray also noted that "A free society is most threatened not by uses of government that are obviously bad, but by uses of government that seem obviously good."[41] James Madison wrote in the *Federalist Papers, No. 10*, that "among the numerous advantages promised by a well-constructed union, none deserves to be more accurately developed than its tendency to break and control the violence of faction." Throughout history, governments that failed to do this introduced "instability, injustice and confusion" into public life, which are "the mortal diseases under which popular governments have everywhere perished."[42]

"Liberalism embraces individual rights and *negative liberty*, or liberty *from* government interference." [Italics mine.][43] "The separation of church and state, the sanctity of the doctor-patient relationship, the lifetime appointments of federal judges, and the exemption of spouses from testifying against one another in court are just some of the examples of . . . attempts to provide insulation from government power and the political process."[44] These observations suggest that government should limit its purview because it is constitutionally mandated to do so. Justice Louis Brandeis offered yet another reason, that "Our government does not now grapple successfully with the duties which it has assumed, and should not extend its operations at least until it does."[45] On the other hand, "one of the pleasant side effects of limited government [is that it] doesn't get blamed for failing to solve problems that are none of its business."[46]

THE SNAKE-OILING OF NEEDS

The concept of need can be separated into:

- "substantive needs," for such items as food, safe shelter, and medical care; and
- "culturally determined needs," which are better defined as desires or expectations.

One analysis of culturally determined needs distinguished four types:

- "*normative need* refers to some condition of an individual that falls below a standard held by the community or prescribed by some knowledgeable authority;
- *felt need* refers to a need that is recognized by the individual in question, it is equated with want . . . and . . . is limited by the individual's awareness of the condition and by the individual's own standard of acceptable functioning;
- *expressed need* refers to a felt need that has been converted into an attempt by the individual to satisfy or fulfill it; and,

• *comparative need* refers to the condition of the individual significantly below the average level of that condition in a group of comparable individuals."[47]

Not only do these definitions stretch the concept of need beyond ordinary perceptions of it; ideologues also claim that needs imply rights. While "rights" in this sense exist nowhere in law, this argument is often effective with legislators seeking excuses to expand government.

"Questions about human needs are questions about human obligations. To ask what our needs are is to ask not just which of our desires are strongest and most urgent, but which of our desires give us an entitlement to the resources of others. . . . Need is the vernacular of justification, specifying the claims of necessity that those who lack may rightfully address to those who have."[48]

Yet social services require an even further conceptual stretch, because social services, as distinguished from concrete services such as direct provision of food and shelter, do not directly meet needs—instead, they provide services that professionals and other experts determine the needy should have. So, while social services have proliferated, people often experience difficulty reaching them and finding a near equivalence between their needs and the programs' services. This search is especially difficult for the poor, the ill or injured, and the elderly—and many people in need have at least one, and often many, of these characteristics. When resources are located, eligibility criteria and other barriers may obstruct access to services. Inquirers may be shunted from agency to agency, and many are so overwhelmed by such impediments as language barriers, inconvenient hours, and remote locations, that they give up altogether. These barriers as well as fragmentation and other inadequacies have prompted one analyst to describe our society as "overserviced but underserved."[49]

Professional ethics, furthermore, require that each client be treated individually, differentially, and holistically.[50] But agencies are loathe to expend resources to help clients who fall outside of their narrow purviews. This results in a conflict between agencies' limited service goals and professionals' relatively unlimited commitments, which is one reason that a relatively small proportion of professionals work in public assistance agencies.[51] It also suggests why professionals often feel justified in stretching the truth so that their clients can be, or can appear to be, eligible for services. Many social workers "are resolved to fight and reform . . . institutional systems . . . and are dissidents and rebels . . . who tend to bend and break rules on behalf of their clients."[52]

Consider what happens when such ideas are "justified" by theory and even written into law, as in the case of the Violence Against Women Act (VAWA), which exaggerated the extent and causes of violence to justify special rights for women victims. The Women's Freedom Network's Amicus Brief opposing VAWA summarized its arguments by stating, "The Violence Against Women Act . . . is an unconstitutional use of Congressional power. Attempts to justify the law's constitutionality are not predicated on sufficient facts that sexual and domestic violence are gender-based." The brief goes on both to note that "the feminist view of rape as a gender-based hate crime does not have wide acceptance in the research community" and to identify five studies published since 1983 which disprove that theory. It further states that "when levels of injury and other factors were taken into account, there was no difference in arrest rates between domestic and non-domestic disputes."[53]

On May 15, 2000, in a 5 to 4 decision, the Supreme Court overturned the only portion of VAWA to reach that level of review. The Court determined that "the Commerce Clause does not provide Congress with authority to enact [VAWA's] civil remedy." This decision invalidated VAWA's mechanism for allowing plaintiffs to sue attackers in civil court without a criminal finding against them.[54]

WHY DOES GOVERNMENT PERPETUATE BELIEF IN SNAKE OIL?

Government is not a monolith. Therefore, different arms of government, at different times, will have philosophies, goals, and priorities that vary from past policies and the policies of other agencies. And this too is significant to note about the sanctification of snake oil. It does not matter which ideological group aligns with which political party to advance its aims. Once it succeeds, the machinery of funding is put into place to advance the ideology; create bureaucratic positions in agencies that fund service, training, and prevention programs; dispense jobs; approve bill payments; define concepts; and otherwise create and perpetuate sanctified snake oil. It can then be used by any group, of any ideology, that aligns with a party in power. As investigative reporter Charles Babcock of the *Washington Post* observed, "there's an industry that grows up around every program [in Washington, DC]."[55]

Government programs in the United States that are targeted to the poor have often been more effective at creating bureaucratic jobs for the middle class than at actually helping poor people, but this says more about how government is run than about the possible effectiveness of government if its priorities were altered.[56]

Mankind . . . makes a poorer performance of government than of almost any other human activity . . . [yet] folly in government has more impact on more people than individual follies, and therefore governments have a greater duty to act according to reason. . . . a limiting factor is too many subjects and problems in too many areas of government to allow solid understanding of any of them, and too little time to think. . . . This leaves the field open to protective stupidity. Meanwhile bureaucracy, safely repeating today what it did yesterday, rolls on ineluctably as some vast computer, which, once penetrated by error, duplicates it forever. . . . the guiding principle in these pursuits is to please as many and offend as few as possible. Intelligent government would require that the persons entrusted with high office should formulate and execute policy according to their best judgment, the best knowledge available and a judicious estimate of the lesser evil. But reelection is on their minds, and that becomes the criterion.[57]

This is not to suggest that government imperfection is merely benign folly. Sometimes this confusion can be exploited for less innocent or accidental ends.

Policy makers are forced into [a] deceptive stance by the culture of autonomy, which says, in essence, that public officials are not supposed to make moral judgments in their official capacity; that their sole legitimate job is to protect the public and individuals from harm. In other words, we first purport to find something to be harmful to others, then on that ground label it wrong. In reality, we often first conclude that something is wrong, then seek evidence that it is harmful. Under these circumstances, it is not surprising that "evidence" is sometimes exaggerated or even manufactured.... The culture of autonomy ... has grown out of the transformation of political liberalism into social liberalism and an expansion of the paradigm governing the relationship between the individual and the state to cover all relationships and areas of social life.[58]

Government has no justification for extending its purview, given not only that limited government is constitutionally mandated but that government has not been effective in any of the areas into which it has expanded; it creates a pseudo-justification for doing so, however, by buying into the public's belief that every problem has a solution, and then spending public resources for whatever programs satisfy constituents. (This is not difficult because "the votes that keep government in office come primarily from citizens who are judging government programs based on their outside perception of them").["59]

As a result, the degree to which government provides rights and services to particular individuals depends far more on current administrators' orientations toward social welfare than on individual or group rights, needs, or government resources. Worse, when budgets are expanded or reduced, politicians scramble to ensure that their constituents' wants continue to be met, with no concern, and usually no awareness, of the effects that this has on truly needy individuals. Thwarting orthodoxy is not condoned—even by those who disagree with the orthodoxy. University of Rochester economics professor Steven E. Landsburg has suggested, in fact, that bipartisanship in Congress is tantamount to an antitrust violation.[60]

Politicians feign ignorance of these issues as they rubber-stamp approvals for services that, despite their ineffectiveness, are desired by their constituents. Even conservative policymakers who recognize that trade-offs will be necessary to pay for these services are happy to jump on a political bandwagon full of constituents who will support those who vote their way. In this age of political apathy, politicians need to show gratitude to any constituency that seems interested in issues and voting records.

These issues appeal to politicians for another reason as well. As long as the public is focused on fixing themselves, there will be less attention on fixing society, or on blaming politicians who have failed in that area. "Treatment" is, despite its association with liberals who support payments for mental health care and drug treatment in lieu of jail for some offenses, a very conservative concept, because it assumes that problems can be solved by changing individuals, rejecting strategies to strengthen communities and institutions that impose problems on otherwise functional people.

In fact, numerous analysts have demonstrated that the neediest always fare worse than less needy but more middle- or upper-class and more highly functional individuals in obtaining public benefits, because being able to access help is in itself a sign of strength.[61] The groups that benefit most are professionals who define and design the services according to their own preferences. Sometimes, too, the benefits serve a social-control function designed more to enforce behavior than to benefit recipients.[62]

Some well-meaning policies are fatally flawed because they establish privileged rights and entitlements that remove critical issues from the give-and-take of the deliberative process.[63] "One important reason Congress has made little effort to control the use of tax funds for political purposes is that there has been almost no pressure from taxpayers to address the problem."[64] It is obvious how these conditions reinforce each other. Taxpayers are satisfied that "issues" are being addressed, without realizing how this is being done. This fact prompted one policy analyst to describe some social programs as "political placebos"—programs that are effective only in convincing the public that "something is being done" about the problems the programs purport to address.[65]

In fact, it is only when a lawsuit or public hearing questions a policy that its fine points reach the attention of the population. This would not be true if the media adequately covered this level of policy making—and if the public rewarded the media for doing so. But government clearly fails to restrain policy making without public exposure. In part, this is in response to the fact that "the American public . . . refuses to believe that some problems simply do not have current solutions, at least not workable ones. . . . The irony is that recent conservative presidents, who have long mouthed slogans about states' rights and local government, have been more zealous than the liberals in denouncing crime, drug use, and the like. They have thus helped keep alive the myth that the federal government can actually do something about the problem. In fact, there is not much the federal government *can* do."[66]

A well-established social problem functions as a resource.[67] One analysis considers social policy a "garbage can" into which policymakers "throw" issues and purported solutions, with the garbage can then becoming a resource—for any that choose to exploit it.[68] This is known as "the bandwagoning effect." According to

Eva Bertram, et al., "Bureaucrats will jump onto promising political bandwagons . . . in order to sustain or increase their budgets."[69] The most obvious result of this is that, as numerous social scientists have pointed out, the government is inherently prone to inflation. Politicians find it easier to yield to demands for more public services than to reject them.[70]

However, this strategy is beginning to backfire as government costs grow and government becomes increasingly bogged down by a range of diverse demands, which make the public dissatisfied because no services seem to operate as effectively as the public believes they should. A *Times Mirror* poll revealed that nearly 70% of the public believes that government services are generally inefficient and wasteful, too intrusive into our personal liberty, and often not worth the trouble. However, the public now believes this largely because it has been lied to so much in the recent past—although most of the lies have come from political leaders rather than from bureaucrats, for whom the public has greater contempt.[71] Politicians' primary concerns are to preserve their positions and to bring attention to themselves. Politicians use crusades to respond to both concerns. Crusades also justify taking resources from other representatives' constituencies and funneling them back into their own.[72]

In view of these factors, it is important to recognize, regardless of one's political view of social benefits, that it is not the amount of money budgeted to a particular social program that will determine its ultimate effects. It is the eligibility for those benefits, the types of services covered, and the circumstances under which they will be provided that will ultimately determine whether citizens will demand that their "right" to these benefits be honored, or whether benefits are forced to be expanded by the judiciary because they are being distributed in a discriminatory fashion. For instance, "Once [the women's movement] could use the law to compel, people no longer tried to persuade. What had been an evolutionary working out of a complicated set of problems became an us-versus-them resentful battle presided over by the bureaucrats and their statistical guidelines."[73]

Matthew Lesko has identified over 1,000 government programs that annually provide more than $190 billion in loans and $287 billion in grants and direct payments. Individuals are eligible for 519 programs; not-for-profit organizations, for 496 programs; and state and local governments, for 796 programs.[74] The recipients of government grants and contracts tend to advocate greater government control over and intervention in the private sector, greater limitations on rights to property, more planning by government, more income redistribution, and more political decision making.[75] Policymakers tend to view the politically powerless as incapable of making correct choices, which rationalizes paternalistic policies that place control over choices in the hands of government officials or other experts.[76] In this way, officials can claim to act on behalf of anything that they can classify as the common good.[77] As one critic observed, "Once government began to see its role as doing good, the sense of what government does well got lost, overwhelmed by the sense of what government ought to *try* to do."[78]

The programs thus created range from *Sex Respect* to VAWA. *Sex Respect* was a curriculum developed by Colleen Kelly Mast of Golf, Illinois, an antiabortion activist with a $300,000 grant that the Reagan administration made to the Committee on the Status of Women in 1986. The committee was later stripped of federal funding for violating the constitutional separation of church and state in making this grant. *Sex Respect* argues against promiscuity and premarital sex. This twelve-week course, which has been used in more than 1,500 school districts, has not been without critics. In Enfield, Connecticut, the program was abandoned when parents complained that it taught children "fear, guilt and shame."[79] On the other hand, VAWA wrote into law theories of Catherine MacKinnon and Andrea Dworkin—a development that Dworkin found so amazing that she commented, "The only possible explanation for it is that senators don't understand the meaning of the legislation they pass."[80] These programs may appear to be widely disparate, but they share the fact that they both constitute sanctified snake oil—they are sanctioned by government but are not based on accurate information, and they are as unconstitutional as they are ineffective.

WHY DOES THE PUBLIC SUPPORT SNAKE OIL?

We live in an age when people believe—with absolutely no evidence—that every problem can be solved. So it should be no surprise that many people choose to believe those who tell them that they have solutions, particularly if their solutions are global enough to solve all problems. In recent years we have heard that all of the problems of society stem from poverty, paternalism, feminism, lack of family values, discrimination, lack of self-esteem, efforts to end discrimination, drug use, the war on drugs, and just about every other single issue imaginable. It is preposterous to believe that any issue *alone* could be the cause of all human difficulties, and even more preposterous to think that a single solution could correct any problem in *any* case, but it is also seductive to believe that finding a single solution could make "all right with the world."

Americans display an unusual willingness to hold onto ideologies even when they fly in the face of incontrovertible facts. While this certainly can occur in other countries, it appears to be most problematic in the United States. "Traditional" countries may base their actions on ideology and ignore fact gathering, resulting in more harmony, even if only because tradition is not challenged. More modern countries can dictate policy based upon facts without fearing considerable opposition because those countries' citizens are more inclined to leave policy making to elites and because elites are respected there.[81]

American populism favors majority opinion over those of "experts"—even when the majority remains ignorant of relevant facts. Few Americans understand how to access data or its sources, and because so much information in this country is presented with a biased slant, many despair of discerning truth and choose sides as if they were selecting ice-cream flavors, by preference rather than research. To make matters worse, although we look to science to "fix" many of these problems, Americans have a general disdain for scientific proof and empiricism. Perhaps this stems from the fact that Americans have less knowledge of science and math than their contemporaries in other First World countries.[82] Yet rather than be embarrassed by ignorance, Americans disdain not only the need for this skill but the skill itself. This suggests that the oppression studies theories are closer to the American mainstream than critics care to admit.

The authors of *Words that Wound* equated debate over affirmative action with "an emerging and increasingly virulent backlash" against women and people of color. "The code words of this backlash," they wrote, "are words like merit, rigor, standards, qualifications, and excellence."[83] Such books as *In a Different Voice* and *Women's Ways of Knowing*, which purport that women have "different" ways of thinking, tell us that rigid, linear, mathematical thinking is just one style of learning information and that other, more "intuitive" styles are equally viable. This is pure nonsense, no doubt concocted by people whose self-esteem is threatened by their ignorance of science, math, and logic. It also insults the many members of racial minorities and women who are successful scientists, mathematicians, and critical thinkers—and intimidates those who might attempt to gain these skills if they were not continually told that they are too "different" to do so. (Ironically, ideologues who have no difficulty identifying their opponents' code words, fail to see that "different" is nothing more than a code word for "inferior," much like "special" when it is used to refer to the developmentally disabled.)

Furthermore, by claiming that objectivity, reason, rules, individual rights, and autonomy are male concepts, so-called victim feminists make women appear unqualified to make decisions.[84] Ironically, one result is that feminists on many American college campuses subvert the tradition of academic traditions. "Intolerance, anti-intellectualism, and ideological policing produce work that is shaped . . . by an ideological agenda. . . . The effort at 'leveling' . . . has led some to observe . . . that the feminist notion of 'empowerment' seems to result above all in the equal disempowerment of each by all."[85]

But consider white males' contributions to this attitude. New York University professor Thomas Bender labeled scholars who insist on accuracy "fact fetishists," and former White House aide George Stephanopoulos, pressed about inconsistencies in remarks made by President Clinton, accused his questioners of "an excess of literalism."[86] As Richard Hofstadter demonstrated in his 1955 classic, *The Age of Reform*,[87] and as Richard J. Ellis more recently demonstrated in his 1998 book, *The Dark Side of the Left*,[88] such ideologies have existed throughout American history and across political spectra. However, today gender feminists are clearly among those who have brought the sanctification of snake oil to the level of an art form. The reason for this is suggested by the fact that feminist bias is not only not discredited, but frequently rationalized by referring to prior biases of men. This is not only irrational, but has been characterized as "emulation of the thing being rejected."[89]

To exemplify several of the previous statements, consider that for at least the past two decades, the government and the media have regarded battered women's advocates as domestic violence experts, resulting in millions of dollars in federal and state funding going to advocacy groups that often conduct officially sponsored training seminars for the criminal justice system. The ideological materials used for training by these groups reflect pseudostatistics which suggest, erroneously, that male violence against women is epidemic. Activists also act as advisors to victims and liaisons with court personnel, sometimes possessing influence and authority rivaling that of district attorneys. In many areas, women who report domestic violence are automatically referred to battered women's groups. Some police officers are even accompanied on domestic violence calls by staff or volunteers of domestic violence programs.[90]

One result of such sanctified snake oil is that funds allocated to domestic violence "services," which many members of the public assume to be shelter or assistance to help women become self-sufficient, are often used to "educate" people not directly involved with domestic violence, using pseudofacts that distort their perceptions of the problem. One such pseudofact was that a 1984 study published in the *Journal of the American Medical Association* demonstrated that 22% of emergency room visits by women were for injuries sustained by domestic violence. On its face, this statistic is ludicrous to anyone who is aware of the incidence of injury, especially as a result of automobile crashes, or anyone who has simply spent time in an emergency room. In fact, the study never made that claim—it asked women in emergency rooms if they had *ever* experienced domestic violence, and 22% responded that they had. In spite of the facts, the misperceived results of the study were spread with extreme speed and little caution by domestic violence and victim advocates, by journalists happy to regurgitate the advocates' press releases rather than investigate the facts for themselves, and by others who should have known better or at least been more cautious. In 1989, when a study published in the *American Journal of Public Health* was similarly misconstrued, this time to reflect a 30% rate of domestic violence injuries, advocates immediately increased their figure. This bogus statistic even found its way into a booklet on workplace violence published by Polaroid.[91]

Research to determine the effectiveness of various interventions with battered women is frowned upon—only research that reflects the ideology of advocates is considered acceptable by them.[92] Recall that Erin Pizzey made a similar observation. Research limited only to self-identified "risk groups" would be intolerable in most other areas of scholarly inquiry. Such studies present one-sided views of very complex issues. Research on batterers is similarly narrowly focused and tends not to make comparisons with normal males. In fact, some ideologues reject the idea that "normal males" exist, instead assuming that battering is an aspect of maleness rather than a pathology amenable to correction. On the contrary, however, significant research demonstrates that batterers are likely to manifest substance abuse and other personality disorders. By discounting or ignoring these factors, however, domestic violence advocacy researchers define maleness itself as pathology.[93]

Some instances of research distortion by gender feminists are now well known. Christina Hoff Sommers detailed the range of statistics on violence against women from different sources. She observed that estimates of women brutalized by men in the United States range from 626,000 per year (U. S. Department of Justice, 1991) to 1.8 million (*Behind Closed Doors: Violence in American Families*) to 3 million (Senator Joseph Biden, 1991) to 4 million (Biden Staff Report, 1992) to 6 million (*Time*, September 5, 1983) to 18 million (National Coalition Against Domestic Violence). Sommers even found cases in which the same source would state a figure both in numbers and time without acknowledging inconsistencies in the two figures.[94] The National Coalition Against Domestic Violence (NCADV) estimated that more than half of married women (over 27 million) will experience violence during their marriage and that more than one-third (over 18 million) are battered repeatedly every year. But when a journalist asked Rita Smith, coordinator of the NCADV, where these figures came from, she conceded that they were "estimates based on what we hear out there." The journalist pointed out that "asking women at a shelter whether they've been hit would be like asking patrons at McDonald's whether they ever eat fast food." Clearly, such responses cannot be generalized to the broader population.[95] Sommers similarly reported that the most common statistics quoted on rape are from Mary Koss' study for *Ms.* magazine, which claimed 15.4% of women had been raped, and an additional 12.1% had been victims of attempted rape. However, Sommers pointed out that only a quarter of the women Koss called rape victims labeled themselves in that way. Instead, 49% labeled their experience miscommunication, 14% labeled it a crime but not rape, and 11% said they hadn't felt victimized.[96] If rape is defined as a loss of power and control, how does one classify a refusal to allow women to control the definition of a situation they experienced?

Although these distortions have caused a rift in the feminist movement between equity feminists and gender feminists, it is important to recognize that the very aspects of feminism that distanced, and in some cases drove away, equity feminists were the very features in which gender feminists took greatest pride. What critics defined as emotional coercion in the classroom was described by advocates as transforming students' consciousness. Where critics identified feminist ideology as distorting scholarship, advocates praised research guided by political commitments. Where the vilified complained about an atmosphere rife with avoidance and shunning, advocates claimed to have found—or created—a sanctuary from patriarchy where they could cultivate women's difference.[97] It is also important to recognize, however, that while feminism may be a hotbed of ideological distortion, it is other feminists who are its most vocal critics—unlike any other ideological faction of which I am aware since the American Left of the 1930s. For instance, it was Erin Pizzey who called for reclaiming the movement from "antimale feminists who ... are helping to perpetuate abusive families" when they reinforce the behavior of women who instigate violent behavior by assuring them that men, not they, are always to blame for violence.[98]

Some contemporary policymakers have replaced empiricism with the ideology that problems would be solvable if only the public would follow the policymakers' one true vision of enlightenment.[99] They are impervious to criticism because they only allow into their inner circle others who share their ideology. They dismiss as isolated anomalies evidence that contradicts their beliefs, or explain it away by a theory without empirical support. Perhaps this is a necessary requirement of the ideology, or any ideology, because if an *opponent* of the prevailing idea could be seen as equally able to care about the group in question, it would suggest that opposing arguments on social policy were arguments about methods and evidence. Perhaps the most fundamental difference between these two perceptions is that those who hold the former see policy making as trade-offs, and in the latter case, in terms of "solutions." If that is the case, then the only remaining question is whether reality is optional.[100]

Those who believe in the "expansive role of government," believe that government should provide for the basic needs of all, presumably starting with the neediest. Part of their ideology stems from the belief that economic redistribution is desirable in and of itself. This idea also emanates from Marxism, which theorized that resources are infinite and that maldistribution alone causes inequality and bias. While Marx rightly pointed out that industrialization provided for more than subsistence, his idea that maldistribution is the *only* reason for scarcity has not only been disproved, but never tested against the concept of "need expansion" in existence today—the translation of needs into "rights." Economists recognize that this ideology makes it easy for people to translate their personal wants (and their perceptions of what others should want) into universal needs.

Although MacKinnon searingly indicts the liberal state, she is surprisingly willing to invest that state with even greater power. Since she sees restrictions on state power are mere disguises for male power, MacKinnon seems to believe that women would be better off in a society without any protections against state power. She fails to acknowledge that women have not fared better in those societies lacking liberal principles and institutions.[101] Individual freedom and social solidarity are not completely compatible, and some compromise of each must be reflected in a just society.[102] The presumption that some people know what is best for most others, however, warrants ignoring democratic preferences and individual freedom. In particular, it allows social workers and other bureaucrats to act on behalf of clients instead of listening to them, which is a clear warrant for abuse and unethical treatment.[103] Note, however, that this can appeal to adherents of all spectra of political ideology on their own behalf. In a liberal democracy, the state may mediate family conflicts and even enforce a solution. "Under capitalism . . . if state intervention in people's personal problems can be seen to produce a better workforce . . . then such an effort may be justified. The state's intervention efforts may even be more justifiable if people's personal problems can be commodified . . . into a new form of marketplace."[104]

So two ideological strains coalesce to "sanctify" snake oil: the belief that problem definitions are political rather than objective, and the belief that some people know what is best for others and have a "moral right" to impose their wills on others—regardless of the facts or majority opinion. This also explains the apparently apolitical nature of sanctified snake oil—and how it binds the Religious Right, who tend to oppose government intervention except to impose their brand of morality, to the economic left, who believe that it is the government's role to meet citizens' needs. These lead ideologues to vie for the right to define needs—the first step in determining how those "needs" will be measured and met.

NOTES

1. Nat Hentoff, *Free Speech for Me—But Not for Thee* (New York: HarperPerennial, 1992).

2. Joel Best, *Threatened Children* (Chicago, IL: University of Chicago Press, 1990), quoted in Daphne Patai, "The Making of a Social Problem: Sexual Harassment on Campus," *Sexuality and Culture* 1 (1997).

3. Stephen Klaidman and Tom L. Beauchamp, *The Virtuous Journalist* (New York: Oxford University Press, 1987).

4. Quoted in Richard Berman, "Junk Research Distorts Public Policy," *The Oregonian* (January 4, 1998).

5. Robert Samuelson, *The Good Life and Its Discontents* (New York: Random House, 1995).

6. Deborah Tannen, *The Argument Culture* (New York: Random House, 1998).

7. "Stop Underestimating Us," *Parade* (July 6, 1997).

8. Howard Kurtz, "Journalist, Heal Thyself," *Washington Post National Weekly* (June 23, 1997).

9. Stephanie Coontz, *The Way We Really Are* (New York: Basic Books, 1997).

10. Susan Smith, *Survivor Psychology: The Dark Side of the Mental Health Mission* (Boca Raton, FL: Upton Books, 1995).

11. Richard Dawkins, *The Selfish Gene* (New York: Oxford University Press, 1976).

12. *Media Monitor,* "'Media Crime Wave' Continues—Crime News Quadrupled in Four Years" (Washington, DC: Center for Media and Public Affairs, January–February, 1996).

13. Peter Johnson, "Crime Wave Sweeps Networks' Newscasts," *USA Today* (August 13, 1997).

14. Howard Kurtz, quoted in Richard Morin, "An Airwave of Crime," *Washington Post National Weekly Edition* (August 18, 1997).

15. Cynthia Crosson, *Tainted Truth* (New York: Touchstone Books, 1994).

16. Lawrie Mifflin, "Crime Falls, but Not on TV," *New York Times* (July 6, 1997).

17. Steven R. Donziger, ed., *The Real War on Crime* (New York: HarperPerennial, 1996).

18. Darrell Huff, *How to Lie with Statistics* (New York: W. W. Norton & Co., 1954).

19. Michael Fumento, *Science Under Siege* (New York: William Morrow and Co., 1993).

20. Accuracy in Media, "The Scandal of News Censorship on TV," *AIM Report* (Washington, DC: Accuracy in Media, September 1997).

21. Dennis King, *Lyndon LaRouche and the New American Fascism* (New York: Doubleday, 1989).

22. Richard Morin, "Public Policy Surveys: Lite and Less Filling," *Washington Post National Weekly Edition* (November 10, 1997).

23. Cynthia Crosson, op. cit.

24. Tom Grant, "Wenatchee and the Media's Reflexive Acceptance of Hysteria," paper prepared for "A Day of Contrition Revisited: Contemporary Hysteria Condemns the Innocent," a conference organized by the Justice Committee, Salem, MA, January 14, 1997).

25. Quoted in Jeffrey S. Victor, *Satanic Panic* (Chicago, IL: Open Court Press, 1993).

26. Debbie Nathan and Michael Snedeker, *Satan's Silence* (New York: Basic Books, 1995).

27. Kenneth Lanning, *Investigator's Guide to Allegations of "Ritual" Child Abuse* (Quantico, VA: National Center for the Analysis of Violent Crime, January 1992).

28. Debbie Nathan and Michael Snedeker, op. cit.

29. Ibid. Also see Richard A. Gardner, "The 'Validators' and Other Examiners," *Issues in Child Abuse Allegations* 3, no. 1 (winter 1991).

30. Debbie Nathan and Michael Snedeker, op. cit.

31. Transcripts of *voir dire* of Eileen Treacy by Dominic Barbara, Esq., in re: Ahmed, July 30, October 26, and October 27, 1987.

32. Debbie Nathan and Michael Snedeker, *Satan's Silence* (New York: Basic Books, 1995).

33. Letter from Dr. Suzanne Sgroi to Martin Stavis re: M. Kelly Michaels' appeal, November 2, 1992.

34. Larry McShane, "Bronx Witchhunt Destroyed Lives," *Denver Post* (December 2, 1996).

35. Carole Paquette, "In Child Abuse Cases, Greater Empathy Espoused," *New York Times* (December 7, 1997).

36. Kathryn Robinson, "The End of Therapy," *Seattle Weekly* (November 13, 1996).

37. Brenda Warner Rotzoll, "Settlement Ends Woman's Ordeal," *Chicago Sun-Times* (November 5, 1997).

38. Ted R. Miller, Mark A. Cohen, and Brian Wiersema, *Victim Costs and Consequences: A New Look* (Washington, DC: National Institute of Justice, February 1996).

39. Charles Murray, *What It Means to Be a Libertarian* (New York: Broadway Books, 1997).

40. Ibid.

41. Ibid.

42. James T. Bennett and Thomas J. Lorenzo, *Destroying Democracy* (Washington, DC: Cato Institute, 1985).

43. Isaiah Berlin, *Four Essays on Liberty* (Oxford: Oxford University Press, 1968), quoted in *The Moral Purposes of Social Work*, edited by P. Nelson Reid and Philip R. Popple (Chicago: Nelson-Hall Publishers, 1982).

44. Thomas Sowell, The *Vision of the Anointed* (New York: Basic Books, 1995).

45. Louis Brandeis, quoted in Alpheus Mason, *The Brandeis Way* (Princeton, NJ: Princeton University Press, 1964).

46. Charles Murray, "Americans Remain Wary of Washington," *Wall Street Journal* (December 23, 1997).

47. Jonathan Bradshaw, "The Concept of Social Need," in *Planning for Social Welfare: Issues, Tasks and Models*, edited by Neil Gilbert and Harry Specht (Englewood Cliffs, NJ: Prentice Hall, 1977), 290–296.

48. Ibid.

49. Risha Levinson, *Information and Referral Networks: Doorways to Services* (New York: Springer Publishing, 1988).

50. See, for example, National Association of Social Workers Delegate Assembly, *Code of Ethics of the National Association of Social Workers* (Washington, DC: National Association of Social Workers, 1996).

51. Burton Gummer, *The Politics of Social Administration: Managing Organizational Politics in Social Agencies* (Englewood Cliffs, NJ: Prentice Hall, 1990).

52. Max Siporin, "Should Professionals Take Action If Their Colleagues Act Unethically?" in *Controversial Issues in Social Work Ethics, Values and Obligations*, edited by Eileen Gambrill and Robert Pruger (Boston: Allyn and Bacon, 1997).

53. Michael Weiss and Cathy Young for the Women's Freedom Network, *Brief of Amicus Against the Constitutionality of the Violence Against Women Act* (Houston, TX: Lawson, Weiss & Danziger, 1996).

54. "Excerpts from the Supreme Court's Decision on the Violence Against Women Act," *New York Times* (May 16, 2000).

55. Charles Babcock, Heard on *Reporters' Roundtable*, C-SPAN, November 9, 1997).

56. Stephanie Coontz, *The Way We Really Are* (New York: Basic Books, 1997).

57. Barbara Tuchman, *The March of Folly* (Boston: G. K. Hall and Co., 1984).

58. Willard Gaylin and Bruce Jennings, *The Perversion of Autonomy* (New York: Free Press, 1996).

59. Daniel K. Benjamin and Roger Leroy Miller, *Undoing Drugs* (New York: Basic Books, 1991).

60. George F. Will, "Politics Without Ideology?" *New York Post* (January 1, 1998).

61. James Galper, *The Politics of Social Services* (Englewood Cliffs, NJ: Prentice Hall, 1975).

62. Frances Fox Piven and Richard Cloward, *Regulating the Poor* (New York: Vintage Books, 1993).

63. Helen Ingram and Steven Rathgeb Smith, eds., *Public Policy for Democracy* (Washington, DC: The Brookings Institution, 1993).

64. James T. Bennett and Thomas J. Lorenzo, *Destroying Democracy* (Washington, DC: Cato Institute, 1985).

65. David Chappell, "Providing for the Victims of Crime: Political Placebos or Progressive Programs?" *Adelaide Law Review* 4, (1972): 294.

66. Lawrence M. Friedman, *Crime and Punishment in American History* (New York: Basic Books, 1993).

67. Joel Best, op. cit.

68. Michael D. Cohen, James G. March, and John P. Olsen, "The Garbage Can Model of Organizational Change." *Administrative Science Quarterly* 17, no. 6 (March 1972), 1–25.

69. Eva Bertram, Morris Blachman, Kenneth Sharpe, and Peter Andreas, *Drug War Politics* (Los Angeles: University of California Press, 1996).

70. Amitai Etzioni, *Capital Corruption* (New Brunswick, NJ: Transaction, 1995).

71. Susan J. Tolchin, *The Angry American: How Voter Rage Is Changing the Nation* (New York: Westview Press, 1996).

72. Michael Fumento, op. cit.

73. Charles Murray, op. cit.

74. Ibid.

75. James T. Bennett and Thomas J. Lorenzo, op. cit.

76. R. Kenneth Godwin, "Using Market-Based Incentives to Empower the Poor," in *Public Policy for Democracy*, edited by Helen Ingram and Steven Rathgeb Smith (Washington, DC: The Brookings Institution, 1993), 163–197.

77. Lewis H. Lapham, *The Wish for Kings: Democracy at Bay* (New York: Grove Press, 1993).

78. Charles Murray, "Americans Remain Wary of Washington," *Wall Street Journal* (December 23, 1997).

79. David Shaw, *The Pleasure Police* (New York: Doubleday, 1996).

80. Andrea Dworkin, quoted in Lynne V. Cheney, *Telling the Truth* (New York: Touchstone, 1995).

81. Pranab Chatterjee, *Approaches to the Welfare State* (Washington, DC: National Association of Social Workers Press, 1996).

82. "U. S. Kids Trailing in Math, Science," *New York Daily News* (February 25, 1998).

83. Lynne V. Cheney, *Telling the Truth* (New York: Touchstone, 1995), also Mari Matsuda et al., *Words that Wound: Critical Race Theory, Assaultive Speech, and the First Amendment* (Boulder, CO: Westview Press, 1993), quoted in Lynne V. Cheney, op. cit.

84. Patricia Smith, *Feminist Jurisprudence* (New York: Oxford University Press, 1993).

85. Daphne Patai and Noretta Koertge, *Professing Feminism* (New York: Basic Books, 1994).

86. Quoted in Lynne V. Cheney, *Telling the Truth* (New York: Touchstone, 1995).

87. Richard Hofstadter, *The Age of Reform* (New York: Vintage, 1955).

88. Richard J. Ellis, *The Dark Side of the Left* (Topeka: University of Kansas Press, 1998).

89. Daphne Patai and Noretta Koertge, op. cit.

90. Cathy Young, *Ceasefire: Beyond the Gender Wars* (New York: Free Press, 1999).

91. Susan Sarnoff, "The NIJ/CDC Study on the Incidence and Prevalence of Violence Against Women: A Case Study in Advocacy Research," *Women's Freedom Network Newsletter* 6, no. 1 (January/February 1999).

92. Cathy Young, op. cit.

93. David H. Gremillion, "Domestic Violence as a Professional Commitment," *From Data to Public Policy*, edited by Rita Simon (New York: Women's Freedom Network and University Press of America, Inc., 1996), 53–59.

94. Christina Hoff Sommers, *Who Stole Feminism?* (New York: Simon and Schuster, 1994).

95. Armin A. Brott, "The Facts Take a Battering," *Washington Post National Weekly Edition* (August 8–14, 1994).

96. Christina Hoff Sommers, op. cit.

97. Daphne Patai and Noretta Koertge, op cit.

98. Donna LaFramboise and David Chan, "Sheltered from Reality," *National Post* (November 23, 1998).

99. J. Israel, *Alienation: From Marx to Modern Sociology* (Boston: Allyn & Bacon, 1971).

100. Thomas Sowell, *The Vision of the Anointed* (New York: Basic Books, 1995).

101. Richard J. Ellis, op. cit.

102. Michael Ignatieff, *The Needs of Strangers* (New York: Viking Penguin, 1985).

103. Ibid.

104. Pranab Chatterjee, "A Market of Human Vulnerability," *Social Development Issues* 3 (1979): 1–12.

Chapter 4

Identifying Sanctified Snake Oil

One thing I have learned in a long life: that all our science, measured against reality, is primitive and childlike—and yet it is the most precious thing we have.

—Albert Einstein

Ability in Mathematics Required.

—Inscription over door of Plato's Academy

When you cannot measure it . . . your knowledge is of a meager and unsatisfactory kind.

—Lord Kelvin

The great problem confronting us today is that we have allowed the means by which we live to outdistance the ends for which we live. We have allowed our civilization to outrun our culture, and so we are in danger now of ending up with guided missiles in the hands of misguided men.

—Dr. Martin Luther King, Jr.

Some forms of snake oil are easy to identify. But the sanctification process makes snake oil more difficult to recognize. Vague definitions, anecdotal "evidence," and disinformation that is perpetuated by government and the media contribute to this problem. The only way to counter these efforts is diligent research to identify the definitions used in particular circumstances and to detect other lies and distortions.

The most common and effective form of sanctification is, however, the manipulation and "cooking" of statistics and other evaluative data. Ironically, one reason for this is that so few Americans understand statistical and other forms of evaluative analysis.[1] "Innumeracy, an inability to deal comfortably with the fundamental notions of number and chance, plagues far too many otherwise knowledgeable citizens . . . [due to] poor education, psychological blocks, and romantic misconceptions about the nature of mathematics. [Its effects include] misunderstanding of probabilities, fearing rare occurrences while taking unnecessary risks in other areas, drawing conclusions from coincidences, not being able to differentiate between correlation and causation, and thereby being unable to effectively prioritize."[2]

Research manipulators do not have to be clever, they simply have to appear sure of themselves and use their "sanctified" channels (agencies that reflect their ideologies) to disseminate this bogus data widely, especially to the media, while ignoring contradictory information. As Christopher Wren observed,

Politicians are said to use statistics the way drunks use lampposts: for support rather than illumination. . . . [Regarding drug use], elected officials, and their constituents, want concrete evidence of what is essentially a shadow legal activity . . . when sensibly vague estimates based on the little that is known won't suffice, law enforcement officials oblige them with numbers that one police officer characterized as "P.F.A.," or "pulled from the air." Left unchallenged, even the wildest guesses take on the certitude of fact.[3]

As already discussed, ideologues stretch concepts and exaggerate statistics in order to make "their" issues appear to be crises. Consider how this is done in regard to the current breast cancer claims that one in nine women will develop the disease. What is true is that one in nine women *who live into their seventies* will develop breast cancer. This does *not* mean that the risk of breast cancer is increasing. What it does means is that because women are living longer, they are more likely to live to the age at which breast cancer becomes a significant risk. Women are also more likely to recognize that they have breast cancer, and to have it treated before it becomes fatal, due to the increase in mammography[4] and other early diagnosis efforts.

The Clinton administration declared victory in its "war against welfare" as a result of one statistic: that 1.4 million people had dropped from the welfare rolls over the past year—despite the fact that many policy analysts note that little follow-up has been conducted of people who have left welfare. As a result, it is unclear whether the economy alone accounts for some of this change—or whether the reduction will be temporary and cause greater problems in the future. A statistician at Columbia University's School of Public Health observed in regard to this that "When numbers are crunched in politics, axes are usually grinding, too."[5]

Government organizations are particularly vulnerable to the lure of statistics and other apparent "facts," because what might result in or constitute success is so unclear. All high-level administrators feel the need to increase certainty, and those whose continued employment depends upon elections and public demonstrations of performance (even if only in charts and graphs) are most likely to believe or endorse the idea that more information means less uncertainty. "Often what they get is instead a torrent of incomplete facts, opinions, guesses, and self-serving statements about distant events."[6]

This chapter will explore the flaws in reasoning that lead people to accept sanctified snake oil and that explain why it is so easy to lie with statistics. It will then discuss how to differentiate science from snake oil.

FLAWED REASONING

"No major ideological battle has been won in this country solely because the victors had the best data sets."[7] This is unfortunately true because data only have meaning for those who make an effort to understand them. This requires first having at least a rudimentary understanding of research and statistics. Then it requires applying that understanding to each new set of information presented.

As noted, many Americans lack even a basic knowledge of research methods. This means that they can never actually understand research findings, but must rely on the often faulty or biased interpretations of research studies that are provided by others. Yet one of the contentions of this book is that, because many purportedly authoritative sources make claims about and even publish research that is flawed, the public is confused about effectiveness. Such trust in others, when it is misplaced, exemplifies one type of flawed reasoning that affects many research "consumers."

Another form of flawed reasoning is category error. In several prominent criminal and civil cases, including the Marv Albert trial, evidence that the accuser had made prior false reports of crime were "shielded" from the jury using the rape shield laws. But the rape shield law protects purported victims' *sexual* histories, not their *criminal* histories. Rape shield laws have also been used to suppress evidence of victims' prior assaults, making it appear as if any traumatic reactions resulted from the present charges. Category error again.

In many cases even people with knowledge of statistics fail to question research that they choose to believe. This is clearly due to wishful thinking, another form of flawed reasoning. Wishful thinking "always succeeds, if not by the original criteria, then by criteria extemporized later—and if not by empirical criteria, then by criteria sufficiently subjective to escape even the possibility of refutation. Evidence becomes irrelevant."[8]

Often, research "findings" are published without mention of the methodology used to obtain them. This makes it impossible to evaluate them without obtaining a copy of the actual study that reported them. In truly fraudulent cases, the actual study may never have been published, or a report purported to be the study may omit key data necessary to analyze it. If the research is published at all, it will be published in a journal that is not rigorous in its demand for research methodology. Belief in such studies is another form of flawed reasoning. In fact, I have observed an evolution in this process just during the time that I have written this book. When I began it, the biggest problem with the presentation of research seemed to be incomplete explanation of methodology or misinterpretation of results. More recently, reports have been released that do not even bother with specifics or even citations.

Another form of flawed reasoning results when statistical differences between or among groups are automatically attributed to intentional or dispositional reasons, without consideration of possible systemic causes, such as age, gender, or cultural differences. Similarly, all-or-nothing reasoning deludes people into believing that all drinking is alcoholism, every domestic disagreement is domestic violence, and extreme differences in degree or kind are, in general, inconsequential.[9] It is precisely such differences in degree that are obfuscated through concept stretching.

Self-fulfilling prophesy results from two other forms of flawed reasoning: hermeneutic reasoning, in which interpretation depends on premises held by the interpreter (satanic abuse exists because I believe in Satan); and representative thinking, or making a judgement on the basis of the degree to which characteristics match a stereotype. (For instance, Richard Jewel was suspected of committing the Olympic Park bombing in Atlanta because he purportedly fit the "profile" of a bomber.)

Investment effect suggests that the more time and other resources people devote to believing something, the less willing they will be to change their beliefs.[10] This suggests why many professionals find it impossible to disabuse themselves of notions that have been disproved, but which have formed the core of their research, teaching, or practice. Expectancy effect is most common when evidence does not clearly point to a single conclusion—even when some of that evidence is less convincing than other evidence. Since people who have invested in a belief tend to be more critical of research that disputes it, they tend to hold contrary evidence to a higher standard, and are then even more convinced that they are right if the evidence fails their test. Persistence of error results from such rigidity. If, instead, people reexamined and rethought their beliefs, particularly in the wake of contrary evidence, they would be more likely to move knowledge forward. Instead, however, human nature leads us to protect our egos and dig in even more firmly when we fear that our ideologies are losing ground.[11]

Peoples' preferences influence not only the *kind* of information they consider, but also the *amount* they examine. Research demonstrates that people believe what they think others believe—and peoples' beliefs affect how they perceive their opinions agree with those of others. It is doubtful that this will ever change, because people prefer coherence in their beliefs to truth.[12] Furthermore, people tend to associate with others who share their opinions, making them believe that their opinions are widely held.

Subsequent success is attributed to prior treatment, which explains the belief in natural healing and spontaneous remission. This belief also explains the inverse, that treatment failure is attributed to failure of the individual to comply with recommended treatment.[13] In fact, one author identified the link between flawed reasoning and bogus therapies by identifying the cyclical nature of many diseases, spontaneous remission, the placebo effect, the psychosomatic nature of some illnesses, the difference between relief and cure, misdiagnoses, derivative benefits, and reality distortion as reasons that therapies may seem to work when they in fact do not.[14]

Another author made this connection between religion and faulty reasoning. He explained that religion leads to the argument *ad hominem*, or the idea that an adversary's view must be wrong because he is wicked. It also encourages the argument from ignorance, that is, that instead of rejecting an idea if it is likely to be false, religion enables people to consider themselves entitled to accept ideas because they are not certainly false. Biased selection of the instances is also common to religion, and especially to religious debate. Any case of a person having a prayer answered, or suffering after doing wrong, is taken as proof of heavenly reward and punishment. Contrary cases are not sought, and if they are incontrovertible, they only attest to the impossibility of understanding G-d's will.[15] Arguing by declaration, from intensity and ubiquity of belief, and from a preconceived conclusion are other examples of this.[16]

Peter Huber, in his 1991 book, *Galileo's Revenge*, coined the phrase "junk science," which he defined as "a hodgepodge of biased data, spurious inference, and logical legerdemain, patched together by researchers whose enthusiasm for discovery and diagnosis far outstrip their skill. . . . It is a catalog of every conceivable kind of error: data dredging, wishful thinking, truculent dogmatism, and, now and again, outright fraud." Huber explained that such "researchers," whom he called "quacks," can be identified because they rely on testimonials and anecdotes as evidence that their treatments or remedies are safe and effective; they fail to use regular channels of communication, such as professional journals, for reporting scientific information, but rely instead on mass media and word of mouth; they offer few facts, relying instead on grand theories and methods that can only be mastered by true believers, and they dismiss mainstream science as reactionary and obtuse.[17] One reason that junk science often goes undetected is that attorneys and other biased consumers of research reject experts who disagree with their contentions and suppress research that conflicts with their agendas.[18]

This is not a wholly modern concept. In fact, in Galileo's time the term *probabilita* meant "meeting with approval."[19] The statistical tricks of sharpening (using a single number instead of a range), leveling (using "as many as" with the most inflated statistic found),[20] and failing to use benchmark figures with which to compare findings are used by "junk scientists."[21]

During the twentieth century, statistics have become a prerequisite to having a cause placed on the political agenda, and to having a claim on public resources.[22] A Gallup poll found that 76% of those asked agreed that a scientific study can be found to prove just about anything—but 86% of them believed that references to scientific research increased the credibility of a story, and 81% believed that statements by recognized experts make a study more believable.[23] Advertisers have long known that buyers consider products defined as "scientific" to be safe, even if "science" is used to describe wholly unscientific surveys, opinion polls, celebrity-expert statements, and even advertising slogans.[24] So despite the pervasiveness of snake oil in purported "research," the public is impressed by numbers and findings described as "scientific," whether or not those terms reflect anything meaningful.

LYING WITH STATISTICS

Probably the best-known book on the topic, Darrell Huff's *How to Lie with Statistics,* has been in continuous print since its publication in 1954. Huff offers many textual and graphical depictions of lying with statistics, and this suggestion: "if you can't prove what you want to prove, demonstrate something else and pretend they are the same thing."[25] The author of an article titled "Even If the Numbers Don't Add Up" noted that "[I]n recent years more and more statisticians and demographers are becoming troubled by the misuse of statistics. As computers and more sophisticated methodology have made data gathering cheaper and more precise, interest groups and businesses are bending and shaping the results."[26]

But again, statistical manipulation is far from new. "The 1840 Census was a cesspool of error, fraud and political machinations largely driven by the slave debate. Much of the battle over Prohibition was fought with finagled statistics. . . . Based on extremely primitive methodology, the temperance movement asserted that half of all sin was caused by intemperance." This continues today in research "adjusted" to fit preconceived patterns by exaggerating positive findings and burying negative ones. Often this manipulation is attributed to researchers who are forced to work with industry to attain the funding of research that is no longer funded by government or private philanthropic entities.[27]

Consider statistics on domestic violence. A 1996 joint publication of the National Institute of Justice and the Bureau of Justice Statistics, entitled *Domestic and Sexual Violence Data Collection,* reported that, "there was a wide variation in how each State defines these offenses, determines what is counted, and measures or reports incidents." Some states, for instance, have written statutes broadly to include all forms of family violence, including child abuse and abuse of elderly family members living in a household. Some states fail to recognize same-sex violence as domestic, or limit definitions to people who are married or have children in common. Another measurement issue is that of thresholds—how particular actions are counted and defined. Is marital rape a sex crime or a domestic crime, for instance? Clearly, these are heavily debated issues about which people have very different views, but in this context, the most significant factor is that without some level of agreement we must be skeptical when comparing statistics.[28] Statistics can also be manipulated more simplistically. Proponents of abstinence training argue that it is the most effective means of birth control because it is 100% effective. But while *abstinence* is indeed 100% effective, abstinence *training* does not ensure abstinence, nor can it boast the same rate of success.

Judith Wallerstein is something of an "expert" at lying with statistics. She has followed a cohort of children from divorced families since the early 1970s and has concluded, much to the delight of pro-family ideologues, that divorce has a severe, long-lasting effect on children.[29] However, Wallerstein's research has never proved what she claimed, because she has consistently failed to compare her results to that of a control group of children from nondivorced families. Therefore, the only thing that can be concluded from her research is that the children she has studied have become more stressed over time. Whether that is true of all children in divorced families, is unique to the group she studied, or has anything to do with divorce is not discernable from her research, which I would call, instead, "snake oil."

SEPARATING SCIENCE FROM SNAKE OIL

"Academic analysis follows where the argument leads, but activism wants only support for a predetermined direction. Academic researchers are intrigued by the structure of arguments, whereas activists only want to win them."[30] Nobel Prize-winning Caltech physicist Richard Feynman defined science as "a way to teach how something gets to be known, what is not known, to what extent things are known (for nothing is known, absolutely), how to handle doubt and uncertainty, what rules of evidence are, how to think about things so that judgments can be made, [and] how to distinguish truth from fraud, and from show."[31] Science may not always be able to prove or disprove a fact at any given time, but scientific questions must be provable, those that are not fall into the domains of religion or philosophy, not science.[32] In fact, what is exciting about science is that it invites imagination, grounded in discipline. It challenges preconceptions and demands consideration of alternative hypotheses. It requires openness to new ideas, even heretical ones, and demands skeptical scrutiny of both new ideas and established wisdom.[33]

"Although it is human nature to seek absolute certainty, absolute certainty is also an impossibility."[34]

What is science is clear. Everything else, until proved fact, is snake oil. As *Skeptical Enquirer* editor Kendrick Frazier explained, "Skepticism is not, despite much popular misconception, a point of view. It is, instead, an essential component of intellectual inquiry, a method of determining the facts whatever they may be or wherever they might lead. . . . All who are interested in the search for knowledge and the advancement of understanding, imperfect as those enterprises may be, should, it seems to me, support critical inquiry, whatever the subject and whatever the outcome."[35] In fact, one way of detecting ideology masquerading as pseudoscience is the certainty of adherents and their resistance to test their beliefs with healthy skepticism.

This difference between science and ideology was recently played out in the media and on the floor of Congress. In July of 1998 *Psychological Bulletin*, a peer-reviewed American Psychological Association (APA) publication, carried an article titled "A Meta-Analytic Examination of Assumed Properties of Child Sexual Abuse Using College Samples."[36] To grossly oversimplify, the article reviewed thirty-six peer-reviewed research studies and twenty-three dissertations on the effects of child sexual abuse, finding that its effects were not as uniformly dismal as has been suggested by the treatment literature. A curiously belated year later, conservative radio commentator Laura Schlesinger, whose comments demonstrated so little understanding that it is doubtful that she read the article, berated the authors for attempting to "normalize pedophilia." Schlesinger's words were echoed in Congress, where Republican House Whip Tom DeLay and others denounced not only the authors, but the APA for publishing the study. Representative Matt Salmon asserted that the findings would encourage pedophilia, and that they could not be true.[37] Child protection advocates jumped on the bandwagon, misquoting and quoting out of context sections of the article to make it seem as if the authors were advocating child sexual abuse.[38] In response, the APA was forced to issue a statement explaining that the claims about the study were distorted.[39]

Ironically, child advocates should have been pleased to learn that child sexual abuse is not as damaging as clinical studies suggest. And the reason should be obvious: clinical samples are obtained from only those people disturbed enough by their reactions to feel the need for professional help to ameliorate them. Furthermore, the research in no way minimizes the moral or legal wrong of child sexual abuse—it only suggests that victims are far more resilient (and therefore less in need of treatment) than the treatment community has worked so hard to make the public believe. Given this fact, it is particularly ironic that the APA published the research.

In addition, erroneous belief that victims always suffer long-term and possibly irreparable trauma is extremely damaging to victims. It could also be devastating if investigators, prosecutors, and defense attorneys buy into the myth, because they might be likely to disbelieve those victims who fail to exhibit signs of trauma. Clearly, understanding what research indicates is best for victims, and best for public policy, in all instances.

UNDERSTANDING RESEARCH AND EVALUATION

It has been observed that the lack of understanding of mathematics and the hard sciences "is producing a citizenry not at all critically minded," and also that probability is at least as important in the so-called soft sciences.[40] In fact, real research is complex, difficult, and costly, and as a result, rare even when it is desired. But advocacy research and politically motivated scholarship have become so common that it has affected our appreciation of good research. Today, reputations are made because shoddy scholarship is championed by advocates and ideologues, rather than because the researchers' research rigor warrants recognition.[41]

Research of human behavior and evaluation of social programs designed to change human behavior are difficult to conduct. This is so not only because human behavior is multicausal, but because concerns about confidentiality and freedom prevail and limit such research. Even when conducted well, caution must be used in drawing conclusions from the results, especially about people who vary in any way from the people studied. Let us review the rudiments of statistical methods, noting the difficulty in applying them to human behavior and social program evaluation.

STATISTICAL METHODS

To study anything, one first has to define it. What may seem to be an easy step is, as examples throughout this book demonstrate, ambiguous, often politically or ideologically motivated, and complex at best. Consider the earlier discussion of domestic violence statistics. Domestic violence is defined differently in each state, both in terms of the severity of abuse that constitutes crime and the relationships included. As a result, one state can appear to have much more (or less) domestic violence *only* because that state does or does not include child abuse or unmarried partners in its definition, or defines less severe forms of domestic violence as crime.

At one time states chose to downplay their rates of domestic violence by defining it narrowly and spending a minimum of effort on "case finding," that is, focusing on efforts to detect crimes and increase reporting. With increased funding available for domestic violence services today, the reverse is the case. States have redirected their domestic violence efforts not only to expand definitions but to identify more cases and, if reporting is tied to funding, to encourage victims to report. In fact, spurred by the VAWA, but experimented with even earlier, states have implemented dual arrest policies, "no drop" prosecutions, and prosecution of cases even when the complaining witnesses refuse to participate in order to increase their domestic violence "numbers."[42] Unfortunately, policies implemented primarily as "numbers games" offer little hope for concrete changes that might, as a result, reduce the incidence or severity of domestic violence.

Another way that advocates play with facts and statistics is to hold public hearings on an issue and then summarize only that part of the testimony that they want reflected in whatever way suits their plans or preconceived notions. The resulting "report" is then circulated widely, without verification of any of its content. The following example will demonstrate how this is done. In January 1996, the New York City Commission on the Status of Women held hearings on domestic violence. Despite the fact that Christina Hoff Sommers had debunked many exaggerated "facts" and statistics on domestic violence in her 1994 book, *Who Stole Feminism?*[43] many of these bogus ideas reappeared in the hearing summary[44]—which was subtitled "Listening with the Third Ear" to suggest that the discrepancies among the statistics reflected not distortions but lack of sensitivity on the part of some researchers, which blinded them to obvious domestic violence that they failed to recognize. In the study, reports of the proportion of women treated for domestic violence ranged from 25% to 60% of all those seen in emergency rooms. These figures reflect studies that used questionable methodology or were limited to single hospitals or cities with unusually high rates of domestic violence, as well as the studies discussed earlier that asked women in emergency rooms if they had *ever* been battered. The only exception to these high figures in the report was a statement that fewer than 1% of the patients seen in the emergency room of New York City's Lincoln Hospital were there for domestic violence during the previous year. But this statement was explained away by claiming that domestic violence victims underreport, when, in fact, it was the only empirical evidence presented in the document. The federal Bureau of Justice Statistics found that nationally, one-half of 1% of women seeking emergency room treatment have been battered.[45] One person who testified used the inflated statistics to determine the cost of domestic violence to New York City employees, hospitals, criminal justice agencies, and homeless services. These figures were then adopted by Polaroid and perpetuated by that corporation in a booklet they produced on workplace violence.[46] This example demonstrates how even debunked statistics can take on a life of their own, but it also demonstrates that the perception of the magnitude of a problem can easily be manipulated by false statistics, resulting in resources being allocated according to a false perception rather than to a real need.

Advocacy statistics work two ways. Consider the debates regarding the number of women who falsely charge men with rape. Some victim advocates claim that such reports are negligible, accounting for fewer than 1% of all reports of rape. But the FBI finds false reports of rape to average 8%–9% nationally—not only higher than advocates claim, but four times as high as false reports of other crimes. On the other hand, some men's advocates who claim that false reports are much higher, cite as their "proof" a study by Eugene Kanin of Purdue University, which found a 41% rate of false rape allegations in the single community he studied (handpicked because of its high rate, as Kanin himself acknowledges).[47] However, it is important to understand that this rate does not disprove the FBI statistics; in fact, it was obtained from FBI statistics. The FBI rate of 8.9% is a national average, which of course means that the actual rate in individual communities is higher or lower. The mistake made by ideologues is to believe that any finding that deviates from the FBI finding disproves the FBI's numbers, rather than that it illuminates a corner that the aggregate FBI statistics cannot.

Kanin, it is important to note, is not himself an ideologue. He did not conduct this study to determine the rate of false allegations; instead, he selected an area with a high rate of false allegations to study the *nature* of false allegations. The area he chose to study, a city in the Midwest which is otherwise unidentified, was chosen because the police there investigate every rape case until it is either founded or the victim recants. Here Kanin points out that it is possible that some victims recant because they "wish to avoid a second assault by the police," but he discounts this, saying that the police "knew" which cases were false from the outset. This argument may, however, be a bit naive regarding police procedures. It is difficult to believe that any police department closes every reported rape case. Even murder, the most frequently closed crime, has only a 66% national rate of closure.[48] To close every case, then, some police officers may force cases into either category just to close them. This may involve badgering some victims (all are polygraphed, for instance) until they withdraw their complaints. It is also likely that some victims would realize after reporting that such careful investigations might unearth things they do not wish revealed. So some actual victims, who may not be completely innocent in their behavior, might recant rather than have something about their behavior disclosed. This is supported by the fact that adolescents are the likeliest group to make false allegations, and adolescents can not only get in trouble for behavior that can similarly be exhibited by adults, but also for things like being with friends their parents do not like, or drinking and having sex, which would not pose similar problems for most adults.

Ironically, rape victims' advocates have long complained that the police fail to fully investigate many rape reports. Kanin's study suggests, however, that many police departments may simply ignore allegations that appear to be false, artificially deflating the number of false allegations reported to the FBI by many communities.

Kanin's most important finding was that 56% of the false allegations served an alibi function, while 18% were made to get attention and sympathy and 27% were made to get revenge. Half of the "alibiers" identified a rapist while all of the revenge-seekers did. Therefore, while 41% of all rape reports consisted of false allegations in Kanin's study, only 22% involved false accusations. This difference is critical because, while false allegations are problems for "the system," they do not result in false prosecutions and possible false convictions. Yet the 41% figure is often misstated as the rate of false *accusations* rather than false *allegations*.

This raises the problem of defining "false" reports. Most communities receive some reports of rape from individuals who are clearly delusional and genuinely believe the reports they make. Some of these people make frequent reports. Sadly, some may have once been assaulted, and may relive that assault over and over again as if it were new. From this situation this question arises: should these cases be counted, and if so, how? Does one person making the same report day after day constitute one report or many?

A different problem exists in regard to the complaints that the police suspect are false. Should they always be investigated to prove that they are false, or should some reports be permitted to remain in limbo, between founded and disproved, if only to preserve police resources? Without common treatment of these cases, the real numbers of false allegations will continue to differ so much that they will be hard for anyone to pin down.

Once a thing has been defined, one must develop a method of measuring it. Here is where studies of human behavior and program success (those that overcome the hurdle of definition, that is) begin to run aground—whether or not researchers admit that this is the case. Short of using such intrusive methods as continual surveillance or urine- or blood-testing (which are generally considered unconstitutional unless they take place in prisons or can be otherwise justified), research of humans must rely on self-reports and other quasi-measures. But people are not always honest in self-reports—and sometimes they are not even aware of all the motivations and incentives that cause them to do things or feel certain emotions.

Stigma also affects people's willingness to self-report. In fact, some experts suspect that the apparent increase in reports of sex crimes may reflect nothing more than reduced stigma that enables more people to admit that these things have happened to them.[49] People are least likely to self-report behavior that could get them into trouble, such as admitting to having committed crimes. For this reason, self-reports about drug use and drunk driving for people in DWI programs are particularly suspect. Alfred Kinsey, in order to find subjects who were willing to discuss their sexual behavior during the 1940s and 1950s (when consensual sodomy was still widely illegal), interviewed disproportionate numbers of admitted homosexuals, male prostitutes, and prisoners because they were willing to discuss their sexual behavior. As a result, he concluded that 37% of men had had at least one homosexual experience and that 10% were practicing homosexuals—proportions now recognized to be inflated 1,000%.[50]

Statistical manipulation and exaggeration can have many causes—and effects. For instance, early in the administration of New York City Mayor Giuliani, he and his then police commissioner, William Bratton, implemented "community policing." They then claimed that the so-called Giuliani Miracle was responsible for the sudden, sharp drop in New York City's crime rate that followed. In truth, the effort did have a serious, and sustained, effect on crime in the city. But, serving on the New York State Crime Victims Board's Advisory Council at the time, I saw another effect of the Giuliani Miracle: an increase in complaints about police officers refusing to write up certain "minor" complaints and charging people with lesser crimes than those they had actually committed, such as harassment instead of assault. This is *not* to suggest that Bratton or Giuliani ordered such actions. Yet calls for major changes in statistics often result in a certain amount of manipulation as well as legitimate effort, because it is understood that evaluators are not actually observing results, but the numbers that supposedly reflect those results. And it often appears that such manipulation "doesn't hurt anyone." This particular effort, however, certainly contributed to revolving-door justice—and something else that only victim advocates could observe. Many New York City crime victims who applied for victim compensation were initially denied because the charges brought in those crimes did not appear to warrant compensation. However, investigation of the injuries they sustained proved that the acts were more serious than the charges tended to reflect.

Police departments have particular difficulties with crime statistics because "although the police are often evaluated by whether crime goes up or . . . down, they don't have the capacity in many ways to control it." Community fear, for instance, is "more heavily mediated by what people see on the 5 o'clock news" than on what the police actually do.[51]

As so much social science research relies on quasi-measures, it is necessary to test the accuracy of the quasi-measure as a reflection of the thing actually measured. This is done by comparing the thing really measured to the quasi-measure, or validity testing, and by ensuring that the "test instrument" (questions, questionnaire) obtains the same results each time, or reliability testing. It must be understood too that these tests rarely, if ever, find complete accuracy—accuracy is measured by degrees. So even a test that is 90% reliable is 10% unreliable.

Reliability and validity tests assume that alternative measures exist against which to test them, but much social science research seeks to measure things that have never before been measured. In these cases, quasi-measures of reliability and validity are developed based on studies of "similar concepts," which results in "quasi-quasi-measurements" even less reflective of what they purport to represent.

A third test of measurement is that of feasibility. Feasibility is the degree to which the study design can be accomplished, given current confidentiality and "Rights of Human Subjects" laws, the skills of the group to be sampled, and the resources available to the researcher. The best research designs, in terms of reliability and validity, are usually the least feasible.

Research today also suffers from the sins of the past. Historic abuses such as the Tuskegee Experiment, nuclear testing in the southwest, and myriad other studies in which people were exposed to dangers and left with untreated effects without their knowledge led to strict limits on the ways that research could be conducted on human beings. Today, research subjects must be fully informed about any research they participate in and must formally consent to participation. Confidentiality rules, which all government agencies have adopted, limit the ways that research of those agencies can be collected, stored, and reported. They also add to the costs of research, and they limit research-design possibilities—for example, by withholding the true purpose of a study until a respondent has concluded participation, or by conducting double-blind studies in which research participants are not told whether they receive the actual treatment or a placebo. While these protections are clearly necessary in medical research and regarding self-incriminating or even embarrassing questions, they may be overly restrictive when applied to more benign social research, adding nothing more than excessive costs to the project, at a great loss to the reliability and validity of the result.

To avoid the problems inherent in self-reporting, alternative data can sometimes be accessed. For example, hospital, prison, or school records might be studied in lieu of questioning informants directly. This method is only as effective as the accuracy of the records in general and the degree to which the records capture the specific data sought by the researcher. Some information (such as age at death) might be accurately reflected in existing documents. But, as the discussion of domestic violence demonstrated, documents may not accurately reflect the concept to be measured, or, even if they do, they may not be comparable to each other.

State-by-state data has the inherent advantage of being complete, but when studying individuals, or most other units of research, it is unfeasible to observe the entire universe of members of the group to be studied. This is when "sampling" becomes necessary. Research has demonstrated that observing only a small selection of all the possible members of a group can produce very accurate results—if the sample is truly representative of the population it represents. But true representativeness is difficult to obtain. Randomness, such as interviewing every third service recipient or reviewing every record ending in the number 7, is the best method of achieving representativeness. This assumes, however, that every third recipient agrees to be interviewed, or that each numbered record contains the data to be measured. Using every tenth crime report to study rape, for instance, would be meaningless because rapes do not occur with similar consistency.

Many researchers claim to have used random samples, only to admit that some informants "self-selected" out. This is particularly problematic with studies that attempt to study "cohorts" over time, because some members of the cohorts inevitably die, move away, or otherwise disappear, at least from the researcher's database. Self-selection out is also common with mailed questionnaires. A researcher may report sending questionnaires to a random sample of informants, but unless there is a 100% return rate (which is unheard of) the responses will not be random. In fact, Harry W. O'Neill, the vice chairman of the Roper Division of Roper Starch

Worldwide, upon receiving the New York Chapter of the American Association for Public Opinion Research's 1997 Outstanding Achievement Award, revealed that "one of polling's dirty little secrets is that the response rate of most, if not all, media polls is below 40 percent."[52] Further, self-reports tend to reflect the opinions of people who feel particularly strongly about the subject of the study.

Advocacy research exploits these facts, as well as the public's ignorance of them. Sometimes advocacy researchers eschew randomness completely, satisfied with "big numbers." For instance, advocacy researchers often publish questionnaires in magazines. This guarantees a high number of returns—and especially high numbers of returns from people whose opinions are most intense. And it further skews the study's results to the "profile" of the readers of the particular magazine(s) in which the questionnaire runs, who, if the researcher is clever, will reflect the thing to be studied in the way the researcher wants it to be viewed.

A further consideration in regard to samples is "domain." A random sample can be assumed to be representative of the population it reflects. That means that what can be concluded about the sample can be concluded about all other members of the population. But it does *not* mean that it can be extrapolated to people beyond that population. So, for instance, a random sample of alcoholics in Wisconsin should reflect things that are true of other Wisconsin alcoholics; but it cannot be assumed to reflect anything about California alcoholics. This is another area where much reported research goes aground.

Even the rare highly accurate research that is conducted must be read with a grain of salt. Perfect research design, if it has ever existed, cannot prevent certain statistical anomalies. For instance, a researcher comparing murder rates in major cities on randomly selected days might have inadvertently identified the date of the Oklahoma City Federal Building bombing as a study date. The study data could then be misinterpreted to suggest that the risk of being murdered in Oklahoma City on any given date would be higher than anywhere else. Only by replicating the study with different dates, and having it conducted again by other researchers and at other times, would this data eventually be shown to be unrepresentative. In this case, it would be acceptable to adjust the errant Oklahoma data, with explanation, by replacing the data with that for the prior or next day. But the ability to adjust unrepresentative data, too, can be abused by advocacy statisticians, who often do so without such justifiable causes. Advocacy researchers sometimes "cook" data by throwing out data elements that fail to reflect what they hope to prove.

PRESENTING AND "CONSUMING" RESEARCH FINDINGS

Most rigorous research results in limited, if any, findings, because effective research takes into account alternate variables that could have produced the same results and discounts the results accordingly. Since few aspects of human behavior have single causes, honest researchers are careful to account for all possible explanations of their results. In fact, unambiguous conclusions in research studies are clear indicators of "advocacy research," as is hyperbole (especially when touting an extreme statistic with terms such as "as many [or few] as)."

One trick of advocacy researchers is to omit the use of a control group, as Judith Wallerstein's research consistently does.[53] A control group is a group that is similar to the study group but receives no treatment, or does not reflect the study variable. It is compared to the study group to determine the degree to which the study group would have changed without the introduction of the treatment or study variable. When observing particular behavior, especially change over time or reactions to a specific type of event, advocacy researchers tend to attribute all of the change to the thing they want to be the cause of the change (divorce, in Judith Wallerstein's research, or treatment in the case of service providers). But we know that a certain amount of change is inevitable. For instance, the stress associated with crime victimization is often the target of counseling (because all states compensate crime-victim counseling). That stress dissipates over time, however, and there is no evidence that counseling is more effective than time alone at dissipating it. Counseling has been shown to reduce stress somewhat faster, but it has never proved to offer a sustained benefit.[54]

Another concern is the "power" of a finding. While statistical significance is a strong indicator of a relationship between two variables, significance refers only to likelihood. There may be many other factors affecting the relationship, so that one variable may have a genuine, but weak, effect on another. In Judith Wallerstein's research on children of divorce, even if she had used a control group and that group had proved a relationship between parental divorce and childhood stress, so many other factors also affect childhood stress that it is unlikely that parental divorce (or any other single variable) could be concluded to be a major cause. Further, as parental divorce can also cause financial concerns, relocation and even the "loss" of one parent, and each of these can cause childhood stress, it can be easy to confuse these factors and attribute all of the result to any one. That one is often chosen for ideological reasons.

It is important to recognize that research incorporates the consideration of error. In fact, an important aspect of research is analysis of the effects of the two possible types of error. A Type I Error concludes that a difference exists that does not, while a Type II Error concludes that a difference does not exist that does. This relates to the power of a research finding (the number of cases that do not reflect the researcher's premise) and the importance of the finding—which is to say, the risk of accepting or not accepting it. So if a study finds a correlation between a particular diet and a fatal illness, it might be worth changing one's diet because the risk of not doing so is great. A danger here is that any report that overemphasizes a particular risk will tend to skew attention and taxpayer support away from other concerns that might be greater or more likely.

Statistical regression is a mathematic method of determining the degree to which each of numerous factors affects a single variable. Computers make statistical regression easy to calculate, but each factor that is singled out increases the minimum size of the sample needed for the study. Not only is much statistical regression conducted on sample sizes too small to be meaningful, but some factors will appear infrequently even in large samples, making their measurement by this method completely meaningless. (Consider a study conducted on a fairly large overall sample, which then attempts to determine the effect of the study variable on green-eyed people. While green is one of only four eye colors, it occurs far less than 25% of the time. If the study sample included considerable numbers of Asians, blacks, or Latinos, green eyes would be even less common.)

In presenting research results, the numbers chosen, and how they are presented, are also important. Aggregate data are commonly presented in "averages." But statisticians understand that there are three types of averages: means, medians, and modes. The arithmetic average is the "mean." The "median" is the midpoint, or the number which signifies that half of all respondents (or values) fall on one side of it and half on the other. The "mode" is the most common single score. Averages offer important information but "discount" extreme highs and lows. Therefore, they are often used to manipulate data.

The single most important reason that people conduct research is to demonstrate causation—that is, to prove that *A* is responsible for the occurrence of *B*. Throughout this book there have been examples of ideologues who claimed that any variety of things "caused" other things to occur. As already noted, however, few phenomena are unicausal.

One of the advantages of pure randomness is that it automatically proves (or disproves) causality; but as has been demonstrated, true randomness is extremely rare, even when it is claimed. With nonrandom samples, it is necessary to prove four separate conditions to prove causality: control of contaminating variables (which is difficult to do for more than a few variables, except by statistical regression, which requires prohibitively high samples to be meaningful); temporal priority, or that the change occurred after the independent variable was applied to the dependent variable; covariation, or that when change occurred in one variable a corresponding change occurred in the second; and correlation, or that the magnitude of change in one variable will be reflected in the magnitude of change in the other. Often, advocacy researchers use any one of these conditions to claim causality. For instance, regarding covariation, "the frequency with which people who have [a given] problem also have . . . a characteristic 'diagnostic' of that problem (say, recall of unhappy incidents in childhood) . . . is *not* equivalent to the frequency with which people who have the characteristic also have the problem. . . . Continually finding association by sampling only those who have the problem, however, often leads professionals to generalize from this select sample of people with the problem."[55] In fact, all "gateway" theories assume that temporal priority proves causality, which is another example of flawed reasoning.

EVALUATING PROBLEMS AND PROGRAMS

Ideologues resent being required to produce statistical evidence of their claims, believing that "their" issues are so worthy and compelling that no right-minded individual could withhold resources from them. When they must produce data, however, they can hardly be counted on to do so scientifically.

Recall that Mary Koss defined rape victims as the women *she* considered to have been raped, defining the concept so as to capture the largest possible response reflective of her ideology.[56] Statistical inflation is a useful way to grab headlines, as well as to support requests for expanded funding, but sometimes it is even more vital to ideologues. It is argued, for instance, that crusaders who oppose the legalization of marijuana have gained the support of the general public because they have been able to count as drug users the millions of people who have "tried" marijuana (always defined as *ab*users, because anti-drug crusaders deny that there can be any acceptable or safe level of use). Without this statistic, crusaders could not make the "drug problem" appear to be much of a problem at all.[57]

These problem analyses can be attributed to bias, but statistical fudging can take other forms as well. Consider the Commonwealth Fund's July 1993 Survey on Women's Health. The survey asked 2,500 women whether they had ever experienced a spouse or partner engaging in behavior ranging from shootings and stabbings to insults and swearing. From their findings, none of these women had experienced threatened or actual shootings or stabbings, nor had any respondents experienced chokings or beatings. The survey results showed that 2% of the women had been kicked, bitten, or hit with fists or other objects. Another 5% had been pushed, grabbed, shoved, or slapped; and 3% had had something thrown at them. So the survey found that 10% of the respondents had experienced violence or intended violence. Another 5% had experienced threats of violence that had not been acted on. So one might stretch the conclusion to claim at most a 15% rate of actual or threatened violence. Yet the survey also found that 11% of respondents had experienced their partners' throwing, smashing, hitting, or kicking something; while 34% had experienced a partner stomping out of the house; and another 34% had experienced being insulted or sworn at. Many references to the survey have counted some or all of the *nonviolent* actions captured in the survey to exaggerate the extent of domestic *violence*.[58]

The worst bias and data cooking are at least usually well intentioned. Not so attempts to confuse goals and processes. True, much of this confusion too is ideological—almost religious in nature. So, people who "believe in" Alcoholics Anonymous (AA), for example, perpetuate the lie that it is the only way to "recover" from the "disease of alcoholism" when, in fact, alcoholism is *not* a disease, there are other ways to overcome it, and almost all of them are more effective than AA.[59]

The government's response to exposés of DARE's ineffectiveness exemplifies another way to "snake-oil" program evaluation. Unable to justify government's spending (at all levels) of some $600,000 each year on DARE with decreases in drug use, the government released a report noting that a "satisfaction survey" proved that DARE attendees and communities "like" the program.[60] However, satisfaction surveys are known to be unscientific—people respond favorably to them simply because they appreciate being asked their opinions and want to be polite. Satisfaction surveys say nothing about the actual effectiveness of a program. In fact, in 1987 "the Central Fact-Gathering Committee of the American Psychoanalytic Association . . . reported that of those who 'completed treatment,' over 96% 'felt benefitted.' " Research is consistent in demonstrating that therapists identify the greatest results from therapy and that their clients tend to recognize improvement to a lesser degree. However, other observers, including family members and friends, often fail to see any improvement.[61] Because researchers know this, it can be assumed that satisfaction surveys are conducted only when desperate program administrators are able to find no other justifications for perpetuating their programs. Of course, the subtle message conveyed by satisfaction surveys is that there are voters out there who approve of the status quo and who fail to understand that defunding a program is not tantamount to opposing the program's goal—often it is the best way to make better progress toward that goal.

This observation of victim programs can be extrapolated to most such politically inspired ones; "few services began as a result of systematic planning; instead, most programs were developed out of the professional or personal experiences of individuals in a community, or in response to a particularly gruesome and well-publicized incident that highlighted the gaps in social service systems."[62] Therefore, capturing the public's imagination is more important to ultimate policy development than getting any of the facts right, no less experimenting with methods until goals are satisfactorily met.

PROGRAM EVALUATION

In his study concluding that federally funded crime prevention programs are largely ineffective, researcher Lawrence W. Sherman of the University of Maryland noted that he was unable to observe measurable results from the bulk of programs funded by the Department of Justice, even though he used a relatively low threshold of strength for the evidence he evaluated. He also noted that many of the program factors that he hoped to study could not be evaluated because little or no meaningful evaluation data had been collected or was required to be collected. It should be noted that the programs that Sherman studied account for billions of dollars in congressional appropriations each year.[63]

When programs are evaluated, they are often evaluated primarily according to their efficiency, which merely refers to their relative cost-effectiveness when compared to other programs that purport similar effects. Furthermore, efficiency is particularly meaningless when comparing social programs, because consumer awareness and choice are limited and measures of effectiveness are complex and difficult to obtain. Instead, surrogate outcomes, such as numbers of clients served or hours of service provided, tend to substitute for assessments of substantive benefits,[64] in part because they vary so much from what researchers actually want to know, but primarily because program directors adapt their operations to play funders' "numbers games" instead of meeting client needs. For example, a recent solicitation for concept papers by the Office for Victims of Crime of the U. S. Department of Justice required "a strategy for measuring the outcome or assessing the impact of the project" but then explained that "the assessment might address items such as the units of service provided, number of individuals trained, number of agencies provided technical assistance, number/type of products disseminated, user satisfaction, and benefit to the field." This is a direct contradiction, because the entire list of examples consists of "input" measures—none address either outcomes or impact.[65] This often results, particularly in bureaucracies, in means being valued over ends, and in following the right rule being more important than achieving the right goal.[66]

Another possibility is to substitute satisfaction surveys or other findings for actual program success. For example, the first of two "dueling" articles in the *APA Observer* noted that "Head Start was designed 'to prevent school failure and improve adult outcomes among low income children' but there is little solid evidence that it does so,"[67] but the second article noted that there had been "gains in the 'accessibility of community-based services for the families involved and . . . higher rates of immunizations' for children in the families," which were touted as benefits of the program.[68] The latter were not program benefits—they were unintended consequences not designed into program goals and probably achievable more effectively by different means.

Given that social programs evaluate so poorly, it might be concluded that service providers would focus on what they can do well, or at least on what minimum standards of service provision dictate. But that is not the case. The "conferral of monopoly power . . . was implicitly conditioned on a 'duty to serve' all members of the community alike. . . . [E]nterprises providing functions and services that are essential and public in character have a common law duty to serve 'a positive obligation to provide all members of the public with equal, adequate, and nondiscriminatory access.' "[69] While this has been upheld in regard to schools and public conveyances, it has not been tested in most other areas of social policy.

In fact, programs continue to operate even when it is understood that they have negative effects that undo their positive effects. Many programs targeted to deviants, for instance, such as criminals and alcoholics, have been found to gather such people into segregated groups, reinforcing their deviant status and giving them opportunities to transmit their skills and attitudes to each other—such programs may even encourage participants to engage in deviant behaviors by exacerbating their alienation from the rest of society.[70] Furthermore, illegal "vice" activity—the very thing most business owners complain is so oppressive that it threatens to force them out of business—is spared government control.

EFFECTS OF SANCTIFIED SNAKE OIL

So now the concept of sanctified snake oil has been explained, and some of the problems caused by it have been explored. However, those examples have focused primarily on unintended consequences and confusions caused by stretched concepts and statistics based on them. Frankly, if these were its worst effects, sanctified snake oil would be a fiscal problem that could be solved simply by cutting funds to it.

But the effects of sanctified snake oil are not that simple. The next two chapters will explore the worst effects of sanctified snake oil: what happens when snake oil is accepted (unchallenged by government, the media, or any other organization that would and should debunk or challenge it) and used in critical decision making in the mental health and criminal systems. Let us first consider some other ways that this has happened:

"New York City now spends over one-fifth of all local social-service dollars in the county. It spends six times the local government average on Medicaid, welfare, homeless services and foster care . . . [and, as a result, spends] less than the national average [on] . . . education, sanitation, parks and roads."[71] This suggests that focusing on the exaggerated claims of sanctified snake oil salesmen has consequences to "traditional" (unarguably necessary) services. Such unintentional trade-offs are not uncommon. As another example, "Education policies instituted in the name of equality have in fact increased inequality."[72] This has happened because programs meant to help target groups instead "cream" the easiest-to-help members of those groups, helping them, but as a result, leaving those unhelped not only worse off, but no longer members of a group identified by its common needs.[73]

Similarly, clashes have occurred among groups with different disabilities. Wheelchair users fought for curb cuts, which then made it more difficult for blind people to locate corners.[74] The Americans with Disabilities Act (ADA) was, in fact, a study in unintended and should-have-been-anticipated consequences. Meant to provide access for people who had overcome physical disabilities, but not the social stigma that others project onto those disabilities, the ADA was written so broadly that it has been used by drug addicts, alcoholics, and people with mental, emotional, and behavioral disorders. This made the pool so large that the physically disabled were literally lost within it. Legislators, administrators, and other policymakers might have prevented this but appeared unwilling to set limits on the ADA or to support them against attack. Instead, like affirmative action and other worker rules that preceded it, all concerns focused on the fear of noncompliance. As a result, workplaces have been required to accommodate people with deficits that make them unable to perform the work assigned to them, or who pose dangers to others in the workplace. These rules are exacerbated by unions that also support workers against virtually any threats to their jobs. This was clearly reasonable when used to avert unjustified firings. Today, however, unions, affirmative-action officers, and advocates for the disabled, among others, often champion the causes of workers who have proven dangerous to coworkers, students, patients, and others with whom they come into contact.

Or consider that a *Wall Street Journal* article on the government's settlement with tobacco manufacturers found "that the measures proposed by the settlement will serve not to diminish but to *increase* smoking." The tobacco settlement requires tobacco companies to spend hundreds of millions of dollars to discourage tobacco use. But emphasizing the danger and deviant nature of smoking will enhance its glamour, especially among adolescents, who are tobacco companies' primary marketing targets.[75] Finally, consider that in 1993, when Andrea Dworkin and Catherine MacKinnon's antipornography statute was finally adopted, not here but in Canada, Canadian customs used the law to seize two "obscene" books—both written by Andrea Dworkin.[76]

These problems are unusual only because of their visibility. More common are the problems dealt with in the remainder of this book: fraud, confusions about real and implied risks, and the effects of sanctified snake oil on the criminal justice system, especially on criminal justice outcomes.

NOTES

1. "U. S. Kids Trailing in Math, Science," *New York Daily News* (February 25, 1998).

2. John Allen Paulos, *Innumeracy: Mathematical Illiteracy and Its Consequences* (New York: Hill and Wang, 1988).

3. Christopher S. Wren, "Phantom Numbers Haunt War on Drugs," *New York Times* (April 20, 1997).

4. Lawrence Garfinkel, Catherine C. Boring, and Clark W. Heath, Jr., "Changing Trends: An Overview of Breast Cancer Incidence and Mortality," *Cancer* (July 1, 1994), 222–227.

5. John M. Broder, "Big Social Changes Revive the False God of Numbers," *New York Times* (August 17, 1997).

6. James Q. Wilson, *Bureaucracy* (New York: Basic Books, 1989).

7. Arnold S. Trebach in Arnold S. Trebach and James A. Inciardi, *Legalize It? Debating American Drug Policy* (Washington, DC: American University Press, 1993).

8. Thomas Sowell, *The Vision of the Anointed* (New York: Basic Books, 1995).

9. Ibid.

10. John Allen Paulos, op. cit.

11. Barbara Tuchman, *The March of Folly* (Boston: G. K. Hall and Co., 1984).

12. Thomas Gilovich, *How We Know What Isn't So* (New York: Free Press, 1991).

13. Ibid.

14. Barry L. Beyerstein, "Why Bogus Therapies Seem to Work," *Skeptical Inquirer* (September/October 1997), 29–34.

15. Richard Robinson, *An Atheist's Values* (Oxford, England: Blackwell, 1975).

16. Wendy Kaminer, *Sleeping with Extraterrestrials* (New York: Pantheon Books, 1999).

17. Peter Huber, *Galileo's Revenge* (New York: Basic Books, 1991).

18. See, for example, Cynthia Crosson, *Tainted Truth* (New York: Touchstone Books, 1994); and Lawrence W. Sherman, *Preventing Crime: What Works, What Doesn't, What's Promising* (Washington, DC: U.S. Department of Justice, February 1997).

19. Peter L. Bernstein, *Against the Gods: The Remarkable Story of Risk* (New York: John Wiley & Sons, 1996).

20. Thomas Gilovich, op. cit.

21. John Allen Paulos, *A Mathematician Reads the Newspaper* (New York: Basic Books, 1995).

22. Cynthia Crosson, *Tainted Truth* (New York: Touchstone Books, 1994).

23. Ibid.

24. Tana Dineen, *Manufacturing Victims*, 2d ed. (Montreal: Robert Davies Publishing, 1998).

25. Darrell Huff, *How to Lie with Statistics* (New York: W. W. Norton & Co., 1954).

26. Steven A. Holmes, "Even if the Numbers Don't Add Up," *New York Times* (August 14, 1994).

27. Cynthia Crosson, op. cit.

28. National Institute of Justice and the Bureau of Justice Statistics, *Domestic and Sexual Violence Data Collection* (Washington, DC: National Institute of Justice and the Bureau of Justice Statistics, July 1996).

29. See, for example, Barbara Vobejda, "Still Feeling the Pain," *Washington Post National Weekly Edition* (June 9, 1997).

30. John M. Ellis, *Literature Lost* (New Haven, CT: Yale University Press, 1997).

31. Richard P. Brennan, *Heisenberg Probably Slept Here* (New York: John Wiley & Sons, 1997).

32. Karl Popper, quoted in Peter Huber, op. cit.

33. Carl Sagan, *The Demon-Haunted World* (New York: Random House, 1995).

34. Ibid.

35. Douglas R. Hofstadter, "World Views in Collision: The *Skeptical Enquirer* vs. The *National Enquirer*," in *Metamagical Themas: Questioning for the Essence of Mind and Pattern* (New York: Basic Books, 1985), 91–114.

36. Bruce Rind, Philip Tromovich, and Robert Bauserman, "A Meta-Analytic Examination of Assumed Properties of Child Sexual Abuse Using College Samples," *Psychological Bulletin* 124, no. 1 (July 1998), 22–53.

37. Kenneth K. Berry and Jason Berry, "The Congressional Censure of a Research Paper: Return of the Inquisition?" *Skeptical Inquirer* (January 1, 2000), 20.

38. Jonathan Rauch, "Washington's Other Sex Scandal," *National Journal* (August 7, 1999).

39. Ray Fowler (Administrative Director of the APA), Memo Re: "Controversy Regarding APA Journal Article," May 25, 1999.

40. Thomas Gilovich, *How We Know What Isn't So* (Free Press, 1991).

41. Susan Haack, "Science, Scientism, and Anti-Science in the Age of Preposterism," *Skeptical Inquirer* (November/December 1997), 37–42, 60.

42. Cathy Young, *Ceasefire: Beyond the Gender Wars* (New York: Free Press, 1999).

43. Christina Hoff Sommers, *Who Stole Feminism?* (New York: Simon and Schuster, 1994).

44. New York City Commission on the Status of Women, *Report of the Committee on Domestic Violence* (New York: Office of the Mayor, January 1996).

45. Michael R. Rand with Kevin Strom, *Violence-Related Injuries Treated in Hospital Emergency Departments* (Washington, DC: U.S. Department of Justice, August 1997).

46. Lindsay Novak, "When Domestic Violence Invades the Workplace," *Chicago Tribune* (October 12, 1997).

47. Eugene Kanin, "False Rape Allegations," *Archives of Sexual Behavior* 23, no. 1 (1994), 81–92.

48. James Alan Fox and Marianne W. Zavitz, "Homicide Trends in the United States" (Washington, DC: U.S. Department of Justice, January 1999).

49. M. Smith and E. Kuchta, "Trends in Violent Crime Against Women, 1973–89," *Social Science Quarterly* 74, no. 1 (March 1993).

50. Ben Wattenberg, "Kinsey: Kinky But Not Unique," *New York [Post* or *Daily News]* (November 22, 1997).

51. Jeremy Travis, *Measuring What Matters, Part Two: Developing Measures of What the Police Do* (Washington, DC: U.S. Department of Justice, November 1997).

52. Quoted in Richard Morin, "Warts and All," *Washington Post National Weekly Edition* (October 13, 1997).

53. Judith S. Wallerstein and J. B. Kelly, *Surviving the Breakup* (New York: Basic Books, 1980); and Judith B. Wallerstein and S. Blakeslee, *Second Chances: Men, Women and Children a Decade After Divorce* (New York: Ticknor and Fields, 1989).

54. Michael J. Lambert and Clara E. Hill, "Assessing Psychotherapy Outcomes and Processes," in *Handbook of Psychotherapy and Behavior Change*, 4th ed., edited by Allen E. Bergin and Sol L. Garfield (New York: John Wiley & Sons, 1994).

55. Robyn M. Dawes, *House of Cards: Psychology and Psychotherapy Built on Myth* (New York: Free Press, 1994).

56. Christina Hoff Sommers, op. cit. Also see Cathy Young, op. cit.

57. Richard Berman, "Junk Research Distorts Public Policy," *The Oregonian* (January 4, 1998).

58. Cathy Young, *Ceasefire: Beyond the Gender Wars* (New York: Free Press, 1999).

59. Stanton Peele, *The Diseasing of America* (New York: Lexington Books, 1995). Also see George Vaillant, *The Natural History of Alcoholism* (Cambridge, MA: Harvard University Press, 1983).

60. "Drug Abuse Resistance Education (DARE)" (Washington, DC: U.S. Department of Justice, September 1995).

61. Tana Dineen, op. cit.

62. Steven Smith and Susan Freinkel, *Adjusting the Balance: Federal Policy and Victim Services* (Westport, CT: Greenwood Press, 1988).

63. Lawrence W. Sherman, *Preventing Crime: What Works, What Doesn't; What's Promising* (Washington, DC: U.S. Department of Justice, February 1997).

64. Neil Gilbert, *Capitalism and the Welfare State* (New Haven, CT: Yale University Press, 1983).

65. Office for Victims of Crime, *FY 1998 Concept Paper Solicitation* (Washington, DC: U.S. Department of Justice [undated, obtained by faxback October 3, 1997]).

66. James Q. Wilson, op. cit.

67. S. Scarr, " 'Head Start and the Panacea Standard,' A Reply to Mann," *APA Observer* 10 (September 1997): 24–25.

68. T. L. Mann, "Head Start and the Panacea Standard," *APA Observer* 10 (September 1997): 10, 24.

69. Charles M. Haar and Daniel Fessler, *Fairness and Justice* (New York: Touchstone, 1986).

70. Kai T. Erikson, *Wayward Puritans* (New York: John Wiley & Sons, 1966).

71. Fred Siegel, "New York: Hooked on Social Spending," *New York Post* (October 5, 1997).

72. Stephen Thernstrom and Abigail Thernstrom, *America In Black and White* (New York: Simon and Schuster, 1997).

73. William J. Wilson, *The Truly Disadvantaged* (Chicago, IL: University of Chicago Press, 1987).

74. Joseph P. Shapiro, *No Pity* (New York: Random House, 1994).

75. Richard Klein, "Prohibition II . . ." *Wall Street Journal* (June 26, 1997).

76. Lynne V. Cheney, *Telling the Truth* (New York: Touchstone, 1995).

Chapter 5

The Ineffectiveness of Treatment and Prevention Programs

Objection, evasion, joyous distrust, and love of irony are signs of health; everything absolute belongs to pathology.

—Friedrich Nietzsche

The right to be left alone—the most comprehensive of rights and the most valued by civilized men.

—Louis Brandeis

There have been a number of excellent books written recently, and not so recently, on the effectiveness, and more often the ineffectiveness, of mental health treatment. Thomas Szasz is probably the best-known, and most extreme, critic of psychotherapy in all of its forms. Szasz suggests that mental illness is a pejorative label used against political and social dissidents, and he offers impressive proof to back up his assertions, which are at least partially true at least part of the time. At minimum, Szasz's criticisms should give pause to any practitioner, as well as to anyone considering treatment—and particularly to anyone who might recommend others for treatment.[1]

Jeffrey Masson's criticisms are different but no less sweeping or justified. He sees the dependent relationship of the client in relation to the therapist as so harmful that it offsets any good that might come from the therapeutic process. Masson is, ironically, the former curator of Sigmund Freud's library, and his book on Freud, *The Assault on Truth: Freud's Suppression of the Seduction Theory*, was one of the catalysts for the "recovered memory" movement.[2] Without accepting blame for his part in that fiasco, he has since repudiated therapy altogether. With his particular insight into past practice, and he, like Szasz, points to the shameful history of mental health treatment to demonstrate how dangerously destructive poor treatment can be.[3] Both also assert that "We must recognize that [psychotherapy] is a less intellectual process than most would suspect. It involves emotional manipulations and coercive forces."[4] Stanton Peele has done for alcohol counseling what Szasz and Masson have done for psychotherapy: he has shown it to be not only largely ineffective but more a means of social control than a technique of personal improvement.[5]

Robyn Dawes, unlike Szasz and Masson, does not suggest that therapy is never effective. He does point out, however, that many trained therapists ignore their training to practice ideologically based rather than scientifically based methods, and that, as a result, professional therapists as a group do not prove to be more effective than unschooled therapists who use appropriate treatment methods. Dawes, a psychologist, also notes that the American Psychological Association creation of the Psy.D. degree in 1971, which permitted students to obtain doctorates in psychology without rigorous training in research, was a major cause of the decline of effectiveness as a practice requirement.[6] Dawes was one of many members of the APA who, in 1988, expressed their dissatisfaction with the American Psychological Association's increasingly unscientific orientation by resigning from it to form the American Psychological Society (APS).[7] As a result, the APS is becoming the professional association for experimental psychologists, leaving the APA to clinicians. One comparison of these groups likened clinical psychology to astrology and experimental psychology to astronomy."[8]

Edward Dolnick in his 1998 book, *Madness on the Couch*, observed that the last branch of medicine to recognize the value of scientific inquiry was psychiatry.[9] A *Washington Post* review of the book observed of the "fathers of psychiatry that "Their sins were large and they are not easily forgiven. Many were arrogant and intellectually lazy. A few were habitual liars. As a group, they lacked the ability to question orthodoxy and to face the terrible threat of competing evidence. Virtually none was a scientist, although all cloaked themselves in the (too) magisterial robes of science."[10]

Tana Dineen's *Manufacturing Victims*, originally published in 1996, with a second edition following in 1998, has already been cited several times in this text. It is one of the newer additions to the critiques of various forms of counseling. Dineen notes that the recent expansion of the number of providers of counseling services has contributed to the fact that practitioners have moved beyond treating the "mentally ill." She demonstrates that through concept stretching and domain expansion (into "grief" work and "trauma" treatment, for instance), coupled with a healthy dose of advertising to "sell" these "new needs" to the public, service providers have created "needs" for their services that never before existed. Dineen suggests three principles on which the modern day mass production of victims relies: *psychologizing*—using psychological constructs to reduce real experiences to theories . . . [enabling] the Psychology Industry [to] pretend . . . to understand the unconscious, to know people better than they know themselves, and, thus, to be able to accurately interpret their experiences; *pathologizing*—turning . . . ordinary . . . people in abnormal . . . situations into "abnormal" people, labeling all victims "damaged," "wounded," "abused," "traumatized," incapable of dealing with it, getting over it or going on with life . . . ; [and], *generalizing*—equating the exceptional and brutal with the ordinary and the mundane; thus ignoring the differences which set victims apart [from one another].[11]

Dineen also notes that it was clinical psychology which created what she refers to as the "Psychology Industry" and that this "discipline" was never grounded in science. She explains that psychology is an immature discipline and that the voices of the few serious researchers in the discipline are drowned out by the "marketing noises" of the Psychology Industry. According to Dineen, psychology promotes its own "germ theory," which attributes psychological problems to abuse or trauma, and which further defines a host of human behaviors, misbehaviors, and life experiences—ranging from shopping too frequently to committing homicide—as psychological problems amenable to therapy; these notions have become common in schools, the political arena, and popular culture. As a result, there is now a tendency to see most people, and women in particular, as "wounded, hurt and damaged, weak and vulnerable, having someone else to blame, and needing to be healed and protected."[12]

At the same time, practitioners have turned away from treating the most seriously mentally ill, whose intractable conditions make them difficult patients.[13] This is clear from the fact that, despite the increase in third-party payments for mental health treatment, and perhaps because of it, the seriously and persistently mentally ill tend to receive brief "stabilization" in hospitals and are then prescribed medication, which they often fail to take, resulting in revolving-door rehospitalization. Worse, prisons are dealing with increasing numbers of mentally ill inmates who are unable to function with the minimal, if any, mental health treatment they are afforded.

At best, research demonstrates that only behavioral and cognitive methods appear to work in the area of "talk therapy."[14] Cognitive methods seem to work best with articulate, self-aware, middle-class people, especially women, because these methods require an ability to express emotional personal information and to comprehend sometimes complex concepts. But this may also demonstrate a particular interest in therapy among this population, or a preference for this type of patient by therapists.[15] Behavioral methods seem more effective when particular types of behavior changes, such as quitting smoking or overcoming phobias, are desired, as well as with less intelligent, less educated and less articulate people.[16]

In stating that these methods work, I mean that in testing them against control groups of patients who received no treatment, these methods have occasionally proved more effective than no treatment. However, many studies have not found a difference, and some have even found that people who receive no treatment have quicker, better recoveries than those in treatment.

Does this prove Szasz and Masson correct? Perhaps. But it is more likely that it proves Dawes and Dineen correct. The fact that there is so much variety in the findings on treatment effectiveness suggests that there is great variety in treatment—and since training in "talk therapy," even across disciplines such as psychology, social work, psychiatry, and even psychiatric nursing, is amazingly similar, it further suggests that the difference is not sanctioned by the professions, but is ignored instead. The work of these writers also makes clear that far more counseling is being provided than is needed. Research demonstrates that 50% of clients improve after eight sessions of counseling, and 75% by twenty-nine.[17] But somewhere between the eighth and twenty-ninth session, improvement is counterbalanced by overdependence on the counselor.[18] As a reflection of how much has changed in this regard, the widely used text *The Handbook of Psychotherapy and Behavior Change* will omit its customary chapter on brief therapy in its 2001 edition, "because almost all therapy is brief therapy now," according to the book's editor, Dr. Michael Lambert."[19]

It is likely that therapy tests so poorly because therapists are not following accepted treatment guidelines, are not correctly diagnosing patients, are creating dependence in patients by keeping them in treatment too long, and, in many cases, are treating people who are not mentally ill, not motivated to change, or whose needs cannot be met by current mental health technology. Therefore, if therapists stuck to what research has proven effective and applied appropriate methods only to the individuals who need and want them and to the extent needed, the approved therapies might consistently test, if not well, then certainly better than they currently do. But we will never know this unless we limit therapy to its proven effective uses and conduct further rigorous research to determine its effectiveness under those conditions.

Mental health professionals are committing malpractice when they use any methods not proved by research to be effective. The use of hypnosis, guided imagery, and the like to "recover" memories are examples of malpractice. They reflect ignorance of the myriad research that refutes these beliefs, as well as a refusal to consider that it is their methods that "create" memories—a refusal which flies in the face of three facts common to memory recovery that should give these practitioners pause: their extreme, often satanic nature (despite the fact that *no* such cases have been documented); their similarity (suggesting that they derive from a common source, i.e., the therapist); and the fact that those in treatment deteriorate as their retrieval of memories increases (people in competent therapy tend to at least stabilize, if not improve, once the cause of their distress is identified).

At best, this is not a strong argument for therapy. The findings related to the control groups on wait lists prove one fact incontrovertibly: most problems diminish over time without help.[20] At best, appropriate treatments effectively applied can speed recovery somewhat, but always with the possibility of creating excessive dependence on the therapist. Dawes noted too that most people who are successful in therapy use multiple methods to achieve mental health. While therapy may well help, successful clients are likely to read self-help books, talk with friends, and otherwise help themselves. When testing for therapeutic effectiveness, however, all progress is attributed to therapy.[21]

Furthermore, there is no evidence that psychotherapy works for all people, or in all instances. In fact, when psychotherapy has failed to achieve improvement for a considerable period (a month or more), it is particularly implausible that additional therapy would be of any help. Dr. Darrel A. Regier, director of the Division of Epidemiology and Services Research at the National Institute of Mental Health, observed that not all diagnosable mental disorders require treatment. Many people have relatively brief, self-limiting illnesses—not enough to warrant treatment. Dr. Regier headed the NIMH study which also found that in 70% of cases mental illness is untreated, and general physicians rather than mental health professionals treat the bulk of mentally ill people who seek help.[22] Yet this very study was used by Surgeon General David Satcher to induce people to seek help and encourage the government to pay for it.[23]

There is also confusion because psychopharmacology once seemed to promise complete relief from mental illness, a promise that was never realized. This confusion was exploited by politicians to deinstitutionalize huge numbers of mental patients, convincing the public that psychopharmacology would serve as its modern replacement. As we now know, psychopharmacology is effective with only a few serious mental illnesses, and then not with all sufferers. Further, once deinstitutionalized there is no way to ensure that patients will continue to take prescribed medication.

Particularly because people have such inflated ideas about the effectiveness of mental health treatment, it is important that policymakers and mental health experts help to clarify the parameters of treatment. The public needs to understand when mental health counseling can help and when it cannot. They also need to understand the circumstances for which effective mental health technologies have yet to be developed, and in which areas they are experimental at best.

Recently, some segments of the population have become more aware of these circumstances, as a result of a number of highly publicized cases of therapist fraud, abuse, incompetence, and other forms of malpractice.[24] The most extreme of these have been cases in which therapists were found to have implanted "false memories." These cases, in which lawsuits have been settled for multimillion-dollar figures and therapists have lost their licenses to practice, have made the public more skeptical of psychotherapy, with some therapists reporting 20% to 50% drops in their caseloads.[25] Also as a result, insurance companies and government agencies have increasingly prohibited payments for recovered memory therapy and states are disallowing court testimony based upon it. Washington State, in 1990, became the first state to provide crime-victim compensation to people who claimed to suffer from "repressed" memories. But in 1996, after public hearings which proved not only that the theory of repressed memories ran counter to all that is known about memory, but that people who entered repressed memory therapy almost always got worse instead of better as a result of the "treatment," Washington State became the first state to specifically eliminate repressed memory therapy from compensation by its victim fund.[26] A study of counseling claims paid in Washington State found that

The crime victim compensation files did not contain systematic information regarding the mental health of the crime victim at the outset and termination of treatment. . . . At times, the evidence for the diagnosis provided by the treating therapists seemed insufficient or inappropriate . . . the current reporting requirements for mental health treatment are not especially useful. The required reports were missing in many cases and the information requested and provided did not appear to capture the true picture of crime victim psychological distress . . . there was no relationship between [prognosis] and treatment length. There were no relationships between planned treatment modalities or use of medication and actual services.[27]

These findings suggest the lax nature of treatment, as well as the lax nature in which government oversees its provision and payment—but an important distinction must be reiterated. "It is different, and clearly unethical, to practice when it is clear that knowledge of an approach demonstrates that it is ineffective, as opposed to absence of knowledge."[28] One therapist observed of his colleagues that "Carried away with our popular acceptance, we have promised far more than we can deliver." He went on to predict what has since been demonstrated, that as clinicians continue to ignore the scientific principles (not to mention ethics) of their profession, the public is unable to distinguish them from "self-proclaimed psychics, new-age healers, religious gurus, talk-show hosts, and self-help book authors."[29] Dineen goes further, equating clinicians with drug dealers who encourage people to become "users" of the services of the Psychology Industry by encouraging their dependence.[30]

Yet mental health treatment continues to appeal to many. This may be less because of its effectiveness than because it purports to explain behavior in ways that appeal to many clients. "The proposition that we are unconsciously controlled by specific events in our histories is a seductive one for prospective patients because it lifts responsibility for seemingly self-inflicted problems off the patient, while at the same time promising to solve problems that may in fact have no satisfactory solution."[31] As a result, $125 billion was spent on mental health and substance abuse treatment in 1993, with 85% of the cost going to inpatient hospitalization, although hospitalization is rarely necessary in these cases. Therefore, the increase in inpatient services is just one indicator that these services are profit- rather than need-driven. Others are that low-cost services (which often served needier patients) were squeezed out by the push for hospital-based (and cost-based) services.[32] Tana Dineen observed that three kinds of "fabricated victims" have been created by the Psychology Industry:

synthetic victims—suggestible, or momentarily vulnerable . . . people who come to believe in what the industry sells and to accept as factual some revised, reinterpreted or fictionalized version of their own lives . . . ; *contrived victims*—who have been diagnosed with some genuine medical problem to which the Psychology Industry attributes a psychological cause . . . ; and, *counterfeit victims*—who turn to the Psychology Industry for a victim identity which they know to be false but which achieves for them some specific purpose, such as gaining sympathy or attention, avoiding blame, seeking revenge or defrauding financial benefit systems.[33]

Perhaps the biggest clue that mental health treatment is largely profit-driven is that "needs" seem to increase exponentially immediately following the creation of a funding stream targeted to those needs. Furthermore, the *Diagnostic and Statistical Manual* (DSM) is used to "prove" the existence of mental illnesses—and to qualify them for insurance coverage. Yet, as Herb Kutchins and Stuart A. Kirk explained in their second study of the DSM,

It is the repository of a strange mix of social values, political compromise, scientific evidence, and material for insurance claim forms. . . . One of the most powerful effects of DSM is due to its connection to insurance coverage: DSM is the psychotherapists' password for insurance reimbursement. . . . It is well known that drug companies provide substantial funding for the American Psychiatric Association's conventions and major scientific journals and reap enormous profits from the expanding market for psychiatric medications. They also fund a substantial number of psychiatric researchers. It is less well known that some pharmaceutical companies have contributed directly to the development of DSM. The companies have a direct financial interest in expanding the number of people who can be defined as having a mental disorder and who then might be treated with their chemical products. For this reason, drug companies are disturbed by the findings of many surveys that have found that a majority of people whom DSM would label neither define their own problems as mental illness nor seek psychiatric help for them. . . . The effects of DSM-driven research on public policy are . . . immediate. Congress and state legislatures use statistics on the number of people in the United States who suffer from mental illness as one basis for allocating public funds to various health programs. They look to public health epidemiologists for those statistics, and epidemiologists use DSM-based categories and definitions to count the mentally ill. To the extent that DSM is flawed, these national counts of the mentally ill are misleading to public policymakers."[34]

The count of the mentally ill has a profound impact not only on therapists' incomes, but on individuals' self-perceptions, on our perceptions of others, and on public policy. Recent legislation requiring parity between medical and mental health coverage, for instance, has caused some employers to cut back on employee medical coverage—but this might have been avoided if more reasonable estimates of the need for mental health treatment had been available.

My own interest in this was sparked, in fact, because I advocated for compensation funds for crime victims when they were meager and hard to come by where they did exist. Once those benefits were expanded, however, instead of going to the victims most in need, and to their greatest needs, these benefits went to those issues that newly self-defined victim "experts" defined—which just happened to be those services the "experts" provided. The experts were particularly adept at working with representatives of the criminal justice system to ensure that their services were recommended, and in some cases even mandated. While I was skeptical, I am admittedly not a clinician and had immersed myself in actuarial science and negligence law for my dissertation on victim compensation. So, although it caught me by surprise, I could not say for certain then whether recovered memory therapy was junk science or a new discovery of which I was unaware. As it took more and more compensation funding, however, I realized that it was imperative that I understand the subject.

The problem did not emanate from greedy therapists alone, however. In fact, beginning with deinstitutionalization and continuing through privatization, the government has encouraged mental health providers to "compete in the market-place," or engage in private practice. The result is that therapists can no longer count on salaries and must more aggressively recruit clients who can pay for their services, either out of pocket or because they are eligible for third-party payments. Entrepreneurial practice is essentially different from agency practice, then, and tends to attract a different type of practitioner.

So how did recovered memory therapy develop, if not through the theory-to-research continuum? It is not clear, but a few possibilities suggest themselves. For one, as noted, "memory retrieval" is used in Scientology to "recall" traumas that occurred during past lives, which are said to affect present perceptions.[35,36] For another, some victims of sexual assault do seem to *spontaneously* recall earlier victimizations only after a subsequent one. But it is important to understand that "spontaneous" recollections are not prompted by reading, journaling, hypnosis, or other "treatment methods"—and that they tend to complicate counseling because these victims tend to confuse aspects of the recent and past assaults and to be less clear about the circumstances of both assaults than are victims of a single assault, recent or past. Further, due to the poor state of research on repression, it is not clear whether these memories were ever really forgotten, or whether they were, instead, ignored until subsequent events made that impossible. And for a third, some counselors may overidentify abuse due to past underidentification, as noted earlier, or to ideological belief in vast, uncounted numbers of victims.

My study of victim compensation benefits suggests a fourth possibility: that recovered memory therapy was invented to enable victims to qualify for compensation benefits after the statute of limitations for reporting the crimes on which their claims were based had passed. Prior to their development, in fact, victim advocates had argued that reporting and filing deadlines should not expire until well after victims of intrafamilial abuse had moved out of the offender's household, but these arguments met with success in only a few states. Next it was argued that people victimized as children should not have their "clock" started until they reached adulthood, but this too was widely rejected. Finally, advocates turned to the fact that some victims seemed to "repress" their memories for some time after their assaults, as discussed above. So victim advocates argued that the "clock" on timely reporting or filing for compensation should not be started until these memories were "recovered." And, presumably because decision makers wanted to approve some form of expanded coverage, some states approved these rules.[37] It can be expected that some of these "recovered" memories will be verifiable, but only because some victims who never forgot their abuse claim that they did to be eligible for compensation. In fact, considering the timing of their development, it could be argued that victim compensation eligibility guidelines were the proximate cause of recovered memory therapy.

This is ironic, because even if it were possible to recover intact memories of repressed abuse, the act of doing so could never be defined as therapeutic. Let us forget for a moment that there is no known technology for recovering intact memories. Let us even forget that it is unethical to break down a patient's defenses, or to provide any service that fails to reduce symptomatology. *If* recovering memories were effective, it would be a criminal justice, not a therapeutic, tool because it purports to identify a crime and the perpetrator of that crime, *not* to reduce the trauma of crime. But recovered memory therapy is not a tool or a method—at best it is a means by which victims of long-past assaults can qualify for compensation despite statutes of limitations; at worst, it is a form of brainwashing at least as abusive as the assaults it claims to retrieve from memory.

No new discoveries had been made or research conducted, and no theory had been developed that would suggest it is possible to recover memories. After it was attacked for this very reason, proponents of recovered memory therapy attempted to publish proof of what were no more than ideological beliefs.[38] They argued that traumatic memories are stored differently from other memories, but offered only a handful of poorly conducted studies which failed to make their case. Even if these studies had proved the ability to repress memories so that they would be forgotten or otherwise lost to conscious thought (studies which are virtually impossible to conduct because the processes of storing, forgetting, repressing, and recalling memories are so poorly understood that we do not even have common definitions of these functions), they would offer scant help in developing methods to retrieve memories that would ensure their accuracy. Yet this is what recovered memory therapy purports to do—using "methods" such as hypnosis, sodium amytal, and guided imagery, well-recognized for their use in "brainwashing" (otherwise defined as "implanting false memories"), it claims to retrieve memories that are so accurate and intact that they can be relied upon not only to prove crimes recalled as a result, but to identify the perpetrators of those crimes so definitively that they led to convictions before their bogus nature was recognized by the courts.

It was only after recognizing the completely bogus nature of recovered memory therapy that I took a second look at the "satanic ritual abuse" cases in which preschool children had reportedly experienced horrible abuse at the hands of daycare center staff. By then, however, more had been written about them and, more importantly, more of it had been written objectively. It soon became clear to me that satanic ritual abuse and recovered memory therapy were not only junk science; they were also drains on funding pools created for legitimate victims, and their very creation undid much of the positive work that victim advocates had done in enabling the public to believe victims.

This is a common result of *medicalization*, in which all sorts of problems and conditions are addressed with the medical metaphors of diagnosis and treatment (alcoholism being an obvious example). Medicalization enables all forms of problems and human vulnerabilities to be marketed.[39] With public benefits and third-party payments, by extension, services are targeted to those who can afford them, rather than those who most need them, and the providers of payments, as well as the recipients of service, can be seen as those vulnerable to exploitation as a result of medicalization.[40]

TREATMENT PRACTITIONERS

One factor that confuses potential patients is that it is not always clear whether a mental health practitioner is a professional. Student interns often pass themselves off as psychiatrists, psychologists, social workers, psychiatric nurses, and other bona fide members of the professions in which they are training, when they are only permitted to practice under the supervision of a professional in their field of study. This is not the same as being an experienced professional. Also, job titles and credentials can mean different things in different jurisdictions. Some states have set standards for the credentialing of marriage and family therapists, for example, while in other states anyone can practice as a marriage and family therapist; and many states bestow the civil service title "social worker" on people in certain jobs, despite the fact that they may have no academic social work training—in fact, they may have no college training at all. The term "psychotherapist," originally coined as a catchall phrase to cover all professionals who practice counseling, is now often used by untrained and uncredentialed "service providers"—the term itself is completely unregulated.

Even the definition of "professional" is debatable. While the appellation is used for every field from psychics to psychiatrists, many experts consider professionals to be only those who hold doctoral degrees, or at least "terminal degrees" in professions that lack doctoral-level training. To many, even those with master's degrees are no more than semiprofessionals.[41] And sometimes professionals falsely claim more education than they have. "Dr." Susan Forward was found guilty of professional ethics violations when she breached the confidentiality of former client Nicole Brown Simpson on national television. Almost by accident it was discovered then that she had never earned more than a master's degree—but her most recent book is again attributed to "Dr." Susan Forward.[42]

It is also common for practitioners unwilling or unable to obtain legitimate advanced training to obtain degrees, including doctorates, from diploma mills—unaccredited schools that have no standards, rarely if ever hold classes, and require little more for "graduation" than payment of a fee. One way to detect bogus "professionals" is to determine whether they hold state licenses and malpractice insurance, which limit provision to graduates of schools accredited in their discrete fields of study. Another clue to these phonies is that they tend to hold one or more "certificates" and "diplomatcies" bestowed by membership groups. And if they claim professional publications, these are books published by vanity presses and articles published in nonpeer-reviewed journals. These diploma mills, groups, and publishers exist only to give the facade of professionalism to fakers and survive only by collecting tuition, dues, and subscription fees from the people whose poses they support. Ironically, these activities usually go undetected because credentials are rarely checked, and these practitioners develop their own "subspecialties," denying that anyone with whom they disagree shares their "field of expertise" (although "fields" are not defined as "subspecialties," but as the generally recognized professions such as psychiatry, psychology, and social work).

Licenses also do not guarantee that professionals will practice according to the standards of their professions. Many mental health practitioners continue to use such untested, poorly tested, or even bogus techniques of recovered memory therapy, biofeedback, and Eye Movement Desensitization and Reprocessing (EMDR).[43] And professional associations, which are, sadly, often little more than public relations agencies for their members, not only tend to ignore these bogus services, but encourage them as means to increase their members' incomes, and thereby their own. For instance, in 1998 the New York State Chapter of the National Association of Social Workers (NASW) listed Clinical Hypnosis and EMDR among the continuing-education programs that it had approved for continuing-education credits.[44] Furthermore, despite the fact that the NASW Code of Ethics requires that social workers "keep current with emerging knowledge . . . and fully use . . . research evidence in their professional practice,"[45] NASW itself has been slow to reflect emerging knowledge in its policy statements, such as that on recovered memories.[46] As a result, many social workers take seminars that present these inaccuracies as fact in order to earn the CEUs necessary for license renewal.

These concerns, while worsened in modern times with the provisions of government payments for these services, are not entirely new. William James criticized Freudian methods because Freudians would forget that their ideas were theories and would listen for information from patients that would support their theories, ignoring contradictory information, which James further characterized as "obsessive thinking."[47]

BIASES OF TREATMENT PROVIDERS

Even properly credentialed service providers often have biases that affect their practice. Speculating why, two researchers observed that the helping professions "by training are not traditionally oriented toward prevention."[48] This brings to mind the adage that if all you have is a hammer, everything looks like a nail. Service providers routinely define the "needs" of others as the services they provide. This makes a mockery of the needs-assessment process considered the first step in any type of program development, and it comes as no surprise that counseling is so often defined as a need, because government agencies and private funders traditionally ask social workers and other counselors to conduct needs assessments. So, for example, although crime victims consistently report that emergency funds and security items (such as locks) are the things they most need after crimes,[49] they instead tend to be provided with more and more counseling.[50] As Osborne and Gaebler pointed out in their influential 1992 book, *Reinventing Government*, "Communities understand their problems better than service professionals.... Institutions and professionals offer 'service'; communities offer 'care.' "[51]

Recall that patient and therapist ratings of therapy outcomes are notoriously biased, with therapists often reporting improvements that go unrecognized by others.[52] Another problem is that service providers often draw conclusions based on preconceived beliefs rather than seeking the truth. For instance, Dr. Bruce Perry 'interviewed' the children released by the Branch Davidians and, after two months, got admissions of abuse from them, although, "the official Justice Department report on the event concludes that the reports of child abuse are false."[53]

THEORY, PRACTICE WISDOM, AND "PROOF"

It has been noted that "Scientific clinical research has little or no impact on the practitioner."[54] If practitioners ignore research, how then do they develop the ideas on which they base their practice? Most base them on theories, either self-developed or developed by others (such as "experts" like Sigmund Freud). Often these practitioners actually believe that their work *is* scientific, erroneously equating theory and even so-called expertise with science. Theory, and its even weaker ancestor, "practice wisdom," are steps on the path toward the creation of science. Unfortunately, however, many more theoretical paths lead to dead ends than lead to science.

Practice wisdom consists of ideas that practitioners develop during the course of their work with clients. It incorporates "clues" about causes and effects of experiences and behaviors and methods that help people overcome problems. Over time, practitioners are likely to see numerous clients who share at least some characteristics or experiences, which lead them to draw conclusions about particular characteristics or experiences and their effects. However, practitioners tend to minimize the extent to which geographical conditions (who lives nearby) and practitioners' own characteristics and contacts affect the particular clients who choose to use their services. Therefore, they may attribute too much to similarities among clients or assume that their caseloads are typical of those of their colleagues. Sometimes, too, practitioners have ideological (or even pathological) reasons to want clients to reflect particular characteristics, and they then project them onto clients who do not possess them.

As a result, "There are alarming discrepancies between therapists' accounts of what takes place in an interview or therapy session and what is demonstrated in video- or audiotapes of the same sessions."[55] For instance, a study of the Pima County Victim/Witness Advocate Program in Tucson[56] concluded that "despite the victims' feelings that the program helped them considerably, the measure of emotional trauma did not indicate any substantial effects."[57]

Practice wisdom, then, is far from foolproof—it is most effective when, as implied, practitioners are particularly wise, which also implies that they have extensive, broad experience. Practice wisdom is particularly useful, for example, when several seasoned practitioners compare notes in order to urge their professional societies to address emerging needs or to bring focus on new, growing, or changing problems.

When practitioners consider altering their practice in response to observations gained through practice wisdom, their next step after identifying the problem (which is the real contribution of practice wisdom) should be to develop these observations into a scientifically testable theory. A theory is, then, more than just an idea or problem identification. It is an educated guess positing that one thing has an effect on something else, which can then be tested and proved or disproved.

Sometimes, if the need for a service appears urgent but science offers no means of meeting the need, practitioners will base treatment ideas on theory or near research; that is, on either untested ideas posited to be effective or research findings about similar populations. Both methods are justifiable if, indeed, there are no better, proven methods available and if such practice is regarded as experimental (and clients are informed of that fact). For example, considerable research has been conducted on crisis-intervention techniques, which have been found helpful in quickly returning clients to their precrisis level of functioning. Most such research was conducted on soldiers returning from battle. However, when feminists began to recognize in consciousness-raising sessions held during the early 1970s that many women had been unwilling to disclose rape (or had done so only to be accused by therapists of "fantasizing"), they suggested using crisis intervention with victims of rape. This theory reflected both the similarity between wartime violence and criminal violence and feminism's focus in the 1970s on women as healthy and able to regain their emotional equilibrium with a minimum of help. However, practice such as this has continued for almost three decades without sufficient research to justify its continued use.

Some advocacy therapists, however, actually reject these cautions. Consider the following excerpt from a chapter called "Childhood Trauma: Politics and Legislative Concerns for Therapists" by Sherry A. Quirk and Anne P. DePrince, which appeared in *A Feminist Clinician's Guide to the Memory Debate*: "As early as May, 1994, [R. Christopher] Barden [founder and president of the National Association for Consumer Protection in Mental Health Practices] stated, 'No state or federal funds should be used for any therapy that has not been shown safe and effective.' Language such as this threatens the very field of psychotherapy. The terms 'safe and effective' and 'scientific,' as defined by Barden, do not include the knowledge base that therapists have obtained from clinical observation. Following this logic, proposals such as Barden's put experimental psychologists and laboratory scientists in a watchdog role over therapists."[58]

Experimental psychologists and laboratory scientists are not "watchdogs"; instead, they can be likened to filters through whom responsible, ethical practitioners subject their practice wisdom and theories in order to reality-test their clinical observations—which hardly constitute a knowledge base! Practitioners who fail to do so are clearly in denial about the possibility that their untested methods could be ineffective or even harmful to their patients, and these very practitioners are among those who promote the pathological nature of denial, as well as the other elements of snake oil.

DRUGS, DRUG "ABUSE," AND TREATMENT

We know that psychopharmacology works effectively for some sufferers of some mental illnesses. Lithium is probably the most effective pharmacological treatment, but it works with only about half of all patients with bipolar disorder (commonly known as manic-depression).[59] Antipsychotic medications are more effective from an institutional point of view, quieting symptoms, than from the viewpoint of patients, who often prefer the grandiosity of their hallucinations to the banality of real life. These drugs also have unpleasant side effects that range from dry mouth to sexual dysfunction. This is probably why many patients stop taking antipsychotic medications soon after they are released from institutional settings.

While Prozac has been hailed as the aspirin of mental health, it should be regarded much more cautiously. Prozac has not been well tested, and not enough time has passed to evaluate its long-term use for any patients. However, Prozac is increasingly being prescribed—even to children. In fact, its maker, Eli Lilly, in anticipation of FDA approval to prescribe it to children, has developed mint- and orange-flavored liquid versions.[60]

Ritalin, on the other hand, is more commonly prescribed for children (and abused by adults), because it appears to enable children with poor attention spans to focus their thinking. But many experts consider Ritalin a way of relieving symptoms without teaching children how to develop the skill of concentration.[61] Even a supporter of Ritalin, Julie Doy, who is president of Children and Adults with ADD (CHADD) and has two children on Ritalin, was quoted as saying, "We are concerned with reports that managed care is forcing quick diagnoses and putting roadblocks in the way of full treatment."[62] Ritalin use more than doubled from 1990 to 1995, and now over 1.5 million people are on the stimulant,[63] which is increasingly being prescribed for adults[64] and used recreationally because of its similarity to methamphetamine.[65]

Prozac and Ritalin are also problematic because they treat depression and Attention Deficit Disorder (ADD), respectively. Depression is the most common psychiatric diagnosis—but it also can be a factor in other diagnoses. Managed care increases the likelihood, however, that diagnoses will be made quickly and will lean toward those illnesses that are cheap and easy to manage. On the other hand, ADD is seriously overdiagnosed—some experts question whether it exists at all. In fact, ADD is often "diagnosed" by elementary school teachers,[66] whose motivation as well as skill in this area is questionable.

In the area of substance abuse treatment, the primary pharmacological success has been methadone, a heroin substitute that allows users to function without impairment. But even methadone is a qualified success, critics considering it a substitute drug rather than a treatment.

We must recognize that the increasing tendency to solve problems with medication parallels the desire to solve problems with drugs that we currently consider illicit. In between are the 10% of hospital admissions attributable to prescription drug abuse, which have a combined social cost ranging from $10 billion to $15 billion per year.[67] Is the answer to reduce drug use, accept it—or, perhaps, to rethink our proclivity for single, simple, sweeping solutions and consider all drug use on a case-by-case basis?

These questions become even more important when we consider illicit drugs. But illicit drug use—and even the definition of "illicit" and "drug"—have been the most frequently snake-oiled issues in the history of this country. As discussed in chapter 2, for a country to offer both freedom and civilization, its citizens must display personal responsibility. For some, this means avoiding any substance or experience that might reduce one's level of functioning or even alter one's mood. For others, it means never admitting such behavior, which, while hypocritical, also ensures a level of discretion about where, when, and how drugs are used, or, in modern terms, a reduction in the "quality-of-life" crimes associated with substance abuse. For still others it means responsible use; that is, use under conditions and limitations that ensure that one's altered state causes no negative effects, at least to others.

Our Founding Fathers saw no need to include drug-use limitations in government legislation, viewing it as an issue of both individual conscience and social control (the latter meaning the opinion of the community coupled with religious and other ideological beliefs, not government acting on behalf of society). The primary drug of the time was alcohol, which, from Colonial times until the Civil War, was used excessively by modern standards.[68] Most Colonists and Early Americans considered alcohol to be a beverage, an intoxicant, and a medicine and were unconcerned about abuse as we define it, although they seriously sanctioned inappropriate drinking behavior and drunkenness.

There were alternative opinions about alcohol even then, however. Dr. Benjamin Rush, a signer of the Declaration of Independence, is considered the "father" of the disease model of alcoholism. "Disease model" proponents consider Rush, as a result, to be a "forward" thinker. But Rush also considered lying, murder, and political dissent to be diseases.[69] And,

among the things he got done . . . were to develop, practice, teach and spread the custom of bloodletting in cases where prudence or mercy had heretofore restrained its use. He and his students drained the blood of very young children, of consumptives, of the greatly aged, of almost anyone unfortunate enough to be sick in his realms of influence . . . [A]s late as 1851, a committee appointed by the State Legislature of New York solemnly defended his thoroughgoing use of bloodletting. It scathingly ridiculed and censured a physician, William Turner, who had the temerity to write a pamphlet criticizing Dr. Rush's doctrines and calling, "the practice of taking blood in diseases contrary to common sense, to general experience, to enlightened reason and to the manifest laws of the divine Providence."[70]

In fact, the reason that Rush believed alcoholism to be a disease was that he believed "excitability of the blood vessels" to be the "single cause of disease,"[71] a theory that dictated his support of bloodletting to reduce the internal effects of external stimulants, as well as his disapproval of excessive drinking.

Early Temperance proponents were religious leaders rather than scientists, and they adopted Rush's disease model (without, of course, considering the theory on which it was based) because it supported their beliefs. This religious fervor, and the equation of alcohol with sin, led Temperance leaders to move from their original stance of moderation to calls for total abstinence. It was the religious Oxford Group Movement on which AA was based; Dr. Robert Smith, the cofounder of AA, had belonged to the Oxford Group Movement before he met cofounder Bill Wilson.[72] Wilson's spiritual awakening had, on the other hand, been gained pharmacologically, when he had been "treated" with the hallucinogen belladonna at Town's Hospital.[73]

As a result, AA was from its inception a "belief system" rather than any form of "treatment regimen." Peele noted that "Although AA proposes a biological explanation for alcoholism, its climate is that of nineteenth-century revivalistic Protestantism. The twelve steps in the AA credo are an obeisance to G-d (G-d is mentioned six times) and the need for taking moral inventory and for contrition."[74] AA has also been observed to have cultlike characteristics such as exclusivity, social isolation, rote repetition of doctrine, blind faith in a leader, rigid rules of behavior, and programmed daily activities.[75] But largely because medical and psychological professionals abdicated their roles toward alcoholics, AA "got the franchise"—by default.[76]

By the 1970s, AA had become the model for all treatment programs and a linchpin in the provision of services for drinking problems in the United States. At the same time, the National Council on Alcoholism (the public-relations arm of the AA movement) convinced Americans that there are millions of unrecognized and unacknowledged alcoholics who require immediate medical and group treatment. As treatment for drugs and alcohol moved away from the self-help concept that AA originally endorsed, it became more coercive, more hospital-oriented, and more expensive.[77]

Because personal motivation and its voluntary nature are the features of AA (and all ideological programs) that make it effective, these changes decreased AA's effectiveness—*if* the coercive, cost-intensive program could be considered AA at all! Peele observed that

Disease concepts of misbehavior are bad science and are morally and intellectually sloppy. . . . Disease categorizations fail at the central goal said to justify them—the possibility of ameliorating the problem behavior by medical therapy. . . . By revising notions of personal responsibility, our disease conceptions undercut moral and legal standards exactly at a time when we suffer most from a general loss of social morality. . . . Disease notions actually increase the incidence of the behaviors of concern. They legitimize, reinforce, and excuse the behaviors in question. . . . Even when [AA members] don't relapse after treatment, they often seem burdened with their alcoholic or addicted self-image to a degree that hinders their functioning.[78]

Another critic of AA noted that "Twelve-step programs offer . . . the antithesis of therapy. There is no cure; the solution provided . . . entails an endless attendance at meetings. An old slogan says, 'You never graduate from Al-Anon,' and you don't; you become addicted to it. . . . Somewhere in the quagmire of the AA movement . . . the meaning of *recovery* was lost."[79]

Peele particularly laments the increase in disease identification among the young, noting that children and adolescents tend to attribute agency and responsibility to forces outside of themselves, a concept reinforced by the disease model. So, for instance, those who curtail drug and alcohol use following treatment tend to attribute their recovery to their group or the treatment and discount their own abilities in the process.[80]

A summary by researchers at the Downstate Medical Center Department of Psychiatry observed that the data fail to support AA's claims of higher success rates than clinical treatment. In fact, they note that when population differences are taken into account, the reverse is true. No study has ever found AA or its offshoots to be superior to any other approach, or even to be better than not receiving any help at all, but other methods that have regularly been found superior to AA and other standard therapies for alcoholism have been completely rejected by American treatment programs.[81] Alternatives to AA are tailored to the individual rather than religious or group- or disease-oriented[82] and are most effective when matched to client needs and are accountable for results.[83] "Nondisease rehabilitation programs—such as those teaching DWIs social skills (like those needed to reject additional drinks), enhanced personal responsibility in decision making, and methods for drinking moderately—*have* shown beneficial results. Yet almost no such nondisease programs for drunk drivers remain in the United States, and these few are under strong attack."[84]

Follow-up studies on alcoholism find that remissions are usually intermittent rather than stable over long periods of time.[85] George Vaillant, in his seminal 1983 book, *The Natural History of Alcoholism*, found that "many long-term studies of the course of alcoholism concur that treatment has little if any lasting effect" and that with or without AA, approximately 5% of the alcoholics sustained abstinence.[86] "AA's undeserved status as a universal cure for alcoholism and the beleaguered state of skill-training approaches for drunk drivers are some of the many indicators that alcoholism practices are based on the prejudices of a few rather than on scientific data."[87] These ideas do not proliferate because they are accurate but because they are ignored by most of the public, and there is no pro-alcoholism or pro-drug abuse movement. As a result, occasional suggestions to rethink drug and alcohol policy go unheard, while unsubstantiated claims about the disease model are perpetuated by members of the treatment industry whose livelihoods depend on it.[88]

Ironically, like mental health treatment, treatment for alcoholism may not suffer from simple ineffectiveness, but from the fact that it is so widely applied to people who may either not be alcoholic or may not be amenable to changing their drinking habits. But we will never know this for certain unless we try to limit treatment to those who need, want, and can benefit from it, and then rigorously research the results of their treatment.

Peele also observed that "Estimates of the number of alcoholics requiring treatment are wildly overblown, and reputable epidemiological researchers find that as little as one percent of the population fits the clinical definition of alcoholism—as opposed to the 10 percent figure regularly used by the alcoholism industry."[89] The newer theories of alcoholism relate the "discovery" of an "early" or "high" bottom, which suggests that younger and less heavy drinkers (as well as drinkers who do not define themselves as alcoholics) can be helped by AA and related treatments.[90] In truth, nearly 80% of Americans adults do not drink at all, or drink so little that they consume only 20% of all the alcohol consumed in the United States. The other 20%, however, consume the other 80% of the alcohol—and half of them, or 10% of the adult population, consume more than 50% of the total amount of alcohol drunk in the United States."[91] Nevertheless,

since the mid-1970s, the emphasis [in alcoholism treatment] has been on recruiting prosperous, functioning individuals who do not appear to be alcoholics. . . . In fact, because these people are so unexceptional, they must often be persuaded of the potential severity of their drinking problems. . . . Since such alcoholics are often judged to be in "denial" and blind to the true nature of their problem, they often need to be forcibly confronted with their alcoholism by loved ones and treatment personnel. . . . This contrasts with the early philosophy of Alcoholics Anonymous, which emphasized that the alcoholic needed to accept his condition voluntarily. The change has meant that coercive tactics are now a regular part of the treatment arsenal.[92]

In addition, one of the largest growth areas in the field of alcoholism is the effort to encourage "codependents" (the spouses of addicts and alcoholics) and their families to seek treatment. It is rivaled only by the effort to recruit "adult children of alcoholics" for therapy.[93] Even so,

In the fall of 1991, at the national conference of the American Association for Marriage and Family Therapy, psychiatrist Steven J. Wolin, a keynote speaker, publicly denounced the ACoA and codependence movements. . . . When a ranking member of the ACoA movement was later asked by a reporter from *USA Today* to respond, he answered, "They're just jealous of all the money we're making." [By the 1980s] the self-help domain had expanded to include just about every compulsive or self-defeating behavior one could think of. It was like an evangelist movement: each program was a part of the larger AA religion, each one reframing reality to conform to the same monolithic culture and belief system . . . sources of information from outside the program are not to be used because they "dilute" the spiritual nature of the meetings. Therapy, therapists, and professional terminology are also taboo topics of discussion, as are other recovery or treatment programs. . . . Such limitations on freedom of inquiry and discussion are common throughout the wider movement. . . . New ideas aren't readily embraced and new methodologies from outside any given program are viewed as a threat.[94]

One reason for this is that AA practitioners tend themselves to be successful AA alumni—who never graduate.

What we "know" about alcoholism . . . has been determined by an active group of prosely-tizers for AA and the alcoholism movement, most of whom are alcoholics. . . . Addictions professional Susan Nobleman, conducting a survey on how addictions counselors enter the field, learned that 71 percent of the professionals she surveyed had entered as a result of a personal need for alcoholism treatment. . . . Emil Chiauzzi and Steven Liljegren noted in a 1993 article in *Substance Abuse Treatment* that the addictions field is one of the few areas of professional endeavor where the counselors and the patients are drawn from the same con-stituency, hence the twelve-step bias. . . . True believers recruit true believers.[95]

Peele observed that "Nowhere but in the United States is a personal history of ad-diction considered essential for helping others combat the same problem. . . . Recovering alcoholics and addicts often move directly from the patient to the therapist role because the treatment setting is the only one with which they are comfortable and familiar aside from a drug-using and drinking one."[96]

As a result of AA's creeping monopoly, AA-type treatment has become the norm for drug as well as alcoholism treatment—even though it has never been in-formed by the differences among substances or their differing effects on health and behavior. But definitions become even more convoluted in regard to drugs, because no level of use is legally acceptable, which is translated by treatment pro-fessionals as all levels of drug use are *ab*use.

Dr. Ronald Siegel, the foremost researcher of the effects of intoxicating sub-stances on animals, observed that

[I]ntoxication with plant drugs and other psychoactive substances has occurred in almost every species throughout history . . . the universal pursuit of intoxication implies the exis-tence of direct connections between the molecular chemistry of the drugs and the chem-istry of the central nervous system, such as opiate receptors in the mammalian brain, a biological investment that is difficult to think of as arising by accident . . . efforts to teach people to control their drug use and avoid excessive amounts or dangerous practices would be more in tune with the reality of a modern complex society in which citizens must learn to control a variety of potentially addicting behaviors including eating, gambling, and tele-vision viewing. . . . Calvinistic pharmacology has prevented us from seeing pleasurable changes in the body or mind as fulfilling health needs.[97]

The University of Michigan Institute for Social Research also found that sub-stance abuse is age- and situation-related—it increases when adolescents leave home and decreases when they take on responsibilities such as a family.[98] Research has shown that serious drug abusers have other serious background problems and that these problems do not disappear when they stop using drugs. That is to say, the problems of drug abusers may be unrelated or only tangentially related to the fact of their drug use.[99] Similarly, research into the relationship between alcohol and violence finds that individuals with particular biological and personality characteristics tend to be both violent and heavy users of alcohol, but that neither behavior causes the other.[100] And while AA appears to work for some drinkers, it appears that particular characteristics of those drinkers and their perceptions of drinking may affect outcomes of AA and other recovery methods.[101]

Total drug abuse spending exceeded $2 billion in 1990, 59% of which was paid for by the public sector due to the limited insurance available to cover this cost. But most treatment is ineffective because patients rarely obtain treatment matched to their needs or circumstances and treatment seekers, particularly those without insurance coverage, are often placed on waiting lists until they have lost their motivation to quit.[102] Like abstinence from alcohol abuse, drug abstinence tends to be sporadic rather than permanent. In 1982, Joseph Califano estimated that at least 90% of New York's heroin addicts were using heroin again soon after treatment. Substantial evidence indicates that addiction is not amenable to medical interventions.[103] Similarly, Dineen noted that "A survey of Fortune 500 companies indicated that 79% recognized that substance abuse was, 'a significant problem,' but, '87 percent reported little or no change in absenteeism since the programs began and 90 percent saw little or no change in productivity ratings.' "[104] Westchester County, New York, limited hospitalizations for drug detoxification to one per person after recognizing that one-quarter of their Medicaid payments were going to 5% of their caseload and that many drug addicts and alcoholics repeatedly entered detox to lower the amount of drugs they need, then resumed usage as soon as they left the facility.[105]

Not only does alcohol and drug treatment prove to have limited effectiveness, but a substantial proportion of alcoholics appear to recover without formal treatment.[106] This suggests, in fact, that at least some of the success attributed to formal treatment actually results from the fact that some alcoholics coincidentally choose to recover at the time that they seek formal help in doing so.

Definition stretching paints all drugs and drug use with the same broad brush. This is so in part because, in October 1969, the Nixon administration transferred the responsibility for ranking drugs according to their danger and potential for abuse from health officials and the surgeon general to the attorney general and his chief narcotics officer."[107] This led to the fact that in the mid-1980s, "Lee Dogoloff and Dick Williams [former drug czar and his assistant] together effected the biggest change in drug policy since Nixon launched the Drug War. They took the leadership away from doctors and scientists and handed it to untrained, emotionally motivated parents. They then directed policy not at the most dangerous drugs, but at the one parents worried about as much for reasons of family politics and culture as health."[108]

This is not to suggest that any drug, even marijuana, is completely benign, especially when used by the young. For instance, marijuana acts as a buffer, which enables users to tolerate problems rather than face them and make changes that might increase the quality of their social functioning and satisfaction with life. Personal growth involves learning to cope with stress, anxiety and frustration, and the many other difficulties that life presents; and drug abuse, especially among the young, can interfere with this process, leading to arrested development.[109] But this does demonstrate how narrowly and ideologically the debate over drugs has become. The debate uses the hyperbole of labeling critics of failed drug policy and those who advocate alternatives as "traitors," even though many advocate more effective drug abuse policies that would reduce the negative effects of drug use.[110] This is also an effect of any policy that defines its strategy in war metaphors.[111] It is ironic, however, that even as society derides drugs because they enable users to escape or deny reality, we increasingly accept and even support efforts to allow people to attribute bad behavior to poor functioning, bad parenting and trauma.

TREATING EMOTIONAL TRAUMA

Trauma, like grief, does not constitute mental illness but is, instead, a normal reaction to a life-threatening event. Its symptoms diminish over time, and there is no evidence that counseling is effective in diminishing it more completely, although cognitive counseling, which helps adult patients understand their experiences and place them in perspective, sometimes helps diminish symptoms more quickly. Therefore, counseling might help some "victims" of trauma whose reactions are so extreme that they risk committing suicide, returning to or increasing drug or alcohol use, or otherwise engaging in dangerous behavior if their reactions are not lessened quickly.[112] On the other hand, medical studies demonstrate that severe trauma can damage the brain, particularly the hippocampus, which is vital to memory and cognition,[113] making counseling difficult if not impossible to comprehend for those who would appear most seriously in need of help.

However, trauma treatment has become 10%–20% of all counseling[114] for a number of reasons. Perhaps most significant is that crime-victim compensation is now available in every state to pay for the counseling of most victims of crime. Yet my own doctoral dissertation analyzing the history, development, and policies of crime-victim compensation agencies suggests that counseling was provided to victims not because they needed or even wanted it, but because victim compensation agencies viewed counseling as a rough approximation of cash for "pain and suffering," payments that they were loathe to provide for fear of fraud.[115] This view was perpetuated by the mental health professionals who designed victim services, probably more out of their own professional preferences than those of the victims whose needs they were supposed to assess and then meet. Dineen observed, in a similar vein, that "As the country's attention has shifted somewhat from 'health and welfare' to 'law and order,' so too has that of the Psychology Industry. Where the secret of success for a psychologist once was to develop a professional association with a physician or psychiatrist, it now is to develop a working relationship with law enforcement or the legal profession."[116]

This view is supported by the fact that use of counseling by victims has been far from uniform. In fact, as noted, half of all victims of rape and child abuse receive counseling, while a scant 1%–4% of other victims do,[117] despite the fact that it has been determined that no more than 25% of victims suffer reactions to crime that warrant counseling.[118] This skew, then, may reflect society's perception of the effects of different crimes, society's (mis)perception of the greater weakness of women and children, or the fact that women are the most frequent users of counseling services, for themselves and their children. It may also reflect the fact that counselors find women and children to be particularly desirable clients.[119]

Many critics attribute the proliferation of counseling in the areas of rape and child abuse to the fact that efforts to encourage detection and reporting of these crimes have created a "victim industry," which zealously "finds" and even "creates" cases to justify its existence. It is undeniable that these are the areas where reporting has increased most, but also where more and more minor and ambiguous cases are entering the system, because there do not appear to be many more serious cases to "find."[120] Critics also contend that sweeping generalizations, like "children never lie about abuse," and misperceptions about the workings of memory have caused innocent people to be charged, prosecuted, and even convicted of crimes that never occurred.

Sometimes these phony cases enter the system through malice, as when mothers claim that their children were abused by their fathers in order to avoid sharing custody. More insidious, however, because they are harder to disprove, are cases concocted by therapists through faulty methodologies. For instance, Richard Gardner, head of child psychiatry at Columbia University, concluded that the use of anatomically correct dolls is such a significant contaminant that he would consider any examiner who utilizes them to be incompetent.[121] This was proved by an extensive study by Stephen Ceci and Maggie Bruck, who found that both abused and nonabused children played with anatomically correct dolls in nearly identical ways.[122] Even so, the Department of Justice currently distributes, in its series *Portable Guides to Investigating Child Abuse*, a booklet titled "Interviewing Child Witnesses and Victims of Sexual Abuse," which describes the use of anatomically correct dolls as investigatory tools. And the Council on Scientific Affairs of the American Medical Association ruled that refreshing memories with hypnosis "can involve confabulations and pseudomemories and . . . appear to be less accurate than nonhypnotic recall."[123]

Coercive methodologies are now recognized as the cause of the allegations that created the satanic ritual abuse scares of the previous decade.[124] They were perpetuated by local "innovations" that discouraged detection of these poor techniques. In

Edenton, North Carolina, parents were told that their child "victims" were eligible for compensation only if they were treated by a handful of doctors and therapists in that city "that were working on this particular case."[125] In San Diego, the same few "approved" therapists "detected" crimes, "treated" their effects, and approved their payment through state funds.[126] Both methods encourage false reports to pad billings and also risk evidence contamination as therapists work with multiple victims of the same case. It is allowed to continue, however, due to government support and lack of media skepticism, and therefore lack of public awareness.

The *Washington Post* editorialized in 1997 that "Children all too often suffer terribly at the hand of perverse and brutal adults . . . children must be protected not only from predators but from counselors of questionable credentials."[127] Or consider the observation of George Franklin, who served almost seven years of a life sentence based on his daughter Eileen's recovered memory that he had murdered her friend decades earlier. Upon filing malpractice lawsuits against Deputy District Attorney Elaine Tipton and Dr. Lenore Terr, the expert whom Franklin claims conspired with Tipton to knowingly present false testimony against him, he commented, "However nutty or even malicious Eileen's accusations were, they would have had little effect on my life if the other defendants in this case . . . had acted responsibly."[128]

MANDATED TREATMENT

The discussion of the ineffectiveness and even negative results of treatment should give pause to anyone supporting mandated treatment for any purpose. But mandated treatment is a cornerstone of both the mental health and criminal justice systems, even though it has never been demonstrated to be effective.[129] It appears that those who support alternatives to incarceration approve of anything that keeps people out of jail, regardless of its effectiveness.

Mandated treatment, however, recalling Szasz's and Masson's view of all treatment, is clearly a means of social control almost as coercive as prison. "Through a creative and brutal system of mandated behaviorism, in which the state uses its immense powers to force targeted citizens and entities to voluntarily accept a violation of their rights and an encroachment upon their liberties—and to pay for this privilege. . . . The two methods, which overlap in practice, are the expansion of the definition of actions as illegal behavior, and the exploitation of this power to win submission through extortion."[130] Involuntary treatment is convenient because it enables psychiatrists to treat unwilling patients, claiming that it is necessary for the protection of society.[131] This can only be done by linking specific behavior with criminality, as in mandated treatment of alcoholics in lieu of prison. But as noted, drinking does not "cause" violence; in fact, several researchers have proved the reverse, that the decision to engage in violence may "cause" drinking.[132]

In addition, "[P]eople learn to associate drinking with certain behaviors, and behave that way even when they *think* they have been drinking but have not."[133]

Mandated treatment is rationalized because the demand for treatment is much lower than the number of practitioners who rely on a steady stream of clients to maintain their incomes. Even some who need treatment either reject it, seek alternative assistance, or are unable to pay for it. Mandating addicts (and others) into treatment substitutes the external coercion of the criminal justice system for motivation.[134] However, many researchers have identified the importance of high initial motivation for successful therapy. One 1963 study concluded that either high initial motivation or a marked increase in motivation during the first sessions was more important than any other patient characteristic. In this study, 85% of the patients who scored highest on the outcome criteria were rated high on motivation. In contrast, 40% of the patients who were rated lowest on motivation showed no improvement.[135] Similarly, a 1980 study that rated motivation found that motivation was predictive of both process and outcome measures.[136]

That mandated treatment is coercive is undeniable. It is also ideological. "Batterer treatment programs to which male domestic violence offenders are referred by the courts are another nexus between the battered women's movement and the justice system. . . . The routine practice of many courts of ordering men into such programs should raise questions about whether anyone can be forced to join a group that promotes a particular ideology. (Some drunk-driving defendants have challenged court-ordered Alcoholics Anonymous attendance on the grounds that AA's religious outlook violates their freedom of conscience, and have won permission to substitute non-religious recovery groups)."[137] Prisoners in Wisconsin and New York sued the prisons in which they were incarcerated for requiring that they attend Alcoholics Anonymous and Narcotics Anonymous programs, arguing that such a mandate violated the constitutional separation between church and state. Both won, although, ironically, part of New York State's argument in favor of prisoners' attendance was the erroneous claim that in a high percentage of cases, those who regularly attend meetings successfully kick the habit.[138] It is unclear whether the state offered any data to prove this point or accepted it as a given. Furthermore, what data exist are based upon alcohol users, because most offenders participating in drug treatment programs are cross-addicted to alcohol, and research on the effectiveness of these programs in treating other types of addiction is meager, but generally suggests poor outcomes.[139]

None of this means that mandated treatment is being discouraged. For instance, in 1996 the Supreme Court ruled that mentally ill prisoners who are likely to commit similar crimes upon release can be remanded to mental hospitals rather than be released upon completing their sentences. The decision was determined not to constitute double punishment because commitment to a mental hospital is in accordance with civil, rather than criminal, law.[140]

Clearly, mandated treatment is encouraged by the treatment industry. After all, the primary source of referrals for alcoholism treatment is now drunk-driving arrests. Furthermore, heavy drinkers have been placed in treatment rather than in prison even if convicted of felonies unrelated to drinking, which range from writing bad checks to child abuse and rape. Employee assistance programs (EAPs) use the threat of job loss to mandate treatment, and parents can "mandate" their children into drug treatment with a signature—sometimes even preventively, when children have only been "exposed" to drug use.[141] Since the majority of drug users use marijuana, and voluntary admissions for marijuana are 8,898 out of 65 million, or 0.0136%, the need for mandating is clear.[142] However, of chronic drunk drivers randomly assigned to psychiatric treatment, AA, or no treatment, 68% of those assigned to treatment and 69% of those assigned to AA were rearrested, but only 56% of those assigned to no treatment were rearrested,[143] and Peele observed that comparative studies of standard treatment programs versus legal proceedings for drunk drivers regularly find that those who receive ordinary judicial sanctions have fewer subsequent accidents and are rearrested less frequently.[144] This demonstrates that mandated treatment is not only less effective but that its use poses risks to the public.

It has been noted that

"to guard against abuses of substantive due process, the criteria for social intervention must be constantly tested for reasonableness and certainty, must be modernized to comport with the latest scientific knowledge, and must be made responsive to democracy's commitment to pluralism and diversity."[145] However, since its earliest days, psychiatry and government have shared mutual economic interests that often translated into political policy overlaid with a moral structure.[146] And mandated treatment is used even within prisons, although, ironically, "There is no association between commitment offense and participation in programs [in prison]."[147]

A federal study of mandated drug treatment in local corrections agencies found such treatment to be largely ineffective, in part because many prisoners were released before completing it. The study concluded that "one response may be to provide substance abuse information to all inmates while focusing intensive treatment efforts on those who are most likely to benefit from and/or to be in need of services."[148] Let us hope that motivation is one of the criteria for services.

Most dangerous of all, some sex offenders are provided "treatment" in prison, although professionals generally agree that there is no known cure for sex abusers.[149] This may be one reason that some sex offenders are offered the option of chemical or surgical castration either in lieu of prison or to lessen their sentences if incarcerated and minimize their postrelease sanctions, such as probation, parole, civil commitment, or community notification.[150] But it is questionable whether any treatment offered in lieu of prison can be considered voluntary.

Furthermore, while chemical and surgical castration lower offenders' testosterone levels, producing "low recidivism rates" if one is to believe self-reports and rearrest records, they are dangerous to offenders and to the public. Chemicals used to reduce or offset testosterone levels cause cancer. But even when castrated, offenders can achieve erections and even orgasms—or they can use implements to simulate penile intercourse. Clever "castrati" can also avoid taking the drugs that cause chemical castration, or can undo the effects of chemical or surgical castration by taking testosterone purchased on the black market or stolen from legal supplies. An all too clear example of this is that fifteen years after he agreed to "chemical castration" as a condition of his probation, a convicted rapist pleaded guilty to new sex crimes and is being investigated in connection with as many as 75 more. The man, Joseph Frank Smith, appeared on *60 Minutes* in 1984 as a success story for chemical castration.[151]

PERSONAL RESPONSIBILITY

Focus on mandated treatment for any problem is not only illogical but counterproductive in that it undermines personal responsibility. Personal responsibility is further undermined when government and the media endorse abuse excuses and the culture of victimhood, with the support of mental health practitioners who find lucrative roles in evaluating clients and testifying on their behalf. "Syndromes are formulaic and politicized in ways that pay insufficient heed in their own rights to the subtleties of reality and individual cases, and unnecessarily compromise the presumption of individual responsibility upon which legal justice and equal citizenship rest."[152]

Drug addicts and alcoholics react to rewards and consequences. Convincing them that relapse is inevitable, however, removes responsibility from the equation. Of course, as already discussed, medicalizing the problem not only reduces the stigma of addiction—and the stigma of relapse—it ensures coverage through medical insurance. If, instead, we defined addiction as a behavior, we would emphasize that people are the instigators of their relapses—but it would also empower them to be agents of their own recoveries.[153] In fact, numerous studies have found that overcoming addictions is far more successful among those people who see themselves in control of situations than among those who see control as an external force.[154]

This, finally, is the crux of personal responsibility: that under American law, both rights and responsibilities extend to individuals. Use of broad "abuse excuses," victimism, disease models, and the "isms" of oppression to explain or excuse behavior not only reject as well as undermine personal responsibility, but treat people as members of groups, personality types, and clusters of symptoms, all of which violate their rights as human beings to be treated as whole, singular, unique individuals. But sometimes people do not want to be treated as individuals, especially when they would be held individually responsible for misdeeds, and sanctified snake oil discourages individual focus because one of its precepts is to stretch definitions to create the perception of ever-increasing numbers of "sufferers."

Rejecting personal responsibility is perhaps most dangerous when it excuses behavior such as drunk driving, attributing it to "treatable" factors and ignoring considerations of personal motivation to change that behavior. This creates a revolving door in a wide range of criminal justice areas, which consequently undermines curtailment of the behavior. This is exacerbated by treatment providers' self-serving acceptance of recidivism (which maintains their livelihoods while further failing to eradicate the behavior).

PREVENTION PROGRAMS

It should come as no surprise that since we know so little about how to treat problems, we know even less about preventing them. Evidence of this abounds. For example, "Hundreds of thousands of dollars were . . . dedicated to campaigns to teach preschoolers to avoid being sexually abused. . . . Eventually, an NCCAN-funded study concluded that the preschool-age prevention instruction was a waste of money and effort."[155] And Megan's Law, an attempt to prevent future child abuse by identifying known past offenders, has been hampered by the poor record keeping and lack of mental health technology that make it difficult to determine which sex offenders are dangerous.[156]

A critique in *Law Enforcement News* of the influential Department of Justice study by Larry Sherman on government-sponsored crime prevention programs found that the country is wasting millions of dollars by funding crime prevention programs that have not been proven effective. In fact, the most shocking finding of Sherman's study was not that so much criminal justice research was inadequate or flawed, but that it is impossible to measure many of these factors because the necessary data were not collected. Congress failed to require effective evaluation mechanisms into its funding guidelines.[157] This is certainly due, at least in part, to the fact that people tend to attribute problems to causes that fit their ideological interpretations of the facts, rather than to research or even to test more global consideration of causation. Despite criticism, in 1996, Congress, the Office of Justice programs, and other federal agencies and trust funds awarded a total of $113.9 million to support ninety discretionary grants for crime prevention, community planning, and other criminal justice programs. These funds included $2,374,776 to Drug Abuse Resistance Education (DARE) programs.[158] The Partnership for a Drug-Free America has been similarly criticized for exaggerating the number of children using inhalants, as part of a decade-long, $800 million attack on drug use, which also makes no distinction among drugs. Such campaigns have been proved to backfire because their messages are simply not credible.[159]

Clearly, society has an interest in assisting people who suffer from mental illnesses and addictions and who have experienced traumas. Yet the greatest need that most such people identify is for concrete services—cash assistance, food, shelter, and daily-care assistance if they are too feeble or out of control to care for themselves adequately. Instead, we offer them "treatment," which is often ineffective, so unwanted that it must often be mandated to be accepted at all, and often paid for with public funds that are then unavailable to help people obtain what they identify as their needs. Rigorous evaluation of services would, then, serve two goals: it would ensure that services are effective (or identify those that are not) and would, if the latter were made ineligible for public funding, free up funds for the provision of concrete services that are clearly effective in meeting needs.

NOTES

1. See, for example, Thomas Szasz, *The Myth of Psychotherapy* (New York: Syracuse University Press, 1988); and *Psychiatric Justice* (New York: Macmillan, 1965).

2. Jeffrey Masson, *The Assault on Truth: Freud's Suppression of the Seduction Theory* (Boston: Faber, 1984); and Mark Pendergrest, *Victims of Memory* (Hinesburg, VT: Upper Access, 1995).

3. Jeffrey Masson, *Against Therapy* (New York: Common Courage, 1993).

4. Willard Gaylin and Bruce Jennings, *The Perversion of Autonomy* (New York: Free Press, 1996).

5. Stanton Peele, *The Diseasing of America* (New York: Lexington Books, 1995).

6. Robyn M. Dawes, *House of Cards: Psychology and Psychotherapy Built on Myth* (New York: Free Press, 1994).

7. Kathryn Robinson, "The End of Therapy," *Seattle Weekly* (November 13, 1996).

8. Margaret A. Hagen, *Whores of the Court* (New York: ReganBooks, 1997).

9. Edward Dolnick, *Madness on the Couch* (New York: Simon and Schuster, 1998).

10. David Brown, "Review of *Madness on the Couch, Washington Post National Weekly Edition* (November 30, 1998).

11. Tana Dineen, *Manufacturing Victims*, 2d ed. (Montreal: Robert Davies Publishing, 1998).

12. Susan Kiss Sarnoff, "Interview with Tana Dineen," unpublished interview.

13. Ibid.; also see Harry Specht and Mark Courtney, *Unfaithful Angels* (New York: Free Press, 1994); Joe Sharkey, *Bedlam* (New York: St. Martin's Press, 1994).

14. See, for example, Tana Dineen, op. cit.

15. Ibid.

16. Michael J. Lambert and Clara E. Hill, "The Effectiveness of Psychotherapy," in *Handbook of Psychotherapy and Behavior Change*, 4th ed., edited by Allen E. Bergin and Sol L. Garfield (New York: John Wiley & Sons, 1994).

17. Robyn M. Dawes, op. cit.

18. Jeffrey Masson, op. cit.

19. Erica Good, "How Much Therapy Is Enough? It Depends," *New York Times* (November 24, 1998).

20. Michael J. Lambert and Clara E. Hill, op. cit.

21. Robyn M. Dawes, *House of Cards: Psychology and Psychotherapy Built on Myth* (New York: Free Press, 1994).

22. Quoted in Daniel Goleman, "More Than 1 in 4 U. S. Adults Suffers a Mental Disorder Each Year," *New York Times* (March 17, 1993).

23. Robert Pear, "Few People Seek to Treat Mental Illnesses, Study Finds," *New York Times* (December 13, 1999).

24. Carol Mithers, "Therapists Have a Bad Day in Court," *New York Daily News* (July 11, 1994).

25. Kathryn Robinson, op. cit.

26. Joe Hallinan, "Debate Heats Up—As State Seeks to Stop Paying Therapy Bills," *Seattle News* (January 5, 1997).

27. Michelle New, Lucy Berliner, and Monica Fitzgerald, *Mental Health Utilization by Victims of Crime* (Seattle: University of Washington, January 1998).

28. George Stricker, "The Relationship of Research to Clinical Practice," *American Psychologist* 47 (1992): 543–549. Also see Paul Meehle, "'Psychology' Does Our Heterogeneous Subject Matter Have Any Unity?" *Minnesota Psychologist* (summer 1986): 3–9.

29. Neil Jacobsen, "The Overselling of Therapy," *Networker* (March/April 1995).

30. Tana Dineen, *Manufacturing Victims*, 2d ed. (Montreal: Robert Davies Publishing, 1998).

31. Richard Ofshe and Ethan Watters, *Making Monsters: False Memories, Psychotherapy, and Sexual Hysteria* (New York: Charles Scribner's Sons, 1994).

32. Joe Sharkey, *Bedlam* (New York: St. Martin's Press, 1994).

33. Tana Dineen, op. cit.

34. Herb Kutchins and Stuart A. Kirk, *Making Us Crazy* (New York: Free Press, 1997).

35. Susan Smith, *Survivor Psychology: The Dark Side of the Mental Health Mission* (Boca Raton, FL: Upton Books, 1995).

36. An interesting aspect of "recovered memory therapy" is that practitioners use it to uncover three types of memories: of sexual abuse, past lives, and alien abductions; and the choice of practitioner dictates the type of "memories" that will be "recovered." See, for example, Ibid.; Ellen Bass and Laura Davis, *The Courage to Heal*, 3d ed. (New York: HarperPerennial, 1994); John Mack, *Abductions: Human Encounters with Aliens* (New York: Charles Scribner's Sons, 1994); and Ronald C. Johnson, "Parallels Between Recollections of Repressed Child Sex Abuse, Kidnapping by Space Aliens and the 1692 Salem Witch Hunts," *Issues in Child Abuse Allegations* 6, no. 1 (1994): 41–47.

37. Refer to the legislative histories of state compensation eligibility guidelines and proposals to expand them; see the bibliography of Susan K. Sarnoff, *A National Survey of State Crime Victim Compensation Programs: Policies and Administrative Methods* (Ann Arbor, MI: University Microfilms International, December 1993).

38. See, for example, Ellen Bass and Laura Davis, *The Courage to Heal*, 3d ed. (New York: HarperPerennial, 1994); and Susan Contratto and M. Janice Gutfreund, eds., *A Feminist Clinician's Guide to the Memory Debate* (New York: Haworth Press, 1996).

39. Pranab Chatterjee, "A Market of Human Vulnerability," *Social Development Issues* 3 (1979): 1–12.

40. Pranab Chatterjee, *Approaches to the Welfare State* (Washington, DC: National Association of Social Workers Press, 1996).

41. Amitai Etzioni, *Modern Organizations* (Englewood Cliffs, NJ: Prentice Hall, 1964).

42. Seth Mydans, "Lawyer for OJ Simpson Case Outs Case," *New York Times* (June 16, 1994).

43. Gerald M. Rosen, Richard J. Nally, Jeffrey M. Lohr, Grant J. Devilly, James D. Herbert, and Scott O. Lillienfield, "A Realistic Appraisal of EMDR," *The California Psychologist* 31 (1998).

44. National Association of Social Workers, New York State Chapter, "Approved Continuing Education Programs," *NYS NASW Update* 23, no. 5 (November 1998).

45. National Association of Social Workers Delegate Assembly, *Code of Ethics of the National Association of Social Workers* (Washington, DC: National Association of Social Workers, 1996).

46. National Association of Social Workers National Council on the Practice of Clinical Social Work, *Evaluation and Treatment of Adults with the Possibility of Recovered Memories of Child Sexual Abuse* (Washington, DC: National Association of Social Workers, June 1996).

47. Tana Dineen, *Manufacturing Victims*, 2d ed. (Montreal: Robert Davies Publishing, 1998).

48. Steven Smith and Susan Freinkel, *Adjusting the Balance: Federal Policy and Victim Services* (Westport, CT: Greenwood Press, 1988).

49. Robert C. Davis and Madeline Henley, "Victim Service Programs," in *Victims of Crime: Problems, Policies and Programs*, edited by A. Lurigio, Wesley Skogan, and Robert Davis (Beverly Hills, CA: Sage Publications, 1990), 157–171.

50. Susan K. Sarnoff, *A National Survey of State Crime Victim Compensation Programs: Policies and Administrative Methods* (Ann Arbor, MI: University Microfilms International, December 1993).

51. David Osborne and Ted Gaebler, *Reinventing Government* (Reading, MA: Addison-Wesley Publishing Co., 1992).

52. Tana Dineen, op. cit.

53. Hollida Wakefield and Ralph Underwager, *Return of the Furies* (Chicago, IL: Open Court Publishing Co., 1994).

54. See, for example, Robyn M. Dawes, op. cit.; Terence W. Campbell, *Beware the Talking Cure* (Boca Raton, FL: Upton Books, 1994); George Stricker, "The Relationship of Research to Clinical Practice," *American Psychologist* 47 (1992): 543–549.

55. See, for example, Terence W. Campbell, *Beware the Talking Cure* (Boca Raton, FL: Upton Books, 1994); Jan Marie De Lipsey and Sue Kelly James, "Videotaping the Sexually Abused Child: The Texas Experience, 1983–1987," in *Vulnerable Populations: Evaluation and Treatment of Sexually Abused Children and Adult Survivors*, Vol. 1, edited by Suzanne Sgroi (Lexington, MA: Lexington Books, 1988), 229–264; Sherrill Mulhern, "Satanism and Psychotherapy: A Rumor in Search of an Inquisition," in *The Satanism Scare*, edited by J. T. Richardson, J. Best, and D. G. Bromley (New York: Aldine, 1991); Ralph Underwager and Hollida Wakefield, *The Real World of Child Interrogations* (Springfield, IL: Charles C. Thomas, 1990).

56. A. V. Harrell, B. E. Smith, and R. F. Cook, *The Social Psychological Effects of Victimization*; final report to the National Institute of Justice, 1985.

57. Robert C. Davis and Madeline Henley, op. cit.

58. Sherry A. Quirk and Anne P. DePrince, "Childhood Trauma: Politics and Legislative Concerns for Therapists," in *A Feminist Clinician's Guide to the Memory Debate*, edited by Susan Contratto and M. Janice Gutfreund (New York: Haworth Press, 1996).

59. Ricki Lewis, "Evening Out the Ups and Downs of Manic-Depressive Illness," *FDA Consumer* 30, no. 5 (June 1996).

60. Barbara Strauch, "Use of Antidepression Medicine For Young Patients Has Soared," *New York Times* (August 10, 1997).

61. Marilyn Elias, "Ritalin Use Up Among Youth," *USA Today* (December 11, 1996).

62. Ibid.

63. Ibid.

64. David J. Morrow, "Attention Disorder Is Found in Growing Number of Adults," *New York Times* (September 2, 1997).

65. Ibid.

66. Ibid.

67. Ronald K. Siegel, *Intoxication* (New York: E. P. Dutton, 1989).

68. James E. Royce, *Alcohol Problems and Alcoholism* (New York: Free Press, 1981).

69. Stanton Peele, op. cit.

70. Jane Jacobs, *The Death and Life of Great American Cities* (New York: Random House, 1961).

71. Robert Merton, "The Sociology of Social Problems," in *Contemporary Social Problems*, edited by Robert K. Merton and Robert A. Nisbets (New York: Harcourt Brace Jovanovich, 1976), 5–43.

72. Charles Bufe, *Alcoholics Anonymous: Cult or Cure?* (San Francisco, CA: See Sharp Press, 1991).

73. Pamela Freyd and Eleanor Goldstein, *Smiling Through Tears* (Boca Raton, FL: Upton Books, 1997).

74. Stanton Peele, *The Diseasing of America* (New York: Lexington Books, 1995).

75. Elayne Rapping, *The Culture of Recovery* (Boston: Beacon Press, 1996); and Marc Galanter, *Cults: Faith, Healing and Coercion* (New York: Oxford University Press, 1989).

76. Ibid.

77. Stanton Peele, op. cit.; and Audrey Kishline, *Moderate Drinking* (New York: Crown, 1994).

78. Stanton Peele, *The Diseasing of America* (New York: Lexington Books, 1995).

79. Michael J. Lemanski, "The Tenacity of Error in the Treatment of Addiction," *The Humanist* (May/June 1997).

80. Stanton Peele, op. cit.

81. Michael J. Lemanski, op. cit.

82. Jack Trimpey, *Rational Recovery* (New York: Pocket Books, 1996).

83. John G. Haaga and Elizabeth A. McGlynn, *The Drug Abuse Treatment System* (Santa Monica, CA: RAND, 1993); National Institute on Drug Addiction, *Principles of Effective Treatment: A Research-Based Guide* (Washington, DC: National Institutes of Health, December 15, 1999).

84. Stanton Peele, *The Diseasing of America* (New York: Lexington Books, 1995).

85. J. M. Polich, D. J. Armor, and H. B. Braiker, *The Course of Alcoholism: Four Years after Treatment* (Santa Monica, CA: January 1980).

86. George Vaillant, *The Natural History of Alcoholism* (Cambridge, MA: Harvard University Press, 1983).

87. Ibid.

88. James T. Bennett and Thomas J. Lorenzo, *Destroying Democracy* (Washington, DC: Cato Institute, 1985).

89. Ibid.

90. James E. Royce, *Alcohol Problems and Alcoholism* (New York: Free Press, 1981).

91. Daniel K. Benjamin and Roger Leroy Miller, *Undoing Drugs* (New York: Basic Books, 1991).

92. Stanton Peele, op. cit.

93. Ibid.

94. Michael J. Lemanski, "The Tenacity of Error in the Treatment of Addiction," *The Humanist* (May/June 1997).

95. Ibid.

96. Stanton Peele, *The Diseasing of America* (New York: Lexington Books, 1995).

97. Ronald K. Siegel, op. cit.

98. Christopher S. Wren, "Maturity Diminishes Drug Use, a Study Finds," *New York Times* (February 2, 1997).

99. Stanton Peele, op. cit.

100. Klaus A. Miczek, Elise M. Weerts, and Joseph F. De Bold, "Alcohol, Aggression and Violence: Biobehavioral Determinants"; Jeffrey Fagan, "Set and Setting Revisited: Influences in Alcohol and Illicit Drugs on the Social Context of Violent Events"; and Joel McCord, "Considerations of Causes in Alcohol-Related Violence," in *Alcohol and Interpersonal Violence*, edited by Susan Martin (Washington, DC: NIAAA, 1993).

101. Elisha R. Galaif and Steve Sussman, "For Whom Does Alcoholics Anonymous Work?" *The International Journal of the Addictions*, 30, no. 2 (1995); and Charles J. Sandoz, "Locus of Control, Emotional Maturity and Family Dynamics as Components of Recovery in Recovering Alcoholics," *Alcoholism Treatment Quarterly* 8, no. 4 (1991).

102. Jeanette A. Rogowski, *Insurance Coverage for Drug Abuse* (Santa Monica, CA: RAND, 1992).

103. Stanton Peele, *The Diseasing of America* (New York: Lexington Books, 1995).

104. Tana Dineen, *Manufacturing Victims*, 2d ed. (Montreal: Robert Davies Publishing, 1998).

105. Joseph Berger, "Westchester to Limit Revolving-Door Care of Poor Addicts," *New York Times* (June 17, 1997).

106. Arnold M. Ludwig, "Cognitive Processes Associated with 'Spontaneous' Recovery from Alcoholism," *Journal of Studies of Alcohol* 46, no. 1 (1985).

107. Dan Baum, *Smoke and Mirrors* (New York: Little, Brown & Co., 1996).

108. Ibid.

109. Arnold S. Trebach and James A. Inciardi, *Legalize It? Debating American Drug Policy* (Washington, DC: American University Press, 1993).

110. Anthony Lewis, "Medicine and Politics," *New York Times* (October 13, 1997).

111. Joel Best, *Random Violence* (Berkeley: University of California Press, 1999).

112. Tana Dineen, op. cit.

113. Daniel Goleman, "Severe Trauma May Damage the Brain as Well as the Psyche," *New York Times* (August 1, 1995), C3.

114. Ted R. Miller, Mark A. Cohen, and Brian Wiersema, *Victim Costs and Consequences: A New Look* (Washington, DC: National Institute of Justice, February 1996).

115. Susan K. Sarnoff, *A National Survey of State Crime Victim Compensation Programs: Policies and Administrative Methods* (Ann Arbor, MI: University Microfilms International, December 1993).

116. Tana Dineen, *Manufacturing Victims*, 2d ed. (Montreal: Robert Davies Publishing, 1998).

117. Ted R. Miller, Mark A. Cohen, and Brian Wiersema, op. cit.

118. Daniel Goleman, "A Key to Post-Traumatic Stress Lies in Brain Chemistry, Scientists Find," *New York Times* (June 12, 1990).

119. Tana Dineen, op. cit.

120. Ibid.

121. Richard Gardner, *Sex Abuse Hysteria: Salem Witch Trials Revisited* (Cresskill, NJ: Creative Therapeutics, 1991).

122. Stephen J. Ceci and Maggie Bruck, *Jeopardy in the Courtroom: A Scientific Analysis of Children's Testimony* (Hyattsville, MD: American Psychological Association, 1995).

123. Council on Scientific Affairs, "Scientific Status of Refreshing Recollection by the Use of Hypnosis," *Journal of the American Medical Association* (April 5, 1985).

124. Debbie Nathan and Michael Snedeker, *Satan's Silence* (New York: Basic Books, 1995).

125. Stephen J. Ceci and Maggie Bruck, op. cit.

126. San Diego County Grand Jury 1996–1997, "Victims of Crime Program in San Diego County," *Final Report* (San Diego, CA: San Diego County Grand Jury, 1997).

127. "Editorial," *Washington Post* (May 24, 1997).

128. Daniel Vasquez, "Repressed Memory Under Fire: Franklin Alleges Trial Conspiracy, Seeks Damages," *San Jose Mercury News* (July 1, 1997).

129. Vicki Fox Weisenthier and Michael Allen, "Forced Treatment Doesn't Work," *Washington Post* (August 5, 1999).

130. Michael Kelly, "A Cold, Cruel New Statism," *New York Post* (June 30, 1997).

131. Lee Coleman, *The Reign of Error* (Boston: Beacon Press, 1984).

132. See, for example, Judith Roizen, "Issues in the Epidemiology of Alcohol and Violence"; Kai Pernanen, "Alcohol-Related Violence: Conceptual Models"; Alan R. Lang, "Alcohol-Related Violence: Psychological Perspectives"; Philip J. Cook and Michael J. Moore, "Economic Perspectives," in *NIAAA Research Monograph No. 24*, edited by Susan E. Martin (Rockville, MD: NIH, 1993), 3–36, 37–69, 121–147, 193–218.

133. See, for example, James J. Collins, "Alcohol Use and Expressive Interpersonal Violence"; David Levinson, "Social Settings, Cultural Factors, and Alcohol-Related Aggression"; Richard E. Boyatzis, "Who Should Drink What, When, and Where If Looking for a Fight," in *Alcohol, Drug Abuse and Aggression*, edited by Edward Gottlieb et al. (Springfield, IL: Charles C. Thomas, 1983), 5–25, 41–58, 314–329; Klaus A. Miczek, Elise M. Weerts, and Joseph F. De Bold, "Alcohol, Aggression and Violence: Biobehavioral Determinants," in *Alcohol and Interpersonal Violence*, edited by Susan Martin (Washington, DC: NIAAA, 1993), 83–119; Mark A. R. Kleiman, *Against Excess: Drug Policy for Results* (New York: Basic Books, 1992), 215–216.

134. Office of National Drug Control Policy, *Understanding Drug Treatment* (Washington, DC: The White House, 1990).

135. D. Malan, *A Study of Brief Psychotherapy* (London; Tavistock, 1963).

136. L. Keithly, S. Samples, and H. H. Strupp, "Patient Motivation as a Predictor of Access and Outcome in Psychotherapy," *Psychotherapy and Psychosomatics* 33 (1980).

137. Cathy Young, *Ceasefire: Beyond the Gender Wars* (New York: Free Press, 1999).

138. James J. Kilpatrick, "Forcing the Faith," *United Press International* (December 27, 1996).

139. D. Gerstein and H. Harwood, eds., *Treating Drug Problems*, Vol. 1: *A Study of the Evolution, Effectiveness, and Financing of Public and Private Drug Treatment Systems* (Washington, DC: National Academy Press, 1990).

140. "Jail Beyond Terms for Sex Predators," *Newsday* (June 24, 1997).

141. Stanton Peele, op. cit.

142. Ed Rosenthal and Steve Kubby, *Why Marijuana Should Be Legal* (New York: Thunder's Mouth Press, 1996).

143. K. S. Ditman, G. G. Crawford, E. W. Forgy, H. Moskowitz, and C. MacAndrew, "A Controlled Experiment on the Use of Court Probation for Drunk Arrests," *American Journal of Psychiatry* 124 (1967): 64–67.

144. Stanton Peele, *The Diseasing of America* (New York: Lexington Books, 1995).

145. Nicholas N. Kittrie, *The Right to Be Different: Deviance and Enforced Therapy* (Baltimore, MD: Johns Hopkins University Press, 1971); and *The War Against Authority* (Baltimore, MD: Johns Hopkins University Press, 1995).

146. Joe Sharkey, op. cit.

147. J. R. Petersilia, *Which Inmates Participate in Prison Treatment Programs?* (Santa Monica, CA: RAND, December 1978).

148. Sandra Tunis, James Austin, Mark Morris, Patricia Hardyman, and Melissa Boyard, "Evaluation of Drug Treatment in Local Corrections," *National Institute of Justice Journal* (June 1997).

149. David Hechler, *The Battle and the Backlash* (Lexington, MA: Lexington Books, 1988).

150. Associated Press, "Castrated Molester Given 26-Year Prison Sentence," *USA Today* (March 4, 1998).

151. Associated Press, "Castrated Rapist Tied to 75 New Sex Crimes," *New York Times* (November 28, 1998).

152. Donald Alexander Downs, *More Than Victims* (Chicago, IL: University of Chicago Press, 1996).

153. Sally L. Satel, "Don't Forget the Addict's Role in Addiction," *New York Times* (April 4, 1998).

154. Charles J. Sandoz, "Locus of Control, Emotional Maturity and Family Dynamics as Components of Recovery in Recovering Alcoholics," *Alcoholism Treatment Quarterly* 8, no. 4 (1991); D. J. Rohsenow, "The Alcohol Use Inventory as a Predictor of Drinking By Male Heavy Social Drinkers," *Addictive Behaviors* 7 (1982); M. P. Naditch, "Locus of Control in a Sample of Men in Army Basic Training," *Journal of Consulting and Clinical Psychology* 43 (1975).

155. Debbie Nathan and Michael Snedeker, op. cit.

156. Todd S. Purdum, "Registry Laws Tar Sex-Crime Convicts with Broad Brush," *New York Times* (July 1, 1997): A1 and A19.

157. "Do You Get What You Pay For? With Criminal Justice Efforts, Not Necessarily," *Law Enforcement News* (May 15, 1997).

158. James T. Bennett and Thomas J. Lorenzo, *Destroying Democracy* (Washington, DC: Cato Institute, 1985).

159. Steven Donziger, "Give Kids Straight Dope on Drugs," *Newsday* (February 6, 1998).

Chapter 6

Snake Oil in the Court System

Perfection may not be demanded of law, but the capacity to correct errors of inevitable frailty is the mark of a civilized legal mechanism.

—Felix Frankfurter

The victim to too severe a law is considered as a martyr rather than a criminal.

—Charles Caleb Colton

False incarcerations are among the worst results of the sanctification of snake oil. As such, they are excellent, if extreme, examples of how the sanctification process works. Sanctified snake oil introduced into trials does not guarantee that false convictions will result; "guilty people who 'beat the rap' because of good lawyers or fine technicalities or intimidations of witnesses . . . far outnumber the convicted innocents,"[1] according to one expert on false convictions. Furthermore, "of all serious offenses reported to the police, only 19.9 percent result in arrests; only 17.1 percent result in charges being filed, only 5 percent result in the person so charged being found guilty, and a mere 2 percent result in incarceration."[2] So system ineffectiveness, rather than system leniency, seems to be the greatest contributing factor in criminal justice failure. These statistics also demonstrate why victim compensation benefits are not limited to cases in which a conviction is sustained—to compensate for systemic inability rather than to corroborate even false allegations.

But sanctified snake oil can set the stage for a series of events that can, in confluence, lead to extreme injustices. Many of the worst examples have occurred in the family court system, which is less punitive than the criminal court system, but which also uses lower standards of proof (and, some would argue, often uses procedures that overlook standards of proof entirely). And because of their supposedly "civil" nature, people subject to family court sanctions are not afforded the right to the same constitutional protections (such as the right to confront accusers) or rights (such as to court-appointed counsel) made available to criminal defendants. As the San Diego Grand Jury reported,

In too many cases, Child Protection Services cannot distinguish real abuse from fabrication, abuse from neglect, and neglect from poverty or cultural differences. . . . [N]umerous medical reports from the Center for Child Protection . . . read, "no physical findings, but history consistent with molest." The *burden of proof, contrary to every other area of our judicial system, is on the alleged perpetrator to prove his innocence* [italics in original]. . . . If a father denies molest and a true finding is made, he suffers the ultimate Catch 22—he can either admit and take a chance that the department will allow him to begin reunification with his family or he can deny and no reunification will occur. . . . Not complying with the reunification plan is grounds for . . . termination of parental rights. . . . One witness to the Jury succinctly stated, "Court intervention investigators don't know the difference between opinion and evidence." . . . we found that some police officers abdicate their role as fact finders to the social worker . . . [or] will integrate elements of the social workers' investigation into their own reports, instead of performing an independent investigation . . . evidence contrary to DSS' position is either excluded or ignored. DSS may weave its case with hearsay evidence and the speculation of "so-called" experts. More than 98% of all petitions are granted.[3]

Ironically, this system was developed because feminists and victim advocates were skeptical of law-and-order approaches to crime and wanted to avoid further traumatizing victims, but the way they did this was to replace police interviews with interviews by social workers who were not trained to do forensic questioning. This was an illegal departure from criminal justice practice, which dictates that interviews be conducted by law-enforcement personnel who have been trained to avoid suggestive and leading questions and to recognize that some allegations are false. It appeared worth the trade-off for the criminal justice system, however, if this new system could save victims trauma and get help for abusers without going through trials that were difficult to win, by encouraging confessions in exchange for lenient treatment. The abdication of the role of police investigators to social workers made it easier for children who had been abused to disclose but provided no means of differentiating them from children who had not been abused. Then, instead of being taught differentiation skills, the social workers were taught untested theories (such as Child Abuse Accommodation Syndrome [CAAS], which holds that children's denials of abuse are indicative of the fact that it occurred) to support their dangerously skewed views. In these cases, legal "reforms" were promoted to make it easier for children to testify and for prosecutors to sustain convictions. Many flew in the face of the Constitution, but because they were rarely used, they raised few concerns. They were primarily used as bluffs, and they apparently worked, because confessions and plea bargains occurred in 75% of cases.[4]

As child protection workers and the general public became convinced by these theories and the increasing number of cases they "detected," demands escalated that more and more intrafamilial cases be criminalized, especially when the accused denied their guilt. And as charges moved out to day-care workers and other nonfamily members, the criminal courts saw more and more of these cases. At first the criminal courts adopted many of the methods of the family courts, which seemed to have had more experience with them. However, review of the cases by appellate courts began to identify the fallibility, not to mention the unconstitutionality, of these methods.

Later, the Appellate Division of the New Jersey Superior Court would rule that

The proper use of child-abuse expert testimony is . . . not as a diagnostic investigative device, as the syndrome does not detect sexual abuse. . . . It would appear that the prospect of designing checklists, inventories and rating scales to provide objective measures of abusive behavior, its antecedents, correlates and consequences, holds promise of yielding information that may be useful both in individual and epidemiological data gathering. Designing and validating such measures, however, depends on theory and research that is currently the focus of much study and controversy. Nowhere is that more evident than in the scientific and legal arguments about whether behaviors exist that are unique to sexually abused children and whether such behaviors fall into patterns and suggest a typical "profile"—or "syndrome" for the child sexual abuse victim. The Superior Court, quoting Suzanne M. Sgroi in the *Handbook of Clinical Intervention in Child Sexual Abuse* (1982), wrote, "Validation of child sexual abuse depends upon recognizing behavioral indicators, the capacity to perform investigative interviewing, the ability to do credibility assessment, recognizing physical indicators and the capacity to perform comprehensive medical examinations. Behavioral indicators of child sexual abuse may be helpful but are rarely conclusive."[5]

Even more important, the existence of these indicators, even when they do reflect abuse, offer no clue to the identity of the abuser. Yet these were precisely the methods used to "prove" many cases of sexual abuse.

Sometimes these poorly trained investigators simply believed reports of abuse without evidence. For example, the report of the investigation into Breezy Point Day School in Bucks County, Pennsylvania, noted that the caseworker and the attending psychologist based their conclusions upon the false assumption that the child had undergone a medical examination that revealed evidence of vaginal trauma. Instead, the family pediatrician contradicted the child's mother's claim of abuse.[6] In other cases, evidence of actual abuse was lost in the morass of incompetent investigations that identified so many offenders and victims that the truth was eventually undeterminable. For instance,

The California Attorney General's office issued a scathing report concerning the conduct of the [Bakersfield] investigation. The report puts much of the blame on one zealot caseworker who virtually took over the investigation from the county Sheriff's Office. . . . Many of the interviews were done by sheriff's deputies who had not received the specialized training required under state law. According to the report, the deputies, "violated basic law enforcement standards and techniques for interviewing young victims. Deputies generally did not question the children's statements and they responded positively . . . only when the children revealed new allegations or said something to reinforce their previous allegations. They applied pressure on the children to name additional suspects and victims and questioned them with inappropriate suggestions that produced the answers they were looking for. . . . [The only exception to this was that, when three of the] children named the social worker, as well as the Deputy District Attorney and a sheriff's deputy, [u]nlike virtually all the other accusations, these led to no arrests."[7]

Some of the workers believed these cases because they believed that children never lie about abuse (and did not comprehend that many of these children were only believed when they were finally coerced to lie). Other professionals believed that statistics "proved" that few cases are false. However, this was often a misapprehension. For instance, Jones and MacGraw's study of 576 Denver cases found that 53% of abuse charges were indicated, 23% were unfounded, 24% reflected insufficient information, 6% were malicious, and 17% were wrong but not malicious. Ceci and Bruck noted that "some commentators have concluded that only a small proportion of reports (around 6%) are false. However, this is a misunderstanding of the data because the percentage of false reports is the entire 23%; 6% are deliberate lies, but the other 17% are just as baseless as the lies, even though they may be honest mistakes. And they can do just as much harm." Ceci and Bruck also observed that these findings correspond with those of two other major studies. A 1990 study conducted by Thoennes and Tjaden, of 9,000 families in custody disputes, found that 50% of charges were likely true, 17% uncertain, and 33% unlikely.[8]

Another of the negative results of this change in the treatment of child abuse was that "Some child welfare experts say that overzealous probes of frivolous allegations lead to *underenforcement* where action is needed most, because the system gets too bogged down in trivial pursuit to single out the serious cases."[9] Still another was that "Law enforcement and the courts fail to differentiate between minor claims of abuse and cases rife with danger signs,"[10] a confusion arising from poor training and overzealousness. As a result, fifty thousand children with severe injuries annually go unreported. One-quarter to one-half of the children who die of abuse or neglect were previously reported to child welfare authorities, but because of insufficient training and coordination and misdirected resources, many children fail to receive essential care.[11] Incompetent workers also err in the other direction, removing children from homes that are not abusive, or not dangerous enough to warrant removal.

The frustrations resulting from such policies create opportunities for those who understand how desperately the public wants "answers," regardless of how doubtful they might be. And the public does not necessarily insist on (or even recognize) correct answers, so instead, it gets answers that make people comfortable and create career opportunities for stakeholders. This has resulted in treatment for families willing to accept it and able to afford it and sensationalism of the handful of cases that attract media attention. What often goes unnoticed is that as a result, cases of physical abuse and abuse against poor children receive few resources and little attention.[12]

EXPERT WITNESSES

As more and more child abuse cases have moved from family court to criminal court, prosecutors have sought to bolster the testimony of child protection workers not only with testimony about professionally developed syndromes, but with the testimony of "experts" who interview children and claim that their evaluative abilities prove the children's abuse. However, many so-called experts lack credentials, present unreliable theories as facts, and intentionally confuse or misrepresent issues and evidence.[13] "Fewer than 100 of the nation's 3,688 colleges and universities may be considered research universities, and more than half of higher education R&D expenditures are concentrated in 40 institutions. Yet 441 institutions offer Ph.D. degrees, and faculty members increasingly define their work as research."[14] No mental health technology enables a practitioner to predict future behavior, but "experts" testify every day to the likelihood that a particular person "will kill again" or "has been rehabilitated" or "has been abused"—and courts act on these spurious claims. Many clinicians who lack research training as well as skills testify based on their own clinical experiences, which tend to be extremely narrow at best.[15] For instance, it has also been observed that the fault is not with children making false accusations, but with faulty evaluators making misdiagnoses.[16] "Experts . . . are not required to cite scientific evidence—a vague reference to their own 'experience' or 'unpublished research' will often do—and they are virtually certain to try to buttress the claims of the lawyers who hired them, no matter how farfetched. . . . Judges are supposed to screen out testimony that is not reliable and relevant . . . but judges are not trained to evaluate scientific testimony."[17]

While mental health practitioners are ineffective in making determinations about human behavior—and least effective in making predictions about future behavior—regardless of the evidence of past activities, what little the mental health industry can offer in the sense of "statistical likelihood" is also prone to identify innocent people as criminals, and criminals as either innocent or not guilty,[18] usually due to some bogus abuse excuse."[19] Fake experts also tend to use tools, such as Rorschach and other projective tests, which have never proved predictive.[20] For instance, Robert Davis, a diplomate of the American Board of Professional Psychology and a consultant to the Oregon Parole Board, uses the "Palo Alto Destructiveness Test" to determine the degree of violence to which offenders are prone. However, no such test exists![21] The most dangerous acceptance of bogus expertise occurs in criminal courts, where self-proclaimed experts present all sorts of bizarre theories as proven facts, sometimes resulting in the false imprisonment of innocent people or the acquittal of guilty ones. The government perpetuates this by funding "training" programs that present unproven theories, disproven theories, and pure ideology as fact.

This type of quackery occurs, as Peter Huber observed, because

maverick scientists shunned by their reputable colleagues have been embraced by lawyers. . . . The legal system has adjusted rules of evidence accordingly, so that almost any self-styled scientist, no matter how strange or iconoclastic his views, will be welcome to testify in court . . . among all the many refractory problems of our modern liability system, junk science is the most insidious and the least noticed . . . people tend to believe what the courts have to say, especially when they say it with large amounts of money.[22]

As a result, "The lawyers with the biggest war chests available [to] spend on expert witnesses usually win."[23]

A related problem with expert testimony is that many courts accept treating therapists as experts in cases involving their own clients, but therapy is based on relationship, so any therapist who has treated an individual for enough time to testify should be assumed to be too biased to act as an expert in that patient's case (not to mention the fact that few treating therapists have the skills or training required of true court experts). Evaluation, which is not based on relationship, is not subject to these compromises.

Some expert witnesses do not simply testify to bogus science, but are outright frauds. In the Breezy Point Day School case, for instance, James Stillwell presented himself as an expert on ritual child abuse and as "the Founder and President of the National Agency Against the Organized Exploitation of Children, Inc." Stillwell claimed that his agency had vast experience in "looking for" and uncovering "satanic stuff," that he employed "in excess of 300 people," and that he had worked with federal and county authorities, including the FBI. An investigation into his background, however, found that he had no such affiliations. It did find, however, that Stillwell had "no formal training or education beyond receiving his High School Graduate Equivalency Diploma" and that he was actually the only employee of his "organization," which operated out of a post office box.[24]

Bogus experts have been divided into four groups:

- *fakes*—whose "credentials" consist of outright lies;
- *sophisticated fakes*—who have degrees from diploma mills and have been published (if at all) in nonpeer-reviewed, self-promoting journals;
- *self-promoters*—who exaggerate their credentials and experience and rehash common knowledge or recognized theories with fancy jargon and as "syndromes"; and

- *ideologues*—who have developed theories around pet ideas that have not been adequately tested or that test poorly.[25]

From 1923 through 1992, federal courts used the *Frye* test for the admissibility of evidence, which was criticized as too restrictive regarding admission of new and emerging theories and techniques. But federal courts that have allowed expert testimony and scientific evidence without adhering to *Frye* criteria have also been criticized—for promoting expert-shopping, litigation-based research, and jury verdicts based on unreliable evidence.[26] In 1993, the U.S. Supreme Court altered its standard of evidence. The new *Daubert* rule, which replaced *Frye*, determined the admissibility of evidence according to whether the underlying reasoning and methodology is scientifically valid and appropriately relevant to the facts at issue. To make these determinations, the Court suggested four general, nonexclusive factors:

1. Whether the theory can be (or has been) tested.
2. Whether it has been subjected to peer review and publication.
3. Whether it has a known or potential error rate.
4. Whether it has gained wide acceptance within the relevant scientific community.[27]

But *Daubert* also required that judges become more involved in assessing experts' credentials and the scientific reliability of their testimony, and the increasingly conservative federal bench has taken this requirement very seriously. For example, in one breast implant case, Judge Robert E. Jones of Portland, Oregon, hired his own experts; and in other cases throughout the country, judges are refusing to allow expert witnesses to testify.[28] Most recently, Chief Justice William Rehnquist clarified *Daubert* by adding that "A court may conclude that there is simply too great an analytic gap between the data and the opinion offered."[29] In response, the American Association for the Advancement of Science has developed a project which will test the possibility of providing the courts with a list of neutral experts. The experts would represent science rather than a particular party or point of view.[30]

However, these efforts are experimental and limited to federal courts. State courts are neither bound by them nor by *Frye* or *Daubert* and generally have much lower standards for the acceptance of expert testimony than do the federal courts. "While many evaluators earn more than $2,500 per case, not all of them have equal skill. Training and techniques vary widely. And critics are particularly wary of the many therapists lured into custody work in recent years because cost-conscious managed health plans have cut into their private practices." Jonathan Gold, a Charlotte, North Carolina, psychologist specializing in custody evaluation, noted that despite the fact that the American Psychological Association set standards for evaluators in 1994, the majority of evaluators fail to follow them. Some critics claim that this is because the guidelines are based on faulty research, are undocumented, and are skewed in favor of mothers.[31] Still, the government continues to fund conferences and publications espousing the unsupported beliefs of such "experts."[32]

POLICE AND PROSECUTORIAL MISCONDUCT

Not all such problems are caused by mental health "experts." A similar case in Jordan, Minnesota, which also started with a plausible allegation that got lost in the hysteria of satanic abuse charges, emanated from the overreaction of a criminal justice official who had recently been "trained" to "detect" satanic ritual abuse. A review by the Minnesota District Attorney General's office with the help of the FBI "found that the Jordan case had been botched in much the same way as Kern County authorities had botched the Bakersfield case.... [As a result, District Attorney] Kathleen Morris was voted out of office and is appealing a 'reprimand' by the State Board of Professional Responsibility."[33] Attorney General Hubert H. Humphrey's report on the Jordan investigation concluded that "There was no credible evidence . . . the many mistakes made by the police and the county attorney had destroyed the opportunity to prosecute successfully those who may have victimized children and had caused suffering of those who may have been falsely accused."[34]

Many of the people who had "made" these cases refused to let them die natural deaths. Some even broke their own newly developed rules in order to perpetuate cases that deserved to be dropped. For instance,

When ritual-abuse cases first surfaced, it was thought vital to preserve children's original disclosures. . . . But instead of revealing heartfelt narratives of children, the recordings [of children supposedly exposed to ritual abuse] starred the interviewers themselves, and showed them working strenuously to lead children from denials to "yes" answers. The same tapes were instrumental in producing jury verdicts favorable to Peggy Buckey and her son, Ray. Similar recordings led the New Jersey courts to reverse Kelly Michaels' convictions. Case investigators soon realized that in ritual-abuse cases, preserving the interviews would create problems for the prosecution. . . . Investigators became so diligent in their efforts to avoid giving exculpatory information to defense attorneys that they apparently have even hidden or deliberately destroyed material. . . . Recantations and statements by the children that would undermine their credibility were also kept from the defense.[35]

In fact, when skepticism began to surface about the "satanic" nature of these cases and the lack of evidence to support these claims, the more sensational aspects of the children's stories were withheld, while the "ordinary" accusations of rape, sodomy, and assault were presented at trial. In many later cases, videotapes were not made, and tapes already made were destroyed.[36]

A trial judge wrongly prevented George Franklin's lawyers from introducing evidence that the details of the killing that his daughter had claimed to have spontaneously recalled had been reported in the press. The prosecution had argued that only an eyewitness could have known the specifics of the murder.[37] And in the high-profile PRACA Day Care Center trials, "it was only later revealed that the first report was made by a mother who was angry with center management over a bill for back tuition." In another PRACA case, prosecutors either lost or deliberately withheld evidence that could have cleared Albert Ramos. As is typical in such cases, the children initially denied being abused; then, after zealous questioning from "therapists," they began to make increasingly more fantastic statements. At one point, one of the purported victims identified the trial judge as his molester.[38]

In the Ohio case of Jenny Wilcox and Dale Aldridge, sentenced to multiple life sentences on several counts of child abuse and jailed for eleven years before they were exonerated, the defense was provided with only eight of twenty-nine pages of police reports. Omitted was information showing that their accusers were coerced and threatened, and one child was held in a juvenile detention facility until he claimed abuse. An expert testifying at their retrial said that "It was the worst incident [of coercive tactics] that [he] had come across."[39] Furthermore, their original attorney did "less than six hours of trial preparation and no investigation whatsoever," and was later suspended from practice. Released from prison in 1996, Wilcox and Aldridge were never reprosecuted, but a court dismissed their claims of wrongful imprisonment in 2000, stating that he believed that they were guilty of at least some of the charges of which they were accused.[40] This is a not a surprise, as governments are often loathe to admit errors that could make them liable for substantial damages, absent such incontrovertible proof as DNA evidence.

A more recent such case occurred

in Wenatchee, Wash., [where] dozens of families were destroyed by a crazed police detective operating hand-in-glove with corrupt child protective service officials and child therapists. . . . The ACLU excoriated Wenatchee public officials for the, "forced incarceration in out-of-state mental hospitals [of children] until sexual abuse allegations are produced," for undocumented and destroyed, "records of interviews with child witnesses," for, "coercive child interview methods," for "collaborating between police and CPS officials in producing allegations from children, for lack of accountability in child protection investigations, and for permitting the lead police investigator to double as the foster parent of the two children who were coerced by the system into making allegations."[41]

The San Diego County Grand Jury observed of the Dale Akiki case, in which a developmentally disabled man was accused of masterminding a ring of satanic abusers, that the prosecutor failed to disclose the fact and result of a surveillance of the accused conducted prior to charging. Furthermore, the investigation of alleged child sexual abuse by a known prior offender, involving a victim related to and occurring near the time of the alleged incidents in the Akiki case, was not disclosed to the defense, and the investigation of that reported occurrence was never pursued. These facts were learned by the defense through an anonymous tip.

The San Diego Grand Jury also noted that the district attorney's office overemphasized conviction to the detriment of its duty of doing justice. Overzealous prosecution led to a lack of objectivity. The U. S. Supreme Court has stated that

> The United States Attorney is the representative not of an ordinary party to a controversy, but of a sovereignty whose obligation to govern impartially is as compelling as its obligation to govern at all, and whose interest, therefore, in a criminal prosecution is not that it shall win a case, but that justice shall be done. As such, he is in a peculiar and very definite sense the servant of the law, the twofold aim of which is that guilt shall not escape or innocence suffer. He may prosecute with earnestness and vigor—indeed, he should do so. But, while he may strike hard blows, he is not at liberty to strike foul ones. It is as much his duty to refrain from improper methods calculated to produce a wrongful conviction as it is to use every legitimate means to bring about a just one.[42]

Police and prosecutorial misconduct are not unique to cases of child sexual abuse, of course. In fact, they have become so commonplace that the U. S. House of Representatives recently convened a Special Committee on Prosecutorial Misconduct; and conservative Republican Governor George Ryan of Illinois declared a moratorium on executions in that state in light of evidence that innocent people had, due to such misconduct, been convicted and sentenced to death. The House Committee proposed requiring new trials whenever it was found that the prosecution had withheld evidence favorable to the defense and to limit the use of jailhouse informants, who have been known to trade questionable testimony for favorable treatment by prosecutors.[43]

"Police and prosecutorial improprieties take on several forms: coaching witnesses at lineups but denying such coaching under oath; obtaining confessions through brutality, threat, force, or guile, and denying any such action in court; planting evidence . . . that will militate against the accused; making threats against potential witnesses for the accused; using rewards and offers of immunity to entice those willing to testify; and suppressing exculpatory evidence even after motions for discovery have been made."[44]

> The [1992 NYC] Mollen Commission found that the most common form of police corruption was the falsification of police records and testimony. . . . [T]he practice was so widespread . . . that officers created a name for it: *testilying* . . . mandatory minimum sentences and truth in sentencing proposals . . . [have] removed sentencing power from judges and transferred it to prosecutors. . . . The budget of the U. S. Department of Justice *quadrupled* between 1980 and 1992. . . . Nationwide, budgets of prosecutors' offices jumped 230 percent

during the 1980s to $5.5 billion. . . . Prosecutors . . . are promoted on the basis of high conviction rates. Prosecutors cannot boast of how often they dismiss trivial arrests or drop charges against innocent people. . . . We need to develop more meaningful criteria for evaluating prosecutors, relying less on conviction rates and more on the quality of prosecutions.[45]

In addition, malfeasance may result from inability, unwillingness, or lack of funds and personnel available to make true and proper investigations. The reason usually given for misconduct is the belief that the person in custody, or under suspicion, is guilty.[46] Other reasons that police officers lie include: to maintain statistics, to make "collars for dollars" (end-of-shift and holiday overtime), to cover up other corruption, and in fear of retaliation by the blue wall of silence.[47] Ronald Hampton, executive director of the national Black Police Association in Washington, noted that "Right after we saw crack on the scene, police officers and politicians started pushing the envelope. Miranda was seen as an obstacle to a safe society. And when you can get people to believe laws stand in the way, then the people who enforce those laws will set them aside."[48]

Judge Burton Katz suggested that rule-breaking by police officers is a common reaction to *Miranda* and exclusionary rules that they claim "handcuff justice."[49] And the use of these rules, as well as the strictness of their interpretation, varies extremely according to jurisdiction.[50]

The incentives for prosecutors, who are elected and therefore must satisfy not only the interests of justice, but the preferences and perceptions of voters, are the "desire to add points to a scorecard, to enhance a reputation as a tough and successful prosecutor . . . or to receive commendation . . . for having . . . solved a difficult case."[51] Crime control policies give prosecutors great power. The American Bar Association observed, however, that "Nobody . . . holds prosecutors accountable for their behavior; rather, they are immune from any attempt at redress or correction. It is a system with all the incentives awarded for making accusations and little interest in the accuracy of the decisions made. It pursues neither truth nor justice, but winning."[52] A rare exception was when "A federal jury ordered Connecticut's top prosecutor [chief state attorney John Bailey] to pay $2.7 million in damages . . . [for] maliciously retaliat[ing] against an employee [Gregory Dillon] who publicly voiced concerns about FBI corruption in a joint state-federal investigation."[53]

The topics in Bennett L. Gershman's classic law tome, *Prosecutorial Misconduct*, suggest the range that these actions can take, including: investigative misconduct (including entrapment), misconduct in grand jury interrogation, impugning the character of a witness, conveying opinions about evidence, misleading, making inflammatory and abusive remarks, threatening or harassing a witness, overbroad subpoenas, overcharging, suppression of evidence, inappropriate comments to the media, misconduct in plea bargaining, delay, misconduct in the presentation of evidence, forensic misconduct, and misconduct at sentencing.[54] Gershman, a former New York State prosecutor who teaches law at Pace University, observed that the problem has gotten more serious as many of the checks and balances designed to prevent the abuse of power have been eliminated by Congress. The courts, once a buffer between prosecutors and the rights of defendants, have become rubber stamps. And defendants are virtually powerless to sue for damages regardless of what offense a federal prosecutor may commit in pursuing an investigation.[55] A former U. S. attorney now practicing criminal defense reiterated that prosecutors have such free rein because the power judges once wielded to mitigate conduct has been taken away.[56] And in 1992 the U. S. Supreme Court ruled in a 5–4 decision that prosecutors have no legal obligation to provide "substantial exculpatory evidence" to a grand jury,[57] virtually ensuring an indictment, which suggests guilt to a trial jury. Lying has become an increasingly significant problem in federal court cases because the rewards to federal law-enforcement officers can be so great and the consequences so minimal. Perjurers are seldom punished; nor are law-enforcement officers who ignore or accept their lies. The *Pittsburg Post-Gazette* found hundreds of cases over the past ten years in which federal officers and prosecutors tolerated or encouraged perjury. In fact, the Justice Department's Thornburgh Rule actually allows federal prosecutors to ignore ethics guidelines in the states in which they operate.[58] While the 10th Circuit Court of Appeals in Denver, 3–0, recently said that promising leniency to witnesses in exchange for testimony amounted to buying testimony, a violation of federal law,[59] this ruling is contrary to actual practice, and the decision only relates to cases in the 10th Circuit.

As a result of the Thornburgh rule, "since a 1963 U. S. Supreme Court ruling designed to curb misconduct by prosecutors, at least 381 defendants nationally have had a homicide conviction thrown out because prosecutors concealed evidence they knew to be false."[60] However, "even when misconduct is clear, federal officials are loath to acknowledge it, punish it, or ensure that it doesn't happen again."[61]

However, it must be noted that not all faulty accusations and convictions are due to system incompetence or malfeasance. Although becoming legally guilty though factually innocent is the result of many factors, faulty eyewitness identification is the most critical and accounts for as many as half of all erroneous findings of legal guilt. These are not new observations, however. As early as 1927, Felix Frankfurter quoted Dr. Morton Prince, professor of abnormal and dynamic psychology at Harvard University, as observing that "Everyone knows that under [suggestive] . . . circumstances, the image of a person . . . may later develop in an observer's mind and become a false memory." Frankfurter also noted that "the identification of strangers is proverbially untrustworthy" and that the English Court of Appeals was created based on such a case, that of Adolph Beck.[62]

These errors alone are usually insufficient against diligent investigation, but when added to overzealousness, bias, criminal justice ineptitude, and pressure for convictions from politicians and the community, they can be more than enough to convict. In addition, where the same people may participate in many arrests, prosecutions, and trials, interactional bonds tend to develop that are hard to overcome. So a single error can be compounded as a case works its way through the system, and there is reluctance to override it at subsequent levels.[63]

False confessions are another leading cause of injustice in America. Police question suspects in private and rarely record the interrogation session in any way. No criminal justice agency keeps any records or collects any statistics on the number or frequency of police interrogations of criminal suspects, so we have no idea how often suspects are interrogated or how often they confess, and even in reported cases it is difficult to establish the "ground truth" necessary to infer the likely truth or falsity of confessions. A confession of guilt is the most damaging evidence the government can present in a criminal trial, so police-induced false confessions are very likely to lead to wrongful convictions. A suspect who confesses will be pressured to plead guilty, and criminal justice officials rarely believe a suspect's retractions. Suspects who confess experience greater difficulty making bail, which also reduces the likelihood of acquittal. If convicted, a suspect who has falsely confessed is likely to be sentenced more harshly. A confession can be so damning that cases have been documented in which suspects have been prosecuted, convicted, and incarcerated even when it would have been physically impossible for them to have committed the crimes of which they were accused.[64] Mentally disabled individuals are particularly prone to falsely confess.[65]

A single training agency, Reid Associates, teaches most of the police officers in the country, using inherently coercive interrogation methods.[66] Its textbook, coauthored by John E. Reid, states that "In dealing with criminal offenders, and consequently also with criminal suspects who may actually be innocent, the interrogator must of necessity employ less refined methods than are considered appropriate for the transaction of ordinary, everyday affairs by and between law-abiding citizens."[67] However, confessions can be a key to proving innocence if the postadmission narrative fails to correspond with the facts of the case and the defense is effective in demonstrating that fact.[68]

Approximately 90% of all criminal cases are plea bargained. In such cases, defendants give up their rights in a process that might be unfair and involuntary,[69] and more likely to catch up a vulnerable individual without knowledge of the law than a savvy criminal. Many innocent defendants are convicted after entering guilty pleas; since many of these "bargains" result in immediate freedom, suspended sentences, or probation, there is no continued aftermath, no investigation, no exoneration.[70] Ironically, juries are rarely informed about the unreliability of eyewitness testimony or the frequency of false confessions, or that the latter are especially common in cases of plea bargains. Similarly, defenses of incompetence can result in the denial of the right to trial, and "incarceration" in a mental facility for an indeterminate period—often longer than the sentence that would have resulted from a criminal trial.

The San Diego Grand Jury observed, too, that

the judiciary blamed many of the problems in the system on attorneys who had not afforded their clients an adequate defense. Appellate attorneys also complained that the record was insufficient upon which to base an appeal. The defense attorney had not made an adequate record of objection.[71]

All of this information, taken together, suggests the fallacy that feminists, or any other group of ideologues, have "taken over" the criminal justice system. Instead, it would appear that the criminal justice system is currently responding to incentives that encourage reports of crime, especially child abuse and violence against women. Further, selective use of "rape shield laws" and other pro-victim policies seem to be used less to help all women victims than to target particular offenders. Herbert L. Packer, in his seminal 1968 work, *The Limits of the Criminal Sanction*, explained that there are two models of justice: the crime control model and the due-process model.[72] Any significant focus on one will tilt the scales of justice away from the other. The 1950s and 1960s saw increased emphasis on the due process model, which expanded the rights of the accused (and made it less likely that innocent people would be falsely convicted). Since the 1970s, however, there have been efforts to tilt the scales back toward the crime control model. "For two decades, the criminal justice system has grown exponentially while our communities are closing libraries, freezing teacher salaries, limiting medical benefits for our senior citizens, slashing student loan programs, and defunding Head Start and other early intervention programs."[73]

However, this increased funding has not been disbursed uniformly. Public defenders received just over 2% of the total spent on criminal justice in 1990. Police received 43%, prisons received 34%, courts received 13%, and prosecutors received 8%. The American Bar Association reported that the underfunding of indigent defense has created a "crisis of extraordinary proportions." In the past five years, over $400 billion has been spent on law enforcement, and spending on prisons has increased by five times since 1980.[74] Emphasis on "putting away the bad guys" and expanding "victims' rights" have, as an unintended consequence, reduced safeguards against false prosecutions. In this climate, sustaining convictions takes on so much importance that it may overshadow the means by which they are obtained.

"When an inquisitorial process replaces or weakens the adversary one . . . presumption of innocence is diminished, the role of investigating officials is vastly enlarged, there is less protection of the rights of the accused, a zealous promotion of vigilance and enforcement measures occurs, and, of course, there is a presumption of pervasive malfeasance in the behavior of the targeted group."[75] As added proof, in 4% of all cases in which the judge believed that a verdict of guilty was unwarranted, that verdict was rendered by the jury. It should also be noted that the damage of false allegations is widespread, because each time an innocent offender is wrongfully convicted, the actual offender remains free to continue victimizing the public.[76]

Criminal justice policy persists because it does not lead to an effective demand for action. Reiman's Pyrrhic defeat theory explains that

the current shape of our failing criminal justice policy . . . is really *three* failures that work together. First, there is the failure to identify as crimes the harmful acts of the rich and powerful. . . . Second, there is the failure to implement policies that stand a good chance of reducing crime and the harm it causes. . . . Third, there is the failure to eliminate economic bias in the criminal justice system, so the poor continue to have a substantially greater chance than better-off people of being arrested, charged, convicted and penalized for committing the acts that are treated as crimes.[77]

But participants in the criminal justice system do not speak out because any societal perceptions that make it easier to anticipate jurors' attitudes and other clues to trial outcomes make it easier to ensure conviction rates. Outcomes are still difficult to anticipate, however, because differences among jurisdictions preempt centralized control, making it impossible to determine, for instance, whether expert testimony that has been accepted in one jurisdiction will be found eligible in another, or whether challenges to particular legislation will similarly carry over in spirit if not in law.

Use of the crime control model may have peaked, however, due to the recent exposés of misconduct that have been found at all levels of the criminal justice system. The Los Angeles Police Department and Los Angeles Sheriff's Department alone have paid out tens of millions of dollars to victims of brutality and their survivors,[78] and in a single New York City case, prosecutors were forced to throw out 125 cases against ninety-eight defendants because their convictions were based on false testimony. About seventy of the defendants admitted in later interviews that they were committing crimes when they were arrested. Prosecutors identified 2,000 cases in which the corrupt officers' testimony tainted evidence, and one-sixth of the officers in a single precinct had routinely stolen drug money and guns and police conducted "key jobs," stealing drug dealers' keys and then robbing their apartments. In addition to conducting illegal raids and stealing and dealing drugs, a dozen officers later admitted to routinely lying under oath. Most admitted committing perjury fewer than a dozen times, but one sergeant admitted to lying on the witness stand in seventy-five trials and hearings. Some officers lied to protect their own drug businesses, while others claimed that they committed perjury to counterbalance the loopholes used by drug dealers to evade the police. At least twenty-five defendants have used that tainted evidence as the ground for lawsuits against the city, and some have won six-figure damage awards. A judge who presided over 3 cases that were later overturned because of police perjury said he still believes that most police officers tell the truth but that many of the jurors in his courtroom do not share that opinion.[79] In Philadelphia, too, police lying and corruption is so common that it is joked that "kids [there] could play cops and robbers at the same time."[80]

In an article in the *Chicago Tribune Magazine* foreshadowing their forthcoming book, *Nine Lives*, David Protess and Rob Warden chronicled the stories of nine men who were erroneously convicted of murder and sentenced to death in Illinois since 1977. They explained that "like the overwhelming majority of the Illinois Death Row population, [the nine men] were indigent and did not have access to legal and investigative resources that could have established their innocence long ago." Carl E. Lawson's conviction was attributed to the fact that his arraignment had been handled by an unsympathetic former prosecutor, and because he was unable to hire an expert to examine the shoe print that eventually was proven to have been left by someone else. Darby Tillis and Perry Cobb were convicted by Judge Thomas J. Maloney, who "was tough on defendants who had not bribed him in order to divert suspicion that he was taking bribes in other cases." Amazingly, in the cases of Rolando Cruz and Alejandro Hernandez, not only were they released, but four police officers and three prosecutors involved in the case were charged with perjury and official misconduct.[81]

In addition, dozens of cases have been affected by problems associated with the FBI lab's work, including sloppy handling of evidence, unreliable processing of the material sent to the lab for analysis, and misuse of the lab's findings. Evidence of such problems was found in such high-profile cases as the Olympic bombing in Atlanta, in which suspicion was placed erroneously on Richard Jewel, in the Oklahoma City bombing, and in the World Trade Center bombing. These errors in the lab are already providing defense lawyers with ammunition to use in some cases. The lab conducts more than 600,000 evidence examinations annually. Among other complaints, scientists at the lab said they were often stifled in a lab run by nontechnical field agents who had little knowledge of science and who regularly altered reports to help prosecutors.[82] The FBI's own study, *Convicted by Juries, Exonerated by Science*, identifies government malfeasance as the cause of 8 cases, or 28% of the cases reported. One serologist was found to have committed misconduct in more than 130 criminal cases handled by his office.[83] Referring to that pathologist, Fred Zain, it was observed that Zain's results almost always favored the prosecution, but this fact was overlooked by those who worked with him at all levels. In another case, in Texas, pathologist Ralph Erdmann was convicted of faking autopsies in more than forty counties. Dr. Erdmann listed in an autopsy report the weight of a decedent's spleen, which had been removed years earlier. An initial investigation turned up 100 fake autopsies.[84]

A 517-page report by the Inspector General's Office of the Department of Justice, the result of an eighteen-month investigation into the FBI laboratory, found that FBI examiners had given scientifically flawed, inaccurate, and over-stated testimony under oath in court; had altered the lab reports of examiners to give them a pro-prosecutorial slant, and had failed to document tests and exami-nations from which they drew incriminating conclusions, thus ensuring that their work could never be properly checked. FBI management, meanwhile, had failed to check examinations and lab reports, had overseen a woefully inadequate record-retention system, and had not only failed to investigate serious and credible alle-gations of incompetence but had covered them up. Management had also resisted any form of external scrutiny of the lab and had failed to establish and enforce its own validated scientific procedures and protocols. "It is quite common to find lab-oratory facilities and personnel who are, for all intents and purposes, an arm of the prosecution," notes James Starrs, a professor of law and forensic science at George Washington University.[85] Similarly, FBI Director Louis Freeh's program to reduce misconduct resulted in the disciplining of 212 employees.[86] A subsequent report by the National Association of Criminal Defense Lawyers claimed that the FBI's DNA laboratory exhibited "prejudice and incompetence" that enabled justice to be perverted by FBI alignment with the prosecution.[87] "Perjury by expert witnesses, faked laboratory reports, and testimony based on unproven techniques . . . although scientific evidence is far superior to other types of evidence, such as eyewitness identifications and even confessions in some instances . . . is also subject to abuse. Too many experts in the criminal justice system manifest a police-prosecution bias . . . too many prosecutors seek out such experts."[88]

However, Judge Katz suggested that misconduct by prosecutors is offset by mis-conduct by defense attorneys.[89] While this may be true when defendants hire high-priced legal teams, it is doubtful that it is the case for most defendants. A U. S. Department of Justice report found that in 1991, 80% of local jail inmates, three-quarters of state prison inmates, and half of federal inmates had had court-appointed defenders.[90] Given the high caseloads, limited resources, and often lim-ited experience of public defenders, however, incompetence may be a greater prob-lem than malicious misconduct in that arena. Perceptions of the police, on the other hand, have improved, primarily because two-thirds of all contacts with police are with victims and witnesses, whose treatment by the police has visibly improved.[91]

Note too that the bulk of misconduct occurs in ideologically charged crimes and against poor defendants who have difficulty countering the superior resources of the criminal justice system. This is nothing new. During Prohibition, agents concentrated their efforts on those too poor to offer them bribes.[92] It was esti-mated that at the height of Prohibition, between one-third and one-half of the entire Chicago police force was "on the take"; nationwide, perhaps as many as one out of ten policemen in major cities received bribes from bootleggers or speakeasy operators. Today, too, the successes racked up by drug enforcement agencies most often come at the expense of fringe suppliers who are unprotected by gang organization. In effect, the enforcement efforts tax unorganized competitors, maintaining the economic viability of organized crime in America.[93] And according to H. R. Haldeman's diary, in 1969 President Nixon emphasized that "the whole problem is really the blacks. The key is to devise a system that recognizes this while not appearing to."[94]

It was not always this way. Until 1967 the federal government had a negligible role in drug enforcement and the Justice Department had no role at all. Then, when Republicans tried to make President Johnson look "soft on drugs," Johnson tried to get J. Edgar Hoover to add drug enforcement to the FBI's mission, which would have brought it under the then Attorney General Ramsey Clark. Hoover refused, recognizing that narcotics enforcement is the type of police work most likely to corrupt cops.[95] The federal budget for the drug war in 2000 was $17.8 billion—and it is spread among forty-four separate agencies with different priorities and skills and no coordination.[96]

Narcotics enforcement also corrupts the criminal justice system as a whole. State and local law-enforcement agencies did not increase their efforts against drugs dramatically until 1984, when a reallocation of resources toward drug enforcement began. One section of the Comprehensive Crime Act of 1984 established a system whereby any local police bureau that cooperated with federal drug enforcement authorities in a drug investigation would share in the money confiscated as part of that investigation. Police in many states whose own laws or constitutions limited confiscation possibilities began to circumvent state laws by having federal authorities "adopt" their seizures. Since 1989 a growing number of states, including Texas, Florida, and New Jersey, have begun to apply their forfeiture laws to any criminal activity.[97] As a result,

Fifty-seven federal departments and agencies now have a piece of what has become America's longest war. Its annual budget climbed from about $1 billion [under] . . . Ronald Reagan . . . to more than $16 billion today. The overall federal, state and local effort has cost nearly $290 billion, according to Drug Strategies, a nonpartisan policy group in Washington, D. C . . . . This proliferation . . . [has] produced monumental turf battles, duplication and waste. Each law enforcement agency has established its own drug intelligence center and database, much of which is off-limits to other agencies. . . . Roughly two-thirds of the drug budget, or $10.5 billion, has been devoted to trying to reduce the supply through law enforcement, interdiction and programs to eliminate production abroad. What's left has gone for treatment and prevention.[98]

However, there is little evidence that this strategy is working. "Drug policy is easily reduced to hyperbole, unrealistic expectations, and denial of the inevitable tradeoffs that accompany public action."[99] While the drug war continues to be the primary growth industry in federal funding, most of the money has been wasted.[100] A recent study by the RAND Corporation, for instance, found that the total impact of the nearly $6 billion spent on coast guard helicopters, Customs Service jets, and radar-equipped blimps succeeded in raising the street price of cocaine in the United States by only 4%. The study also estimated that for each 2% hike in the street price of cocaine, an additional $1 billion per year will have to be spent on protecting our borders from smugglers. Inspecting every one of the steel cargo containers that are used to bring in 90% of America's imports would require the full-time services of more than 300,000 customs inspectors, and would bring the country's international trade to a grinding halt. Even if this could be done, the United States still has more than 12,000 miles of coastline and 7,500 miles of land bordering Canada and Mexico.[101] Furthermore, cocaine supply-control strategies that seize and destroy 70% or less of production, without limiting the total level of production, also have little impact on the market.[102] Illegal drugs are a classic Third World product: cheap to manufacture, easy to transport, and sold on street corners at a huge markup. It costs $100 to produce a kilo of cocaine that can be sold for $30,000. The markup is so great that drugs are overproduced for the demand probably by 2 to 1 or 3 to 1.[103]

Many law-enforcement bureaucracies created misinformation in order to exaggerate the potential benefits of a drug war.[104] Early in the Reagan administration, it became clear to U.S. Attorney for San Francisco Joseph Russianello that the new Justice Department was using the drug problem as an excuse for increasing the power of the prosecutor.[105]

Unintended consequences inevitably result from such snake oil policies. Arrests for drug crimes now exceed 1 million per year, and the number of people imprisoned has doubled in a decade. Drug offenders make up more than 60% of the federal prison population and nearly 25% of state prisoners.[106] However, most of the people arrested on drug charges are otherwise law-abiding citizens; one study recently completed by researchers at Florida State University revealed that more than three-fourths of all people arrested on drug charges had no prior criminal record and that the typical American who goes to jail on drug charges is a casual user.[107] Studies at Harvard Medical School and at Carnegie-Mellon University for the RAND Corporation found similar results and concluded that incarcerating people for drug crimes because it would prevent violent and property crimes is misguided.[108] Yet six hundred thousand Americans were arrested for marijuana crimes in 1995, an all-time record.[109]

These illegalities and excesses have spawned what *Atlantic Monthly* termed a "prison-industrial complex"—an industry built around not only building prisons but serving the needs of prison officials, prisoners, and their families. California now has the biggest prison system in the Western industrialized world, a system 40% bigger than the Federal Bureau of Prisons. The United States prison population exceeded 2 million in 2000,[110] more people than any other country in the world. Throughout the first three quarters of this century the nation's incarceration rate remained relatively stable, at about 110 prison inmates for every 100,000 people. In the mid-1970s the rate began to climb, doubling in the 1980s and then again in the 1990s. Meanwhile, the proportion of offenders being sent to prison for violent crimes has actually fallen.[111]

Ironically, criminals of all types are now generally convicted on fewer or lesser counts and receive lighter punishment due to plea bargaining. Most people arrested as felons are not prosecuted and convicted as felons; in fact, the odds that a person arrested for a felony will be sentenced to prison are 1 in 108. And consider that Los Angeles County made arrests in only half of its 2,000 annual homicide cases, compared with 4 out of 5 twenty-five years ago.[112] Prosecutors pointed to a lack of staff and to police failure to secure items of evidence or lists of witnesses.[113] But this also suggests that the number of drug crimes have overpowered the criminal justice system, rendering it less effective in all areas. This parallels Prohibition, when the murder rate hit record levels, rising to a level 25% above the years preceding 1920. When Prohibition was finally repealed, the murder rate declined for eleven consecutive years. Assaults with firearms followed a similar pattern, rising sharply with the onset of Prohibition and falling abruptly with its repeal.[114]

Recognizing the failure of these costly policies, not only in terms of dollars but in terms of their drain on the resources available to handle serious, violent criminals, many judges are in individual and organized revolt over the injustices of the drug war, especially those imposed by mandatory minimum sentences. Some surveys have shown that more than half of the people whose property is forfeited are never charged with a crime. And there is concern that precedents set in the drug war can ultimately affect any American who comes to the attention of our increasingly powerful law-enforcement agencies.[115] The urge to rethink the drug war is derived less from libertarian theory than from prudence, grounded on the observations that some illegal drugs are not very harmful and that the prohibition of others has passed the point of diminishing returns.[116]

It is ironic that prosecutors of child abuse and drug offenses have both lost sight of priorities in "numbers games" that build careers and feed ideologies at the expense of taxpayers—and at the expense of justice. But it is clear that overwhelming a system will bring it to its knees faster than a revolution—and cause the public to lose faith in that system as well.

While it is impossible to know how many of those inmates are incarcerated falsely, whether as a result of police or prosecutorial misconduct, faulty lab work, erroneous eyewitness identification or other factors, the tide is beginning to turn. Sadly, this is not the result of enlightenment on the part of representatives of the criminal justice system. Instead, it is due to improved forensic methods, particularly the increased use of DNA evidence, which has proved that even death row inmates have been convicted wrongfully—possibly in as many as 2 out of 3 cases.[117] This has resulted in a call by the then president-elect of the American Bar Association, among others, for a moratorium on the use of the death penalty.[118]

NOTES

1. C. Ronald Huff, Arye Rattner, and Edward Sagarin, *Convicted But Innocent* (Thousand Oaks, CA: Sage Publications, 1996).

2. Michael J. Ross, *State and Local Politics and Policy: Change and Reform* (Englewood Cliffs, NJ: Prentice Hall, 1987).

3. San Diego County Grand Jury, *Analysis of Child Molestation Issues. Report No. 7* (San Diego, CA: San Diego County Grand Jury, June 1, 1994).

4. Debbie Nathan and Michael Snedeker, *Satan's Silence* (New York: Basic Books, 1995).

5. *State of NJ v. JQ*, 130 NJ 554, 617 A. 2d 1196 (1993).

6. Alan M. Rubenstein, *Report: Investigation into Breezy Point Day School* (Doylestown, PA: Office of the District Attorney, March 1990).

7. Richard Wexler, *Wounded Innocents* (New York: Prometheus, 1995).

8. D. Jones and J. M. MacGraw, "Reliable and Fictitious Accounts of Sexual Abuse in Children," *Journal of Interpersonal Violence* 2 (1987), cited in Stephen J. Ceci and Maggie Bruck. *Jeopardy in the Courtroom* (Washington, DC: American Psychological Association, 1995).

9. Cathy Young, *Ceasefire: Beyond the Gender Wars* (New York: Free Press, 1999).

10. Richard Gelles, cited in Cathy Young, *Ceasefire: Beyond the Gender Wars* (New York: Free Press, 1999).

11. Lela B. Costin, Howard Jacob Karger, and David Stoesz, *The Politics of Child Abuse in America* (New York: Oxford University Press, 1996).

12. Ibid.

13. See, for example, Richard B. Schmitt, "Who Is an Expert? In Some Courtrooms, the Answer Is 'Nobody,' " *Wall Street Journal* (June 17, 1997), A1 and A8; Lawrence W. Sherman, *Preventing Crime: What Works, What Doesn't, What's Promising* (Washington, DC: U. S. Department of Justice, February 1997); and Peter Huber, *Galileo's Revenge* (New York: Basic Books, 1991).

14. Jon C. Straus, "College Costs Too Much, Fails Kids," *USA Today* (July 17, 1997).

15. Margaret A. Hagen, *Whores of the Court* (New York: ReganBooks, 1997).

16. Diane Schetky, "Resolved: Child Sexual Abuse is Overdiagnosed: Affirmative," *Journal of the American Academy of Child and Adolescent Psychiatry* 28, no. 5 (1989), 789–797.

17. Marcia Angell, "Trial By Science," *New York Times* (December 9, 1998).

18. Robyn M. Dawes, *House of Cards: Psychology and Psychotherapy Built on Myth* (New York: Free Press, 1994).

19. Alan M. Dershowitz, *The Abuse Excuse* (New York: Little, Brown & Co., 1994).

20. See, for example, Robyn M. Dawes, op. cit.; and Margaret Hagen, op. cit.

21. William F. McIver II, "Behind the Prison Walls," *Issues in Child Abuse Allegations* 9, nos. 1/2 (1997), 16–24.

22. Peter Huber, *Galileo's Revenge* (New York: Basic Books, 1991).

23. Richard B. Schmitt, "Who Is an Expert? In Some Courtrooms, the Answer Is 'Nobody,' " *Wall Street Journal* (June 17, 1997), A1 and A8.

24. Alan M. Rubenstein, op. cit.

25. Tana Dineen, *Manufacturing Victims*, 2d ed. (Montreal: Robert Davies Publishing, 1998).

26. R. Christopher Locke, "Expert Testimony in the Post-Daubert Era," *CPA Expert* (spring 1996).

27. Ibid.

28. Richard B. Schmitt, op. cit.

29. Frank J. Murray, "Justices Curb 'Junk Science,'" *Insight* (January 26, 1998).

30. Ellen Goodman, "Court Program Could Trash Junk Science," *The Statesman Journal* (February 24, 1998).

31. Steve Johnson, "Custody Calls Anger Parents," *San Jose Mercury News* (November 26, 1998).

32. See, for example, David Lloyd, ed., *A Judicial Response to Child Sexual Abuse* (Huntsville, AL: National Children's Advocacy Center, 1990). Grant 90-CA-1359 from the National Center on Child Abuse and Neglect, Office of Human Development Services, U.S. Department of Health and Human Services.

33. Ibid.

34. David Hechler, *The Battle and the Backlash* (Lexington, MA: Lexington Books, 1988).

35. Debbie Nathan and Michael Snedeker, op. cit.

36. Ibid.

37. Tamar Lewin, "Judge Upsets Murder Conviction Focused on "Repressed Memory,'" *New York Times* (April 5, 1995).

38. Larry McShane, "Bronx Witchhunt Destroyed Lives," *Denver Post* (December 2, 1996).

39. Marianne McMullen, "Cry for Justice," *Dayton Voice* (February 21, 1996).

40. Wes Hills, "Aldridge and Wilcox Molested at Least 2 Children, He Rules," *Dayton Daily News* (September 2, 2000).

41. Paul Craig Roberts, "Benching the Witch Hunters," *Washington Times* (September 13, 1996).

42. San Diego County Grand Jury, *Child Sexual Abuse, Assault, and Molest Issues, Report No. 8* (San Diego, CA: San Diego County Grand Jury, June 29, 1992); also *Berger v. United States* 295 U.S. 78, 79 L.Ed. 1314, 55 S. Ct. 629, 633 (1935), cited in the aforementioned 1992 SDCGJ Report No. 8.

43. Maurice Possley and Christi Parsons, "Lawmaker Goes After Prosecutorial Misconduct," *Chicago Tribune* (June 15, 2000).

44. C. Ronald Huff, Arye Rattner, and Edward Sagarin, op. cit.

45. Steven R. Donziger, ed., *The Real War on Crime* (New York: HarperPerennial, 1996).

46. C. Ronald Huff, Arye Rattner, and Edward Sagarin, *Convicted But Innocent* (Thousand Oaks, CA: Sage Publications, 1996).

47. Jack Chin, presentation at the Conference on Wrongful Convictions and the Death Penalty, Northwestern University, November 13–15, 1998.

48. Jan Hofman, "Police Tactics Are Chipping Away at Miranda Rights of Suspects," *New York Times* (March 29, 1998).

49. Burton S. Katz, *Justice Overruled* (New York: Warner Books, 1997).

50. William Tucker, "Crime and No Punishment," *New York Press* (March 11–17, 1998).

51. Ibid.

52. American Bar Association Task Force, *The Judicial Response to Lawyer Misconduct* (Chicago: American Bar Association, 1984).

53. "Judge Orders Prosecutor to Pay," *New York Times* (November 26, 1998).

54. Bennett L. Gershman, *Prosecutorial Misconduct* (Deerfield, IL: Clark, Boardman, Callaghan, October 1991).

55. Associated Press re: *Pittsburgh Post-Gazette* article (10-part series) (November 21, 1998).

56. Quoted in Bill Moushey, "Calculated Abuses," *Pittsburgh Post-Gazette* (December 7, 1998).

57. Bill Moushey, "When Safeguards Fail," *Pittsburgh Post-Gazette* (December 6, 1998).

58. Bill Moushey, "Wrath of Vengeance," *Pittsburgh Post-Gazette* (December 8, 1998).

59. Bill Moushey, "The Damage of Lies: Zeal for Convictions Leads Government to Accept Tainted Tips, Testimony," *Pittsburgh Post-Gazette* (November 29, 1998).

60. Ken Armstrong and Maurice Possley, "The Verdict: Dishonor," *Chicago Tribune* (January 8, 1999).

61. Bill Moushey, "Failing to Police Their Own," *Pittsburgh Post-Gazette* (December 13, 1998).

62. Felix Frankfurter, *The Case of Sacco and Venzetti* (Boston: Little, Brown and Co., 1927).

63. C. Ronald Huff, Arye Rattner, and Edward Sagarin, op. cit.

64. Richard A. Leo, *False Confessions and Miscarriages of Justice Today*, paper prepared for "A Day of Contrition Revisited: Contemporary Hysteria Condemns the Innocent," a conference organized by the Justice Committee, Salem, MA, January 14, 1997.

65. Robert Perske, "The Unusually Vulnerable—Persons with Mental Disabilities," paper presented at "A Day of Contrition Revisited," Salem, MA, January 14, 1997.

66. Richard Ofshe, Conference on Wrongful Convictions and the Death Penalty, Northwestern University, November 13–15, 1998. Citing Fred E. Inbau, John E. Reid, and Joseph P. Buckley, *Criminal Investigations and Confessions*, 3d ed. (Baltimore: Williams & Wilkins, 1986).

67. Fred E. Inbau, John E. Reid, and Joseph P. Buckley, op. cit.

68. Richard A. Leo and Richard J. Ofshe, "The Consequences of False Confessions: Deprivations of Liberty and Miscarriages of Justice in the Age of Psychological Interrogation," *The Journal of Criminal Law and Criminology* 88, no. 2 (winter 1988), 429–496.

69. Robert Elias, *Victims Still* (Beverly Hills, CA: Sage Publications, 1993).

70. C. Ronald Huff, Arye Rattner, and Edward Sagarin, *Convicted But Innocent* (Thousand Oaks, CA: Sage Publications, 1996).

71. San Diego County Grand Jury, *Child Sexual Abuse, Assault, and Molest Issues, Report No. 8* (San Diego, CA: San Diego County Grand Jury, June 29, 1992).

72. Herbert L. Packer, *The Limits of the Criminal Sanction* (Stanford, CA: Stanford University Press, 1968).

73. Steven R. Donziger, ed., *The Real War on Crime* (New York: HarperPerennial, 1996).

74. Ibid.

75. Daphne Patai, "The Making of a Social Problem: Sexual Harassment on Campus," *Sexuality and Culture* 1 (1997), 219–256.

76. C. Ronald Huff, Arye Rattner, and Edward Sagarin, op. cit.

77. Jeffrey Reiman, *The Rich Get Rich and the Poor Get Prison*, 2d ed. (New York: Macmillan Publishing Co., 1984).

78. Farai Chideya, *Don't Believe the Hype* (New York: Plume, 1995).

79. David Kocieniewski, "New York Pays High Price for Police Lies," *New York Times* (January 5, 1997).

80. Michael Kramer, "How Cops Go Bad," *Time* (December 15, 1997).

81. David Protess and Rob Warden, "Nine Lives," *Chicago Tribune Magazine* (August 10, 1997).

82. David Johnston and Andrew C. Revkin, "Report Finds FBI Lab Slipping from Pinnacle of Crime Fighting," *New York Times* (January 29, 1997).

83. Edward Connors, Thomas Lundregan, Neal Miller, and Tom McEwen, *Convicted by Juries, Exonerated by Science: Case Studies in the Use of DNA Evidence to Establish Innocence After Trial* (Washington, DC: U.S. Department of Justice, June 1996).

84. Paul C. Gianelli, "The Abuse of Scientific Evidence in Criminal Cases: The Need for Independent Crime Laboratories," *Virginia Journal of Social Policy & the Law* (winter 1997), 439–478.

85. John F. Kelly and Phillip K. Wearne, *Tainting Evidence* (New York: Free Press, 1998).

86. Michael J. Sniffen, "FBI Fired 19 Employees Last Year for Misconduct," *Associated Press* (December 9, 1998).

87. Richard Willing, "FBI's DNA Lab Accused of Bias, Incompetence," *USA Today* (November 26, 1997).

88. Paul C. Gianelli, op. cit.

89. Burton S. Katz, *Justice Overruled* (New York: Warner Books, 1997).

90. Steven K. Smith with Carol J. DeFrancis, *Indigent Defense* (Washington, DC: U.S. Department of Justice, February 1996).

91. "Police Abuse Rare," *New York Times* (November 23, 1997).

92. Edward Behr, *Prohibition* (New York: Arcade, 1996).

93. Daniel K. Benjamin and Roger Leroy Miller, *Undoing Drugs* (New York: Basic Books, 1991).

94. Alexander Cockburn, "Why the Drug War Works," *New York Press* (June 17–23, 1998).

95. Dan Baum, *Smoke and Mirrors* (New York: Little, Brown & Co., 1996).

96. U.S. Department of Justice, *DEA Briefing Book* (Washington, DC: U.S. Department of Justice, October 1999). See also, Robert Dreyfuss, "The Drug War: Where the Money Goes," *Rolling Stone* (December 11, 1997).

97. David Rasmussen and Bruce Benson, *The Economic Anatomy of a Drug War* (Lanham, MD: Rowman & Littlefield, 1994).

98. Glenn Frankel, "The Longest War," *Washington Post National Weekly Edition* (July 7, 1997), 6–8.

99. David Rasmussen and Bruce Benson, op. cit.

100. Glenn Frankel, op. cit.

101. Daniel K. Benjamin and Roger Leroy Miller, op. cit.

102. M. Kennedy, P. Reuter, and K. J. Riley, *A Simple Economic Model of Cocaine Production* (Santa Monica, CA: RAND, 1994).

103. Glenn Frankel, "The Longest War," *Washington Post National Weekly Edition* (July 7, 1997), 6–8.

104. David Rasmussen and Bruce Benson, *The Economic Anatomy of a Drug War* (Lanham, MD: Rowman & Littlefield, 1994).

105. Dan Baum, op. cit.

106. Glenn Frankel, op. cit.

107. Daniel K. Benjamin and Roger Leroy Miller, *Undoing Drugs* (New York: Basic Books, 1991).

108. Carey Goldberg, "Study Casts Doubts on Wisdom of Mandatory Terms for Drugs," *New York Times* (November 25, 1997).

109. Michael Pollan, "Living With Medical Marijuana," *Sunday New York Times Magazine* (July 20, 1997).

110. David Ho, "U.S. Imprisoned Population Exceeds 2 Million," *Chicago Tribune* (August 9, 2000).

111. Eric Schlosser, "The Prison-Industrial Complex," *Atlantic Monthly* (December 1998).

112. *USA Today* (December 2, 1996).

113. David Rasmussen and Bruce Benson, op. cit.

114. Ibid.

115. Arnold S. Trebach and James A. Inciardi, *Legalize It? Debating American Drug Policy* (Washington, DC: American University Press, 1993).

116. Richard Brookhiser, "Why Won't This Nation Go to Pot?" *New York Observer* (November 17, 1997).

117. Fox Butterfield, "Death Sentences Being Overturned in 2 or 3 Appeals," *New York Times* (June 12, 2000).

118. Associated Press, "ABA Leader Seeks Moratorium on Death Penalty," *Chicago Tribune* (July 10, 2000).

Chapter 7

De-Sanctifying Snake Oil

In differentiation, not in uniformity, lies the path of progress.
—Louis Brandeis

Nothing is more destructive of respect for government and the law of the land than passing laws which cannot be enforced. It is an open secret that the dangerous increase of crime in this country is closely connected with this.
—Albert Einstein

Legal philosophers from Mill to the present have argued that to give priority to individual liberty, one must accept some version of the demonstrable harm requirement as a condition for acceptable laws.
—Jeffrey Reiman

Elimination of all snake oil would be a worthy goal, but elimination of the sanctification of snake oil is vital to public policy for many reasons: because it unfairly skews criminal justice outcomes, wastes tax dollars and other resources that could be allocated to real problem solving, facilitates fraud and corruption of benefit systems, distorts the nature and magnitude of social problems, and, for all of these reasons, undermines public trust in government. Successfully de-sanctifying snake oil, however, requires efforts in several diverse areas. Most significantly, these include reducing outright fraud; enabling the public, including the media, government, and other groups that inform and make decisions for the public to make more accurate assessments of risk; and making the public (including the specific groups mentioned above) aware of the various alternatives to sanctified snake oil that would better meet their goals if only they understood them.

FRAUD

Experts believe that fraud, abuse, and incompetence are rampant in public benefits and private insurance. As much as $346 million has been paid to people who made false claims against federal agencies alone in recent years.[1] The first full audit of Medicare found that hospitals, doctors, and other health-care providers had been overpaid by $23 billion, or 14% of the program's total budget, in a single year.[2] Home-care groups alone are guilty of billions of dollars worth of Medicare fraud. One study found that between 25% and 40% of home-care billings to Medicare were fraudulent. (In a single year, Medicare covers $20 billion in home care for the elderly and disabled.)[3]

The investigation found a single "computational error" of $4.5 billion in Medicare's estimate of unpaid claims. Cases were also found in which hospitals and doctors were overpaid and checks were signed by unauthorized people. Payments were made for services that were not covered by Medicare or did not have the necessary medical documentation proving their necessity. Inadequate record keeping, bookkeeping, and other internal controls frequently prevented proper audits[4] and made it impossible to collect many erroneous overpayments. In fact, the Medicare audit reported that "the Government had no reliable way to prevent or detect improper Medicare payments, and no reliable estimate of what it might owe on unpaid claims for services already provided," because its financial and other records were in such disarray. New York City was required to refund $9.5 million to Medicare for providing ambulance service to patients who did not need it, in one of the rare cases in which a paper trail enabled determination of a refund.[5]

So it is clear that this is not a crime committed only by brilliant system analysts who have overridden complex prevention methods to obtain illegal funds. Ironically, Medicare officials long bragged that they spent only 2% of their budget on overhead. Now that figure is used to demonstrate how shockingly unsupervised the program has been.[6] Furthermore, Harvard economist Malcolm K. Sparrow has reported that fraud control in the health-care industry is woefully inadequate and that "institutional denial of the scope and seriousness of fraud losses is the norm. Fraud control policies tend to be shortsighted and scandal-driven."[7]

Since so much fraud has been found in public benefit systems that pay for services, it should come as no surprise that similar fraud has been detected in the service delivery systems they fund. For instance, the *New York Times* reported widespread financial corruption in mental health and substance abuse treatment in fall 1991, stating that treatment facilities "systematically misdiagnosed, mistreated and abused patients to increase profits from insurance claims."[8] Treatment facilities also charged for hours of therapy that exceeded the hours of the day or were otherwise unreasonable, and doctors who subsequently quit for-profit psychiatric hospitals "reported changed diagnoses, drugs administered without doctors' approval, quota pressure, [and] pressure to 'rediagnose' patients to fit new benefit categories."[9] Children were often medicated only because failure to do so was a signal to insurance companies that the child might not be seriously ill enough to require inpatient hospitalization.[10] Children were also separated from their parents so that the children would not talk their parents out of hospitalization.[11] National Medical Enterprises actually paid premiums anonymously for newly unemployed patients whose benefits were about to be cut off, and moved patients to different units with different diagnoses after their admitting psychiatrists had discharged them.[12] A former auditor for National Medical Enterprises admitted that "violations of state, federal, IRS and accepted business practices occurred, but raised no questions from insurers or the IRS."[13] Fraud has been detected at the University of Pennsylvania Health System and SmithKline Beecham PLC as well as among con artists. "[E]ven Medicare's fraud-busters have been busted for fraud."[14] Tenet Healthcare was forced to repay $100 million to settle 700 Texas claims made by former psychiatric patients who were victims of malpractice as well as false imprisonment so that they could be hospitalized until their insurance benefits were exhausted.[15] And most recently, as of this writing, Columbia/HCA Healthcare Corporation agreed to pay $475 million in civil penalties to settle charges of having cheated federal health care programs.[16]

Defrauders have been creative. One California national toll-free suicide hot line, listed in telephone directories around the country, has since been characterized as a front for gathering leads on potential patients who had insurance that covered mental heath treatment. Leads were then sold to local recruiters at private psychiatric hospitals. Perhaps the best evidence that so much of this treatment was fraudulent was first, that in nearly all cases, the dates that patients' insurance ran out were the dates of their discharges, and, second, that a 1991 study by the Texas State Insurance Department found that eleven of the twenty-five U. S. health insurance companies had a total of $1 billion invested in psychiatric hospitals and facilities.[17] Robert P. Stewart, former president of the National Association of Social Workers, cautioned that "There is a fundamental difference in the application of free-market principles to products and services in the usual realms of commerce, as contrasted with their application to services responding to human suffering and distress. The extraordinary vulnerability of many consumers of mental-health services opens the potential for exploitation almost beyond imagining."[18]

Of all unintended consequences, the greatest was probably that "during the 1980s, consumer medical groups tried to point out that mandates for mental health and substance abuse coverage were a primary cause of dwindling access to health care,"[19] not simply because coverage was provided, but because more and more "diagnoses" were being "identified" by mental health practitioners, lower thresholds of difficulty were being determined to require treatment, and more and more mental health services were being provided on an inpatient basis. As Dineen observed, "The growth of the victim-making industry, with the proliferation of information about psychological conditions and the growth of services that cater to them, may be leading to an epidemic . . . of 'playing sick.' . . . The victim-making capacity of the Psychology Industry has facilitated the rapidly growing business of financial claims based on psychological injuries. Like the 'soft tissue damage' claims . . . psychological damages are invisible and only established through the statements of victims."[20] So, while not all benefit fraud consists of sanctified snake oil, sanctified snake oil confuses those who might otherwise cut the funding pipeline that enables such fraud to proliferate.

These problems are as old as public benefits. For example, within a year of British Parliament's passage of the Campbell Act in 1846, the first law compensating victims and survivors of railway injuries, "juries awarded over three hundred thousand pounds to people claiming [such] injuries."[21] British physician Herbert W. Page, writing in 1883, noted that "the British public was fully aware of the provisions of the Campbell Act, and people involved with railway accidents were now unable to think of injuries in isolation from their possible monetary significance." Page advised doctors who were diagnosing people with "trivial or invisible injuries" to consider "the possibility that the patients' state of mind might be affected in 'wholly unconscious ways' by a desire for compensation." Page further remarked that "Even in perfectly genuine cases . . . compensation acts as a potent element in retarding convalescence, as evidenced in numberless instances by the speed with which recovery sets in as soon as the settlement of pecuniary claims has been accomplished."[22]

False claims, however, are only part of the problem. For example, some agencies so broadly construe medical recommendations that they will okay medical procedures based upon the recommendation of a mental health expert that lack of such treatment would be psychologically traumatic. Taxpayers have paid for the organ transplants of illegal aliens, and "New York's Medicaid rules—long considered among the most generous in the country—have permitted coverage of sex-change operations for more than 20 years."[23] Costs of penile implants and cosmetic surgery have also been government funded by this means.

By far the most extreme fraudulent behavior is reported by Ken Dornstein in his 1996 book, *Accidentally, On Purpose*,[24] and by Denis Hamill.[25] Both discuss "accidents" that were staged for monetary gain: "lawsuitin' " in the vernacular Hamill quotes. Dornstein's coverage of one such "accident," which resulted in a fatality, led him to research similar claims dating from the development of the railroad in

America to today's staged automobile crashes. He even identified a town in Florida where so many men have lost limbs to staged gunshot and mangling injuries that it goes by the nickname "Stump City."[26] Florida is not alone. Between 1993 and 1998 suspicious accidents increased by 848% in New York State and deliberately staged "accidents" increased by 180%.[27]

So it seems that fraud—even fraud so desperately extreme as to create injuries to be convincing—seems to go hand in hand with the provision of benefits based on such injuries. Insurance experts have found that many people feel justified in committing insurance fraud, because they believe that private and governmental benefit agencies overcharge and overtax them.[28] In fact, exaggerated claims by victims were the historic reason that governments initially entered the compensation process. Some victims also "double-dip," or obtain multiple payments based on the same injuries. This occurs because benefit providers often fail to screen for alternative benefit eligibility and fail to collect funds advanced to claimants on the condition that they reimburse that agency if they later recover the funds from another source.[29]

Insurance fraud may exist in places that we fail to look. For example, one of the factors that linked the McMartin PreSchool with several other prominent—and later disproved—"ritual abuse in day-care center" cases that were early targets of allegations was that they were all valuable or particularly well insured. Civil suits were filed by the parents of each accusing child against the teacher, the teacher's aid, and the owners of Breezy Point Day School. This was one of the few cases that was thoroughly debunked before it ever got to a grand jury, as the result of an extensive investigation by Buck's County District Attorney Alan Rubenstein.[30] In the Fells Acres Day Care case in Massachusetts, the fact that the day-care center had $300,000 per year per child in insurance coverage has been cited as one of the reasons that the parents of the purported victims may have brought false charges. Eventually, eighteen families stand to collectively receive $20 million over their lifetimes from this policy alone.[31] After the first wave of day-care scandals, the lawsuits alone guaranteed that all future day-care centers would have to be well insured or forced out of business. Recall that in the PRACA Day Care Center case in the Bronx, it was later revealed that the first report was made by a mother "irate at center management over a bill for six weeks back tuition."[32] Nevertheless, to date, most benefit agencies have limited their cost-containment methods to fee schedules and caps and have not investigated even obvious incentives to commit fraud in these cases.

Several books, including the popular book for survivors of incest, *The Courage to Heal*, encourage retribution through suing abusers. In 1992 the National Organization of Women distributed *Legal Resource Kit on Incest and Child Sexual Abuse*, and in that same year, lawyers Joseph and Kimberly Crnich published a book on how to sue in these cases. One lawyer went so far as to suggest that because the "real purpose" of such lawsuits was "therapeutic," legal fees should be paid by Medicare. A 1993 examination of more than 500 cases in which the *only* evidence was a recovered repressed memory found that 15% of the cases were criminal suits and 85% were civil. Since 1994, however, it became more likely for such claims to be dropped, dismissed, or withdrawn than to go to trial.[33]

U. S. District Judge William Jarvis expressed in his ruling in *Laura Knuckles Seaton v. Kenneth Marshall Seaton*, "extreme discomfort with the sweeping nature" of VAWA, which permitted women claiming rape or battering to sue their alleged abusers civilly without filing criminal charges. Judge Jarvis noted that this aspect of the law "opens the doors of the federal courts to parties seeking leverage in settlements rather than true justice." The Women's Freedom Network's *amicus* brief supporting a Virginia judge's opposition to VAWA in the *Brzonkala* case observed that the law offers limited help because few perpetrators have adequate financial resources if they are targeted. This idea was echoed by an attorney in an unsuccessful VAWA challenge, who described the law as "a litigation weapon for upper-middle-class and wealthy women in divorce cases."[34] But the concern raised by the *Brzonkala* case is more than that practical concern—it is that without the standard of evidence demanded by a criminal court, these civil suits can invite abuse by women who have not been crime victims. And, indeed, the *Brzonkala* case was overturned by the Supreme Court on May 15, 2000.[35]

Benefit fraud engenders other types of fraud, such as a black market for identity cards. As agencies tighten fraud checks, limiting the types of documentation they will accept to prove eligibility, for instance, the cost of forged or other illegal cards has increased, and more and more "inside jobs," in which motor vehicle clerks and other government employees who provide such documents do so illegally, have been reported.[36]

With the increase in benefits provided to victims of crime, benefit fraud has added a new wrinkle: some defrauders actually make false criminal charges in order to obtain benefits. This adds new problems to those already resulting from fraud. For one, when false charges go undetected, as they often do, these cases artificially inflate crime statistics. In some cases, too, they can cause people to be falsely accused—and even falsely convicted—of criminal charges. Similar lawsuits are brought, and threatened, against a range of people accused of committing or aiding in a range of crimes, the mere accusations of which stigmatize those accused. Often this constitutes "extortionate litigation," lawsuits that the litigants expect to be settled out of court, regardless of their merit, to avoid such stigma.

For example, Desiree Washington, whose accusation that Mike Tyson raped her resulted in his conviction, lied on the witness stand about having an agreement with a lawyer to handle a civil lawsuit. While this does not prove that she lied about being raped, it clearly suggests that she had a motive to do so—a motive common to people who make reports against the rich and famous in particular.[37]

The Ohio case of Ron Tijerina, which demonstrates how benefit incentives can lead to fraud, began when Tijerina's adolescent brother-in-law, Dan Mohr, was being discharged from a drug rehabilitation facility because his mother's insurance had run out. Mohr, who had been sexually abused as a child, was told that he could be transferred to the facility's mental health unit if he "admitted" being abused, in which case the state's crime-victim compensation program would pay for his treatment. He did so, and as mandatory reporting guidelines dictate, the therapist reported his abuse allegations to the state hot line, which in turn reported them to the police in the county in which the report had been made. When questioned, Mohr named several "abusers" but was vague on details, and it was decided not to pursue his criminal report because it was not believable. However, one of the people he had named as an abuser, Tijerina, was disliked by Mohr's parents. As the abuse by Tijerina was alleged to have occurred in two counties, the parents reported it in the second county—omitting that other abusers had been named as well, and that the first county had concluded that the report was not credible. Not only was Tijerina charged, but he was found guilty, largely because information about Mohr's prior abuse and multiple accusations was withheld from the defense. Mohr has since recanted to his sister, Tijerina's wife, and Tijerina is currently seeking an appeal based on the discovery of evidence withheld from the defense in the first trial. It is significant that the withheld information was in the file of the county's victim assistance worker, who had nonetheless assisted the Mohrs to obtain victim compensation based on the case.[38] In an even more tragic instance, "A muddled rape accusation from a troubled girl—who later admitted to police she lied . . . devastated two Brooklyn families," when the girl's father killed the accused rapist.[39]

" 'Recovered memory therapy' has generated the most attention; it is "the first psychology 'product' in history that made people aware of how harmful a psychological service can be."[40] It is so harmful, in fact, that in Britain the chairman of a group that studied memory recovery for the Royal College of Psychiatrists, Dr. Sydney Brandon, called for the governing body of the British medical profession to disqualify all psychiatrists who continue to use the practice, and for those who have used it to contact their patients and explain that their memories were invented.[41]

Malpractice lawsuits based on recovered memories have resulted in settlements as high as $10.6 million, and resulted in sanctions against numerous practitioners. Among the most prominent is Bennett Braun, M.D., who was expelled from the American Psychiatric Association for "provid[ing] incompetent medical treatments, unsupported by usual standards of practice," among other charges.[42] In Texas, the first criminal charges against five mental health professionals were filed against staff members of Spring Shadows Glen Psychiatric Hospital. The sixty-count indictment charged that the five engaged in a "scheme to defraud by falsely diagnosing multiple personality disorder caused by participation in a satanic cult."[43] Here, as in the NME fraud case discussed earlier, the hospital also paid insurance premiums for patients about to lose benefits.[44]

The fact that both the Child Abuse Prevention and Treatment Act (CAPTA) and VAWA have encouraged "detection" and "case finding" to increase reporting also makes it easier to make false reports—and have them "lost" in the avalanche of cases developed by these means. CAPTA long ago shifted its focus from physical violence against children, which is relatively easy to detect, to sexual and other types of abuse that are more difficult to identify—and failed both to develop technologies to detect such abuse and to provide adequate training and salaries to lure well-trained professionals into the field. Yet both VAWA and CAPTA key their funding to "detecting" cases, encouraging zealous "case creation." This is demonstrated both by the great increase in such cases that have been "identified" since these acts were passed and by the much smaller comparative increase in cases that have resulted in convictions.[45]

One such case was that of Jim Wade, accused of raping and sodomizing his eight-year-old daughter, Alicia. Claiming that she had been abducted by a stranger who climbed through her bedroom window, Alicia was nonetheless removed from her family, placed in foster care, and repeatedly questioned by her foster parents and a marriage, family, and child counselor assigned by the state to obtain evidence against Jim Wade through Alicia's statements. They did eventually convince Alicia to accuse her father, even though the counselor was aware that other abductions—through bedroom windows—had occurred at the Wade's apartment complex around the same time. Wade was cleared when DNA proved not only that he could not have committed the crime, but that the DNA of the man who had already been arrested for the similar crimes did match the DNA found on Alicia after the assault.[46] The counselor has since surrendered her license to practice in California (on the eve of disciplinary hearings to remove it).[47]

CAPTA originally provided full immunity to anyone who reported alleged child abuse. As a result, malicious charges could be made without fear of reprisal. One woman who was falsely accused of child abuse five times is suing the state of Connecticut, claiming that "her constitutional right to confront her accusers is at least as important as the state's interest in encouraging child abuse complaints." Connecticut claims that 70% of its child abuse complaints are substantiated. This number is very high—in New York only 27% of abuse reports are substantiated, while this is true of 34% of New Jersey's reports.[48] Studies suggest that from one-third to one-tenth of reports are baseless or intentionally false,[49] and that more may be caused by mistakes or exaggerated concerns.

In 1991 officials in Westchester County paid $187,500 to settle a suit after a federal judge described a social worker's actions as official "outrages." The social worker had made what the judge said was an intrusive investigation of a Scarsdale family based on a mistaken address. In 1996 the Idaho legislature rejected a measure which would have barred social service officials from beginning a child abuse investigation based on an anonymous report. And across the nation in recent years, legislatures (including Connecticut's) have made falsely reporting child abuse a crime. Under the Connecticut law, anyone making a false report of child abuse can now be sentenced to up to a year in jail.[50]

False reports are more common than victim activists care to admit. In fact, the Army received so many false reports on its sexual harassment hot line, primarily as acts of vengeance, that it prematurely curtailed its operation.[51] One of the jurors in the O. J. Simpson trial was dismissed because she had earlier reported to the police that she had been a victim of domestic violence. When confronted with her report, which she had not disclosed during jury selection, she admitted that she had made false accusations of battering and marital rape, noting that "It was just a part of a custody dispute; nobody believed that."[52]

The San Diego Grand Jury found that a parent who makes false allegations of child abuse during a custody dispute is very likely to be believed, enabling the accusing parent to obtain sole custody and sometimes even to prevent visitation by the accused partner. Defense attorneys admitted to the jury that they encourage clients to plead to minor charges even when they are certain that the clients are innocent in order to reunify the family and avoid trial. They consider this in the clients' best interest because of public sentiment about abuse allegations.[53] The jury also identified a conflict of interest in that many of the programs evaluate victims to determine whether they were abused; treat those whom they determine were abused; and verify that the abuse constituted a crime reimbursable by the state victim compensation program.[54] In some programs victim advocates even appeared to coach victims' testimony.[55]

For example, the California Victims of Crime Fund will pay at least $200,000 for therapy for children and their families who accused Dale Akiki of molestation. Akiki was, however, vindicated of those charges. The fund approved 200 claims for payment—all to only a handful of mental health counselors working with all of the families. Akiki's attorney, Kathryn Coyne, criticized what she termed the board's "lack of effort" in investigating the claims based on the Akiki case, calling it fiscally irresponsible and probably amounting to malfeasance. She noted that the jury did not believe the district attorney, but did believe the experts who testified that the interviews of the children by therapists were experimental and unproven and had deviated from professional standards and contaminated the children's statements.[56]

In the case of Larry Champney, who was accused by his paranoid wife of sexually abusing their daughter, investigators found no signs of abuse, but had the eight-year-old interviewed by Dr. Kathleen Coulborn Faller of the University of Michigan mental health clinic. The doctor's zeal to find abuse led to an unsuccessful lawsuit for emotionally abusing the little girl in an effort to produce an accusation against her father.[57] Faller and her staff were cleared, but this was apparently because the jurors saw them as "good, hard-working professionals trying to take care of children," according to the university's attorney. However, that staff clearly behaved in a biased manner, asking leading questions, using anatomical dolls, and even allowing the child's mother to participate in the interview[58]—a contaminant in any case, but particularly egregious considering that the mother was the source of the allegations. Faller, it should be reiterated, conducted a study which found that one-third of allegations of child abuse in divorce cases were false, but she dismissed her own findings simply because they failed to match her preconceived ideas.[59]

Although gender feminists deny any increase in false reports during divorce, studies have found that between one-quarter and one-third of such allegations are likely to have been false.[60] And no lesser feminist than Erin Pizzey, the founder of women's shelters, charged that "the shelter movement has been 'hijacked' by anti-male feminists . . . many . . . abused women . . . [are] 'violence prone' people [who are violent] toward their husbands and their children." Today, most shelters—including the one Pizzey founded—are operated by feminists who stereotype men as aggressors and women as victims, arguing that even when women are abusive, it is only to defend themselves against male "primary aggressors." Pizzey laments that these stereotypes not only prevent shelters from helping violent women overcome their destructive behavior, but reinforce these behaviors by assuring women that they are not to blame. Pizzey noted that she "knew that once we were getting any form of recognition, but above all, any funding, we would be in serious trouble . . . because the feminist movement was hungry for funding."[61]

As a result of cases like this, however, California claims related to child abuse increased more than 225% in a decade, making them the leading draw on the that state's Victims Fund. So much of this money had gone to counseling payments that state lawmakers, admittedly worried about therapists' abusing the fund, limited individual maximum payments for therapy to $10,000. Child abuse cases reflected 27.2% of the compensation paid from the Victims Fund, as compared to 18.5% for families of murder victims or 6.9% for robbery victims.[62]

Despite the questions raised by these cases, they continue to receive payments with few questions from the government agencies that provide them. State agencies are clearly under political pressure to fund the services constituents want and rarely conduct the kinds of oversight of funding or treatment more typical of private insurance companies, but failing to do so exposes children who have not been abused to abuse by treatment professionals or parents who coerce them to claim abuse that never happened. This is not hyperbole. In one New York State case, in which a father had been charged with sexual abuse of his child, Nassau County District Attorney Denis Dillon's office, after determining that the allegations were both false and malicious, charged the mother and her mother with custodial in-

terference and endangering the welfare of a child. The latter charge was made because the false allegations caused the child to be "subjected to a series of physical
and mental exams that were not necessary."[63]

Ironically, these abuses have resulted in calls to eliminate victim compensation,
or to at least withhold it until a conviction is sustained. But victim compensation
assists a wide range of victims—and is particularly helpful in enabling victims to
pay for necessary medical, funeral, and other services when they are needed, as well
as in assisting victims whose assailants are never caught. Instead, agencies might
follow the lead of Washington State, which eliminated payments for recovered
memory therapy, finding it both unscientific and the cause of further pathology in
patients that undergo it, by requiring corroboration of memories, which is, of
course, impossible to produce. They might also coordinate with district attorneys
after case disposition to ensure that fraudulent cases result not only in criminal
charges, but in civil actions to regain misappropriated funds. Just a few such actions would discourage many potential defrauders, alert the public (especially
those calling for an end to victim compensation) that the system had gained integrity, and enable legitimate victims to continue to receive timely payments.

The focus on "believing the victim" has removed healthy skepticism as a quality
to be encouraged in all of those who work with victims. While it might have rel-
evance early in the treatment process for those who provide only treatment services, it is completely inappropriate in those whose role is detection or verification
of criminal matters or compensation claims. That compensation fraud may be ex-
ceptionally common in the areas of child and adult sexual assault claims is also
suggested by the fact that these services receive the bulk of program funds (76%,
considerably more than the 30% mandated), and also receive a significant portion
of direct compensation (30% of awards and 18.7% of funds),[64] suggesting how
numerous claims based on these allegations are. In addition, increasing numbers of
"retractors" are publicly acknowledging that their former allegations of recovered
memories were misguided, and usually induced, or even coerced, by therapists.

One reason that these cases often go undetected is overzealous or incompetent
use of the rape shield law, which has resulted in calls for its repeal. But most of the
complaints do not attack the purpose of the rape shield law, which is to disallow
irrelevant information about victims' sexual histories to be brought up at trial.
Instead, they attack its misapplication, for example, hiding the fact that the victim was sexually victimized prior to the assault alleged at trial (which would raise
doubt that reactions of the victim that are typical of sexual assault victims were
caused by the defendant).[65]

The rape shield law has also been misapplied to withhold the fact that an accuser has a history of making false allegations, as in the Marv Albert case.[66] Yet a
history of prior false allegations is common among fraudulent claimers, as in the
case of Albert's accuser and that of ex-stripper Nina Shahravan, who falsely

claimed to have been gang-raped by two of the Dallas Cowboys at gunpoint and was charged with filing a false police report. Her estranged husband disclosed that his wife had falsely charged him and a former fiancé with sexual assault as well.[67]

One response to these charges is that they are so few that they do not warrant notice, because "victims don't lie"—especially about sexual abuse. Yet even the FBI has observed that 8%–9% of all reports of sexual assaults are false, as compared with fewer than 2% of other crimes. "FBI statistics indicate that eight to nine percent of rape reports are 'unfounded'—closed because the complainant recants or investigators conclude that no crime was committed, [while] the rate for all crimes is around two percent."[68] Even former Manhattan sex crimes prosecutor Linda Fairstein acknowledged the occurrence of false reports, noting that they make it more difficult for legitimate victims to be taken seriously."[69] The FBI figures translate into more than eight thousand false rape reports each year,[70] and thousands of false reports of other crimes as well. The discrepancy between false reports of sexual and nonsexual crimes may inadvertently support the stereotype that women are likely to lie about sexual assault when, instead, the system's own incentives may be at fault.

Or yet another cause is possible. As the research of Rita Simon of American University has demonstrated, as women have gained equality, their opportunities to commit crime have increased as well. The crimes women are likeliest to commit are white-collar crimes, such as benefit fraud, because many women know how to access benefit agencies, because they have been either recipients or employees. Furthermore, this is a crime women can justify to themselves, particularly if it enables them to support family members as they could not otherwise.[71] Take the example, casually mentioned in an article on entrenched Appalachian poverty, that "many parents urge their children to try to go to special education classes at school as a way to prove that they are eligible for disability benefits."[72] If this is the case, the Wellstone-Murray Amendment to the 1997 federal welfare law changes, which permits waivers to the five-year cutoff for benefits for battered women, will only encourage false reports of battering to qualify for extended public assistance.

Another example of fraud is the investigation of Chicago victim advocate Beverly Reed, a victim of child abuse herself, who created a victim group and organized fund-raising for Girl X, the victim of a particularly brutal rape who remains in a coma as a result of the attack. Reed reportedly raised $300,000 for her Girl X fund but spent only $800 on the victim, and an accounting of the remaining funds remains in dispute.[73]

Even hate crimes have been falsely reported. Nearly 100 cases of false hate crimes have been recorded since 1990, with most having occurred after 1994.[74] A particularly extreme example was that of a wheelchair-bound African-American lesbian who, with her white partner, faked 21 hate crimes against themselves in an effort to obtain sympathy and more concrete rewards.[75] If two women could commit so many serious frauds before being caught, it seems likely that many more such crimes have gone completely undetected, particularly if the defrauders make only one or a very few reports (and if they stagger them over time and geography). That these reports, and the inflated statistics that make the false claims believable, are rarely questioned is perhaps the best proof of the existence of sanctified snake oil in this area.

Not only is it imperative that such fraud be punished, but also it is imperative that the sanctified snake oil that enables it to have these effects be exposed. Criminal fraud charges should be brought against police, prosecutors, and forensic "experts" whose misconduct is designed to sustain wrongful convictions. In addition, misrepresentation of professional credentials, expertise, and research should be similarly prosecuted as criminal fraud. Other areas of fraud that need to be more seriously addressed include overdiagnosis and overtreatment by service providers and advocacy scholarship by researchers (and its promotion by advocacy groups).

RISK

As the examples demonstrate, provision of insurance (or insurance-like benefit) coverage is no panacea. It may in fact put those with generous policies at risk of unnecessary treatment.[76] Opponents of mandated insurance also observe that people may take greater risks when they know that those risks have minor if any financial consequences,[77] or when provided with new forms of protection from risk, a concept called "risk homeostasis."[78] And demanding the "right" to safety may lead some people to take chances that they otherwise might not, as if the desire for a right, or even the fact of one, negates all possibilities that that right might be infringed upon.[79] Furthermore, there may be less emphasis on determining the causes of social problems and preventing them if their costs are routinely compensated.

Ironically, "The risks that kill people and the risks that scare and anger people—and therefore prompt government action—are frequently (and surprisingly) very different."[80] Many modern-day risks can only be reduced by collective action. Risks to and from the environment could be reduced by improving public transportation, raising gasoline taxes, and promoting electric cars, for instance. But risk reduction has costs, in dollars, jobs, inconvenience, and infringements of privacy and liberty. Clearly, our collective risk dollars should prioritize the most serious risks, and expenditures should roughly equate the risk reduction achieved. Instead, what we spend on a particular risk depends more on its visibility in the media and its appeal to well-organized ideologues.[81]

A broader problem is the responsibility of individuals to insure themselves against potential risks. But skewed or inaccurate perceptions of risk, as well as perceptions that a "government safety net" exists to provide for people who fail to provide for themselves, make it less likely that people will attribute accurate weight to the risks most likely to affect them or will purchase proportionate insurance to protect themselves adequately against the likeliest risks. And one of the ironies of government benefit provision is that, although it is provided to many, few recipients find that it adequately meets their expenses.[82]

On a public policy level, focus on unrealistically broad "risk reduction" (such as the belief that anti-drug laws actually reduce the availability of drugs) also takes the emphasis away from "harm reduction," which can be more easily and completely effected by government. For example, if all efforts to curb drinking were concentrated on reducing drunk driving, it could be virtually eliminated. However, Prohibition taught how unlikely it is that a program to eliminate drinking could succeed.

Furthermore, the reasons and manners in which people engage in risky behavior vary, changing the actual risk for each. Today, with many people of the middle and upper classes living into their eighties and beyond, behaviors that take their toll later in life, such as cancer and heart disease, appear to be greater concerns because people have the luxury of living long enough to experience them. But people's expectations of life span vary, as well, so who is to weigh which behaviors that have very long-term effects should be avoided, without knowledge of the life spans that individual people will live?

Or consider the perceived risk of domestic violence. Surveys have found that 2%–3% of domestic violence incidents are severe, as defined by requiring medical attention. Yet ideologues add in mutual and minor violence as well as threats and insults to inflate these statistics definitionally. Such distortions create unnecessary fear in the public and inaccurately persuade victims that their numbers are legion. Perhaps if victims of severe battering knew that they were only 2% of the population rather than 50% they would be more inclined to leave their dangerously abusive relationships. Furthermore, if resources were targeted to that 2% (allowing them more time in shelters, or even entitling them to low-cost housing), the most severe abuse might be lessened.

Victim "advocates" have been using the same statistics for decades—only altering them when they learn of a study that increases the figures. What does this say about the money and time that government and private funders, professionals and volunteers, have devoted to providing services and changing legislation to benefit these victim groups? If advocates feel that it has all been wasted, and that the problem has not diminished in the least as a result, can further requests for funds, at least for similar services, be justified? It would appear that they cannot be, but appearances are as deceiving as the statistics used to create those appearances. A further consideration is relative risk. Yet, by making it seem as if every woman has the same chance of being raped, high-risk victims, and the measures that would be needed to increase *their* safety, are ignored. Worse, these concerns are buried by rape ideologues who consider it more important that the risk of rape *seem* universal than that all victims, and especially the most vulnerable victims, receive the kind of help they need.

Why would ideologues be so misguided? The current "victim feminist" ideology dictates that all men are potential rapists; therefore, all women are in danger of victimization all the time. Recognizing that risk changes according to victims' ages, lifestyles, circumstances, incomes, prior histories, and a variety of other factors would also force them to admit that women have some control over their risk of being raped. It would similarly force them to admit that men have a differential likelihood of committing rape—and that most men are unlikely to commit rape under any circumstances. But perhaps most significant is that, if ideologues admitted these facts, they would also have to admit that their analyses of the problem, and therefore the solutions that they have developed, have been misguided.

The stigma of rape is not a monolith. It varies from victim to victim as well as over time, and depends on many factors, but particularly on attitudes that the victim has about rape, as well as attitudes that society has about the circumstances under which particular rapes occur. Victims who believe, or whose families believe, that virginity is the complete value of a woman are likely to find rape most stigmatizing. On the other hand, society tends to stigmatize victims whose lack of caution or other personal factors or choices contributed to the crime. If feminism has had any positive effects on society, one is surely that a woman who has been raped does not lose her "worth." And if feminism has had any impact on the law, it is that rape victims are much less likely to have their backgrounds or behavior mentioned in court, unless it proves relevant to the crime.

So it would appear that rape *is* less stigmatizing than it once was, at least to most victims. One indication of this is that victims are now far more likely to discuss their rapes openly, not only with counselors and close family members, but in training and prevention programs, at conferences, and even in the media. Rape victim advocates argue that rape victims are treated differently from other victims, particularly by the police. Marge Piercy even wrote a poem imagining a "Mr. Smith" who, on reporting a robbery, was asked why he had been carrying so much cash—was he asking to be robbed? But the truth is, the police often question victims of robbery in just that way!

By trying to "universalize" rape, feminists have done at least two things that impede further improvement of the societal response to rape victims:

- First, they have scared many women who are unlikely to be raped. Let me be very clear about this. All women bear *some* risk of being raped. (Men have a similarly differential risk of forcible sodomy, although overall rates are lower except among children and prisoners.) But income, age, and lifestyle (access to a car, the need to work or travel at night) raise or lower that risk considerably. Illegal activity not only raises the risk of rape, but makes it more dangerous for the victim to report for fear of self-incrimination. So women who have no high-risk characteristics should be less fearful, and women with many can lower their risk by changing those characteristics that they can, or by taking greater precautions.

- Second, they have deflected concern from high-risk women. This is also part of the "universalization strategy," which is rationalized, when it is recognized, by claims that public sympathy is best aroused if a problem is perceived as endangering one's wife, mother, daughter, or sister. However, because services have been developed with those wives, mothers, daughters, and sisters in mind, they often fail to meet the special needs of prostitutes, institutionalized women, and other high-risk victims. As just one example, the recent National Institute of Justice and Centers for Disease Control and Prevention study on violence against *women* found that more than half of all sex crimes occurred to *women* under the age of eighteen. Cleverly, the study co-opted child sexual abuse as violence against women.

There is yet another way that domestic violence is misperceived. Women are far more dangerous criminals than society acknowledges, despite rhetoric suggesting that most women criminals are usually unwilling accomplices of controlling men. Data on homicides in Chicago between 1986 and 1996 demonstrate, for example, that the Chicagoans at greatest risk of being killed by an intimate partner are African-American men, at twice the rate of African-American women and five times the rate of white women. In Chicago during that time, 18% of black men killed were killed by their mates. These men were most at risk when the women were in their teens or twenties. The risk of being killed by a female partner in any racial group peaks when the women are in their twenties and then decreases sharply. Whether these men provoked their killers or not, assaulted them or not, appears quite variable. Of the men killed by women in Chicago, 65% had no recorded history of domestic or other violence. In eighty-six cases, the women killed their partners when they tried to leave; in sixty cases, they killed men who had left; in eight, their victims were female lovers; and in twenty-four, they used accomplices or hit men. Indiana criminologist Coramae Richey Mann studied females who committed homicide in six major U. S. cities and found that 30% had from one to thirty previous misdemeanor arrests.[83] Rita Simon's aforementioned work supports the idea that as women's opportunities have expanded, one such opportunity is that to commit crime. She observed that "The rate of severe assaults by men on women in the home fell by almost 50 percent between the first National Family Violence Survey in 1975 and the most recent update in 1992. It dropped from 38 per 1,000 couples per year to 20, but the rate of dangerous female assaults on males in the home stayed essentially static over that period—45 per 1,000 couples—and is now twice as high as the male rate."[84] Not only are women violent more often than is generally acknowledged, but men are abused more often than is usually recognized as well.[85]

In a similar vein, a recent study of rapists and child molesters found that 62% had been sexually abused when they were young and had been abused by female caretakers as well as male. Studies of wife-batterers frequently reveal a majority who were abused as children, and in these cases, as in all nonsexual assaults of children, mothers are the perpetrators far more often than fathers. Research on the correlation between child abuse or neglect and female criminality shows that twice as many girls who were mistreated were later arrested for adult crime. Men and women who were abused are much more likely to fatally assault or neglect their own children.[86]

ALTERNATIVES AND COMPARISONS

Finally, let us consider some of the ways that de-sanctification could improve public policy. By defunding snake oil, wasted resources would be saved, which could then be allocated to other public priorities (education, infrastructure, deficit reduction, or tax cuts, for example). This would improve citizen confidence in government, because currently, as columnist William Raspberry has observed, "What we are seeing is not a lack of desire to solve these dreadful problems . . . but doubt that the funds we're asked to provide will solve them. What we call laziness, selfishness and bigotry are frequently nothing more than the people's transcendent doubt that anything they do will make any real difference."[87] Let us explore how each of the subjects discussed in earlier chapters could assist in this de-sanctification effort.

Media could assist the public to better recognize sanctified snake oil by covering issues in greater depth. Media could limit the use of single cases to exemplify broader issues. When they use cases, they could use typical, rather than extreme, ones and use numerous cases to avoid distortions. Media outlets could regain the skepticism that should be a cornerstone of their field, rather than acting as public relations representatives for ideological groups, public officials, and providers of inadequately tested treatments, drugs, or anything else. To do so, reporters would need to improve their knowledge of statistical and evaluative methods and devote more time, space and attention to these issues.

Reporters could provide context for the discussion of issues, by placing information in historical perspective and making appropriate mathematical comparisons (absolute numbers and percentages, for instance). Controversy about information could be reported, and opinions of the author or interviewees could be clearly identified as such. When reporting on research findings in particular, the methodology used, and any flaws, could be discussed, and the qualifications, expertise, and possible bias of the researchers could also be stated. When corrections are published, they could be given the same prominence as the original stories in which they appeared. Media could also report on a much wider selection of topics, using more objectivity and far less sensationalism.

The media could devote more print space and airtime to poll stories in order to give readers or viewers more information with which to evaluate a poll. They could also provide more context, in the form of results from previous polls that used similar questions, and they could place more emphasis on the complex attitudes that most Americans bring to issues of policy.[88] The media could, in this way, educate the public about the history of policies and the research methods that led to results. They could report on negative as well as positive results of scientific studies, particularly if positive studies of the same subject have been well publicized. Reports on research should disclose not only the sponsor but also the cost of the research and how the research outcome might affect the sponsor.[89] Some few newspapers, including the *Wichita Eagle*, the *Charlotte Observer*, the *Tallahassee Democrat*, the *Portland Press Herald*, and the *Minneapolis Star-Tribune*, have begun to practice "public journalism," which focuses political coverage on in-depth analyses of issues that interest local voters. They also address other citizen-defined concerns and organize neighborhood round tables and living-room discussions.[90] Journalists who do so find inspiring examples of local success[91]—and eager audiences to read of them.

In public policy, we need to learn to "disagree without being disagreeable" by limiting criticism to issues rather than extending it to issue proponents. Criticism is least useful when it polarizes and most useful when it allows the public to more fully understand and compare alternatives.[92] We should therefore require that any policy statements (from legislators and activists as well as media) reflect context and completeness—and we should judge policymakers and issue proponents by their ability to prove that they understand opposition to their judgements.

One of the purposes of snake oil advocacy is to drown out voices of disagreement, which might present alternative analyses of problems or alternative solutions for them. For example, the availability of sexually explicit material has been found to be greater in places where gender equality is more pronounced,[93] despite the fact that gender feminists have tried to have pornography banned *because* it causes men to commit rapes.[94] Furthermore, although feminist analysis presumes that any female who alleges rape is telling the truth, black women remember all too many cases in which black men have been lynched as rapists simply on the say-so of a white woman.[95] As noted, women are involved in twice as many incidents of child abuse as men. Ignoring abuse by women, or discounting it as "provoked" by men, endangers children and prevents intervention into the cycle of abuse.[96] The focus on child *sexual* abuse, the one type of child abuse more frequently committed by men, also takes focus off the physical abuse and neglect of children, which is more often committed by women and is more likely to cause psychological as well as physical damage to children.[97] Focus on men as abusers or women and children as victims may interest academic gender theorists, but child abuse will only be addressed when we concentrate our resources on identifying serious abuse and abusers and preventing further damage, instead of trying to fit abuse to preconceived ideological theories.

Or consider David Gelertner's alternative view of victimization:

Those of us who hate today's victim culture don't hate it because we are Teddy Roosevelts aiming to build character and toughen people up . . . we hate it because it inflicts harm. When you encourage a man to see himself as a victim of *anything*—crime, poverty, bigotry, bad luck—you are piling bricks on his chest. . . . The victim culture is bad because it is demeaning and discouraging to people who are stamped "victim." . . . In many classrooms nowadays, students are taught to see society as a victimization machine and themselves (particularly if they are not white and male) as likely targets.[98]

Gelertner is no Teddy Roosevelt, nor is he a curmudgeon with no experience in these areas. He is a Yale professor who was a victim of one of "Unabomber" Theodore Kaczynski's package bombs, which permanently damaged his right hand and his vision.

In yet another example of counterintuitive (or at least counterideological) results, it has been found that enforcement of illegal immigration does not discourage immigrants from coming, but does discourage them from going home, making what would have been a seasonal flow permanent.[99] Substance abuse also suggests alternative views, although these too are often attacked, when they are not suppressed. For instance, in contrast to current AA lore on alcoholism, Bill Wilson, the cofounder of Alcoholics Anonymous, said at the 1960 National Clergy Conference on Alcoholism that "We have never called alcoholism a disease because, technically speaking, it is not a disease entity."[100] And in regard to marijuana, Vermont Representative Fred A. Maslack was quoted as describing hemp legalization as "a classic Republican issue . . . getting government out of the way so people can go out and make money." Maslack is part of a network of legislators from nearly a dozen states who support relegalizing hemp, noting that every other industrialized country grows and makes money from it. He resents the Federal Drug Enforcement Administration's lobbying of state governments to prevent legalization of *Cannabis*.[101]

Harvard researcher Lester Grinspoon, a leading expert on medical marijuana, testified before Congress on the unusual safety of *Cannabis*. He noted that "About half of the patients treated with anti-cancer drugs suffer from severe nausea and vomiting. In about 30 to 40% of these, the commonly used antiemetics do not work . . . the nausea and vomiting are . . . a threat to the effectiveness of the therapy. Retching can cause tears in the esophagus and rib fractures, prevent adequate nutrition, and lead to fluid loss." In 1982 a committee of the National Academy of Sciences recommended further research on the medical uses of *Cannabis* for the treatment of nausea and vomiting in chemotherapy, asthma, glaucoma, seizures, and spasticity. Under federal and most state statutes, marijuana is listed as a

Schedule I drug, which means that it has no currently accepted medical use and cannot be used safely even under medical supervision, a designation that is impossible to justify given the strong medical evidence of marijuana's medical uses and its clear safety for use under medical supervision.[102]

Yet the federal government blindly refuses to consider changing its policy toward any form of marijuana, for any purpose. It prefers to believe, perpetuate, and sanctify bogus and costly snake oil. One of the many ironies about the nation's drug war is its inherent, hypocritical inconsistencies. None of these is greater than the illogical contrast between women's hard-won right to choose what they do with their bodies regarding pregnancies and the complete lack of rights for adults to choose what they wish to take into their bodies in the form of illicit substances.

Along these lines we need to recognize how easily political correctness feeds intolerance and repression. While debate should be more civil, debaters should not shy away from facts that may identify a particular group or set of circumstances as prone to a particular social problem. Instead, research should be scrutinized to clarify such links (because many are spurious or misconstrued), and increased tolerance of, or at least reduced sanctions against, practices that are not proved harmful to others, from eating meat and smoking cigarettes to wearing fur and using currently illegal drugs, should be encouraged.

In drafting legislation, efforts should be made to anticipate costs and consequences. Services should also be evaluated in order to identify and counter unintended consequences and to recognize how incentives can encourage overattention to some issues and consequent underattention to others. For instance, the disabled are not a single group, but people with different needs and differing degrees of need. Neither providing benefits alone nor jobs alone would serve the needs of all disabled people, although policy toward them, as with so many other groups, has followed pendulum swings rather than differentiating among needs and abilities. One of the ways that unintended consequences could be reduced is by simplifying rules[103] so that people would have a clearer understanding about when they are eligible for benefits or when they are breaking laws. Innovations might include limiting the number of times a person could be treated for drug or alcohol abuse at public expense, to increase motivation; outlawing mandated treatment; allowing more individual choice of services; and targeting services not only by treatment matching but by triaging services: providing more services to those in greatest need, but denying services where they are either unnecessary or would fail to provide enough help to be worthwhile.

While intervention by the mental health and social service systems should never be imposed, assistance should be offered to those clearly at risk. However, these risks should not be accepted as excuses, and those who commit crimes that harm others or put others at risk should be punished, not offered endless chances to reform. One way to change this would be to shift government funding away from treatment and toward concrete assistance, and to increase the salaries of those who do this work. Another reason to shift government funding from treatment is that people should not be made to fear government intervention in their lives, except in extreme circumstances. Instead, they should be helped to assess the real risks that their behaviors pose to them, and then act on that reality—or suffer the consequences of their actions. While this may sound cruel, it is far more cruel to hide from the public the real effects of bad behaviors by not permitting them to see the people who suffer their results. The economic left might be persuaded to support such a shift if it can be made to understand how funding treatment instead of basic needs prioritizes behavioral conformity and support of the professional classes over that of the needy. Along these lines, we need to narrow definitions of prevention but recognize efforts to improve life circumstances as self-justified.

To prevent concept stretching in program and benefit eligibility, definitions of recipients should be written into legislation, and changes to eligibility should be subject to public notice and comment. This would not deter legitimate expansions and acknowledgment of newly recognized needs but would ensure that the public supported these changes. Legislators (and others) who rush to propose legislation in response to single, isolated cases should be harshly criticized—and those who propose and support unconstitutional laws and policies should be severely sanctioned.

Public policymakers need to recognize the potential for service provisions to be self-serving to proponents and providers. They need to learn to differentiate between need and service and target help to those in need rather than to their helpers. Similarly, they need to be able to differentiate between problems that require personal motivation and individual action and those that require community or broader efforts.

We need, above all, to examine every policy and ask whether government needs to be responsible for the activity. This would be facilitated by judging government by its results rather than its goals, and by conducting feasibility studies on such alternatives as drug prohibition versus drug control. The government needs to be more realistic about the goals it sets. Alexis de Tocqueville documented how, long before government had expanded its purview into all areas of American life, Americans innovatively and spontaneously created self-help and religious-based programs to meet a wide range of human needs. These programs were quickly and effectively adapted to changing local needs, and because workers who carried out the programs were familiar with community members, it was not necessary to conduct investigations into their character—nor could these workers be easily conned by fakers. But these programs were also often short rationed and judgmental.[104] If we could remedy these last two problems (by encouraging charitable contributions, supporting volunteer efforts through tax and workplace incentives, making not-for-profit financial information more accessible so that donors could

make informed contributions, accepting diversity, and supporting travel or relocation to meet uncommon needs), many ideological groups would be encouraged to
provide services. And lowering taxes (by defunding snake oil) would leave citizens
with more disposable income to donate to causes they choose to support. This
would free the government from responsibilities it should not have and cannot
meet as effectively as can community groups, and would remove the implied sanction of government from programs, as well.

Government must also be realistic and responsible enough to refuse to pass legislation that funds goals when methods to meet them do not exist. Instead, funding targeted to goals should be limited to research and research-oriented treatment
programs. In turn, such programs should be carefully monitored, patients should
be informed of their experimental nature, and under no circumstances should such
programs be used in lieu of prison or other sanctions. One way to implement this
would be to differentiate clearly between scientifically tested methods that have
been proven effective to a high degree (such as fingerprinting and DNA analysis)
and that should not only be mandated, but subject to national standards; and programs, treatments, or methods that are experimental or only marginally helpful (to
a small degree or with a limited number of individuals) and should never be mandated, standardized, or federalized. Instead, experimental programs should be
funded *only* as research projects, and service recipients should be paid for their participation in them, as is usual with research subjects. Refunding should be predicated only on further evaluation, improved standards or increased differentiation
of clients, and enhanced treatment matching. An indication that this is happen-
ing, albeit in a small way, is that, as of July 1, 1998, all drug prevention programs
must prove their effectiveness to qualify for the federal funding that is distributed
through the states.[105]

As public policy can be no more effective than the quality of the research on
which it is based, we need to focus research on meaningful issues and set high-
strength thresholds for its acceptance. Researchers, again, should be judged by the
honesty and completeness of the presentation of their findings in addition to the
effectiveness of their methodologies. The funders of research and their agendas
should also be incorporated into all research reports. Those who conduct advocacy
scholarship or present advocacy statistics should be sanctioned by defunding and
reporting to professional ethics boards—which should become far more active in
this area.

Professional associations that represent mental health providers need to enhance their self-regulatory mechanisms, or relinquish the regulation of their
members. Professional associations should be in the forefront of encouraging skill
enhancement, evaluating programs and treatments, setting treatment thresholds
and parameters, and sanctioning members who commit malpractice or other
forms of fraud. Sadly, professional associations presently focus on expanding their

members' scopes of practice to the exclusion of ensuring that their members possess competency in these areas, or that competency is possible in some cases. Professional associations, government officials, and service providers need to identify the incompetence and fraud in their midst to ensure that services are improved rather than done away with entirely. They must also demonstrate that they are not colluding with these efforts but are victims of scams and the unintended consequences of meaning well but having insufficient information, technology, and resources to do good.

Professional associations and government must pay particular attention to the nexus of the treatment and criminal justice systems to ensure that treatment is not used as a substitute for punishment when the former is ineffective as well as when the latter is warranted. For instance, several states have passed laws requiring that certain sex offenders undergo treatment in specialized treatment facilities after they've served their prison sentences. They can be confined until courts determine that the risk that they pose to the public has been reduced. These laws have come under attack because they keep people imprisoned after they have served their sentences, a clear violation of their constitutional rights. Proponents of the laws, however, say that they are not meant to punish, but to help offenders and protect the public, and that civil commitment differs from criminal penalites. The American Civil Liberties Union (ACLU) counters that the laws would be unnecessary if that were true, because civil commitment laws currently allow dangerous people to be locked up. Another, arguably more important, issue is whether this treatment works. The American Psychiatric Association is just one of the organizations that has questioned whether sex offenders' behavior can be changed.[106]

Policy in regard to mental health and other forms of treatment should reflect how payment structures act as incentives to treatment providers, how explanations of problems can undermine the effectiveness of help, and how treatment can be separated from other needed forms of help. Program evaluation should not only be improved but broadened to incorporate more feedback from service recipients, taxpayers, and even opponents rather than just from service providers, politicians, and others with vested interests in program perpetuation. It is especially important to evaluate programs by results rather than by goals or inputs alone. Programs that fail to meet these criteria should be defunded to make room for better programs. Program evaluation should focus on replacing punishment for systemic problems with assessments (postmortems) to reduce the possibility of recurrence, as in medicine.[107] But programs that perpetuate disinformation or *ad hominem* arguments should be defunded on principle.

Again, there should also be a clear differentiation between ideologically based and concrete services, with more emphasis on the latter, in the form of housing, jobs, food, and health care, than on the less-tangible former services, such as counseling and prevention education. Social work training is particularly useful in enabling workers to assist people in locating appropriate services such as housing, home health assistance, and other services which directly meet basic needs (and prevent further problems). Unfortunately, the social work profession has been particularly ineffective in encouraging those trained in social work to conduct this important work, because most graduates want only to provide "therapy," which tends to be the most lucrative area of the field. A capitalist society should not be surprised at a correlation between salaries and interest in jobs, but it can use this incentive to lure workers to other areas by changing its priorities.

Above all, service providers should never be permitted to promote ideologies in programs or require ideological orientation as a criterion for service provision. Ideologically based services should be required to rely on grassroots funding and other support. As a general rule, in fact, policy should prioritize what can be done well within existing resource allocations and without rights violations. This requires adequate funding of those services deemed necessary by society, including upgraded training and qualifications of professionals, especially if their work has the potential to determine the fate of others in any way. A clear difference should also be made, and explained to the public, between professionally-provided, treatment-oriented services, which should be eligible to receive third-party payments and must be evaluated for effectiveness, and mutual-aid self-help groups made up of fellow-sufferers (such as cancer patients, crime victims, and alcoholics), which are appealing because of their unprofessional, unpaid, and voluntary nature.

Government must develop more stringent and uniform criteria for approving the funding of treatment, prevention, experts (in and out of the courtroom), training, and research. This might include, for example, coordinating all benefit and funding agencies with state licensing boards to ensure that funded services are provided by appropriate, competent professionals, and to enable agencies to cut off funding to providers who commit fraud or malpractice against any agency. These agencies might, as some few have, monitor treatment plans, develop peer-review committees to oversee counseling, limit payments to qualified professionals who use modalities of treatment appropriate to the needs of their clients, and hire "care managers" to ascertain that all treatment paid for by the agency is necessary and appropriate. It is important, however, that care managers understand treatment, and not serve only as gatekeepers to keep costs down.

Checks should be conducted of all service providers to ensure that all of the services they provide are necessary, and that they are qualified to provide them. While most benefit agencies review medical charges in some way, counseling costs do not appear to be similarly monitored. Not only might this save money, but also it could generate income if agencies were empowered to fine, and collect the fines of, providers who improperly treat or charge benefit agency third-party payers or clients themselves. It is a very appropriate role for government agencies to protect citizens from professional fraud and malpractice.[108] In fact, principles of common law state that service providers must describe the major risks of their service and that "service provider[s are] liable if harm occurs because the providers' practice was not in accordance with ordinary standards of good practice."[109]

In 1994 Dr. R. Christopher Barden created the National Association for Consumer Protection in Mental Health Practices because, as he stated,

Patients across America are being subjected to experimental and dangerous forms of "psychotherapy" at taxpayer expense . . . without any warning of the serious risks involved. To stop this national tragedy we must enact legislation . . . that will require full disclosure of the risks and hazards of mental health treatments to patients *before* the therapy begins and ban federal, state and private insurance funding for any psychotherapy procedure that has not been proven safe and effective by valid and reliable scientific methods . . . [this] legislation is [also] necessary to stem the flood of bogus pseudoscientific testimony by mental health professionals in courtrooms across America. Expert witnesses should be required to state the scientific research support for their positions and explicitly include any known limitations on their methodology or conclusions.[110]

As a result of Barden's efforts, the Indiana legislature unanimously passed a law in 1997 that requires all patients to be informed of their therapists' training and credentials. Other states have similar legislation pending as this book goes to press. The law also requires that mental health providers inform their patients of the "reasonably foreseeable risks and relative benefits of proposed treatments and alternative treatments," and of their patients' right to withdraw consent for treatment at any time.[111]

Additional methods of protecting mental health consumers are also being developed. On November 7, 1996, for example, Massachusetts became the first state to make information about medical malpractice available to the public through a toll-free hot line. The profiles list those malpractice claims that have resulted in payment, along with disciplinary actions against doctors and criminal records. It also compares doctors within a specialty and classifies each liability payment as average, above average, or below average for that specialty. Other states are considering similar disclosure laws.[112] And in February of 1997, the New York State Board of Regents placed licensing information for the 610,000 professionals under its purview, including disciplinary action, on the Internet.[113] Medical societies in two states are also preparing to punish doctors who testify as experts in malpractice trials if their testimony proves false or misleading, and some state medical associations have set up peer-review panels to judge whether expert testimony meets accepted standards.[114] Another egregious form of sanctified snake oil seems to be on the wane. The False Memory Syndrome Foundation reported in its September 1997 editorial that "We are increasingly called upon to help families in their struggle to reconcile, to assist former patients and to help all parties in their efforts to hold those who have harmed them accountable."[115]

Unfortunately, these efforts represent reactive steps taken to undo the damage of past social policies. The government must now take proactive steps to ensure that snake oil will no longer be sanctified by its own agencies.

To begin, there should be reevaluations of the criteria used for government appointments and employment in all government-funded not-for-profits. Above all, employment should be predicated on professional qualifications, rather than political or ideological ones. Ethics rules should require ideologues to publicly disclose their ideological leanings, so that conflicts of interest can be identified, the first step in avoiding them. For instance, Nassau County, New York, District Attorney Denis Dillon has been criticized for his outspoken opposition to abortion. However, Dillon has been careful not to prosecute cases such as attacks on abortion clinics, instead trading them with prosecutors in adjacent counties for cases they would prefer to have prosecuted out of venue. While Dillon has been criticized for espousing political views, it is clear that his honest expression of his beliefs, coupled with means to ensure that they will not interfere with the requirements of his office, have better-served his community than would denial of those beliefs.

Government could also add oversight mechanisms to all funding areas, such as appointing citizen watchdogs, as well as appointing representatives of taxpayer groups and even opponents of certain aspects of services to advisory boards and other monitoring bodies that oversee these allocations. For example, CAPTA has recently added citizen-review panels to conduct postmortems in child death cases. What it lacks, however, is a parallel panel to review cases proven false. Similar watchdog groups of research experts could review all funded research and applications of research (in grant proposals, research, legislation, and the like).

Enhanced fraud prevention, another form of oversight, could be facilitated by creating incentives for reporting fraud, creating feedback mechanisms to prevent "double-dipping" and repeated acts of fraud by the same individuals or organizations, and issuing mandatory *Miranda*-like warnings about the penalties of fraud whenever people apply for benefits or report crimes. The federal government has recently required the home health-care industry, which has a history of defrauding Medicare and Medicaid, to post bonds seizable by the government if further fraud is detected.[116] Similar bonds could be required of all government-reimbursed providers. One way to prevent the worst kind of fraud is to decouple services from victim status, so that it would never be necessary to falsely report a crime in order to obtain benefits.

Many of these abuses could be curtailed if the states adopted a coordinated system of benefit eligibility. In such a system, a medical practitioner would first determine the medical needs of applicants and whether their injuries or illnesses limit their ability to return to work temporarily or permanently. Then a benefit specialist would determine which benefit, or combination of benefits—public and private—the applicants are eligible to receive. Claims would then be forwarded

to the appropriate benefit agencies for payment, with collateral payers clearly identified to prevent redundant payments. (This would not only prevent "benefit shopping," but would serve as a double check of the benefit specialist's assessment.)
Finally, if claimants are unable to return to their former employment, they would
be referred to state vocational centers to determine whether they could be re-
trained for alternative work. This last step might be waived if a claimant is near
enough to retirement age so that early retirement would be cheaper.

Such a system would not add costs to the present system—medical practitioners and benefit analysts currently working in existing benefit agencies could simply be redeployed to the coordinating agency. Private insurers could have the
option of operating a parallel screening mechanism or paying the government to
perform this task for them. In addition to curbing benefit fraud, a coordinated system would encourage greater uniformity in benefit eligibility and coverage. And
by coordinating paperwork, such a system would lower the administrative costs
that currently make up one-quarter of health-care costs in America.[117]

The most important advantage of such a system, however, would be that legitimate benefit claimants would no longer have to become benefits experts in order
to have their expenses met. By creating an information "gateway," deserving
claimants would be sped on their way to benefits for which they are eligible—
while "benefit shoppers" would be stopped at the gate.[118] With such a system, too,
claimants would not have to hire, or agencies pay, attorneys merely to direct
claimants to benefit agencies. Attorneys' fees could then be targeted to complex,
adversarial, and test cases, as well as to appeals, where they are most needed.

Lack of such national coordination of health care can be attributed to two
camps: those who feel that the nation will go bankrupt unless government health
care is seriously reduced; and those who feel that national health care must cover
every possible health-care cost for every American, a plan so grandiose that it
could not be implemented successfully even if it could earn widespread support.
On the other hand, many analysts recognize the provision of some minimum of
health care as a right.[119] In fact, Congressional Budget Office (CBO) projections
of future costs of health care are based on current cost structures, eligibility formulas, and usage except when specific changes are recommended. CBO accoun-
tants can only base their projections on existing costs or by manipulating the
specific variables they are directed to manipulate. As a result, numerous alternatives have never been explored, nor their effects on costs considered.

The escalating costs of health care have produced such positive effects as tech-
nological advances and increased life expectancy, whether they are attributed to
public money or private enterprise. Yet many of the factors that contribute to the
costs of health care are only negative. The range of public and private benefits,
and the limitations that encourage insurers to dump unprofitable claimants onto
alternative systems, make the costs of administering our system the highest in the

world. This complex administration can also delay treatment, causing conditions to worsen and require more care than if addressed earlier.

The irony of the fear that national health care will force taxpayers to pay for the health care of others is that this occurs now in Medicaid, Medicare, and a range of other public programs. Yet Medicaid requires no prior or current contribution by recipients, and Medicare too covers many people who have never paid taxes or contributed to the Social Security system. Therefore, it would be less costly to cover those individuals in an administratively more efficient national system—and nothing would prevent such a system from assessing premiums from all recipients, even if premiums were subsidized for the poor.

Such a system would also enable policymakers to identify the causes of the greatest costs to the system, so research and prevention efforts could be targeted more effectively. (Currently, these costs are obscured because they are paid by so many diverse providers.) Such a system would not have to displace private insurers, and it might enable insurers to provide the national package of benefits and to offer optional benefits, at additional cost, as well. Further, a national system could save money by capping provider costs, improving quality standards, and conducting public education to improve public health and reduce unnecessary and excessive treatment.

Such a system could bring attention to social conditions and behaviors that contribute to poor health. For instance, people who live in the streets (as opposed to the broader group of "homeless") are often hospitalized for conditions brought on by malnutrition, exposure, and poor hygiene. The costs of such treatment can run up to hundreds of times what it would cost to feed and clothe the patient for years. National health care might be predicated on a responsibility to maintain a certain level of self-care—making it easier, and less arbitrary, to require street people to live under some degree of supervision if they fail to take reasonable care of themselves without such monitoring. (This would also be a more direct and less coercive system than having people determined "mentally incompetent" and then forcing them to accept "treatment.")

Finally, government should clearly identify the needs it will meet and define parameters and eligibility for having them met, eliminating false hopes and lawsuits for "crimes" that people are unaware of committing (such as esoteric forms of sexual harassment). In line with this, government should adopt a policy which ensures that social thought dictates law, rather than law dictating social thought. This would ensure, for instance, that definitions of rape, sexual harassment, child and spouse abuse, and the like reflect genuine attitudes about these issues rather than the extreme beliefs of a handful of ideologues who devote their lives to seeing their unique views reflected in law.

As noted, there is a great need for oversight of mental health treatment, and moreover, great need for penalties against providers who overdiagnose and over-treat. Eliminating mandated treatment and defining substance abuse more narrowly than *any* use would be a healthy first step in this direction. Improving treatment and prevention services so that they are more effective and more attractive to recipients would help to lure people to services before they are identified through the criminal justice system. If people are so identified, however, they should not be rewarded for then entering treatment, but instead should be punished more severely for not having sought treatment before being arrested.

The criminal justice system must be evaluated by different measures of effectiveness, so that winning at all costs is no longer an incentive. The most meaningful reform that could be made to the system would be to reduce its size to make it more manageable. Creating alternative responses to many nonviolent crimes (including decriminalization of "victimless" crimes such as prostitution, gambling, and drug use) and creating alternative sanctions for all young and mentally ill criminals would be a good start. From there it would be possible to begin to redefine the roles of the police, caseworkers, and mental health providers in the criminal justice system to make more appropriate use of the specific skills of each. Family court and civil proceedings, particularly in regard to child protection, should be subject to the same standards of evidence as criminal proceedings and to the same right to indigent defense as well. Public defenders should be paid for their services more equitably, and compensation for investigators and experts hired by the defense should be on a par with that available to the prosecution. (In cases in which defendants are represented by high-profile attorneys, the reverse might also be implemented.)

Misconduct by any participant in the system should be severely punished, and defendants should be protected from negative results of such misconduct even if it is erroneous rather than malicious. Such misconduct would be more easily detected, and more effectively dealt with, if all interviews were videotaped without interruption, if all relevant evidence were preserved for as long as there is the possibility of an appeal or review, and if all coerced and jailhouse confessions were rendered inadmissible and all confessions were made in the presence of a judge. Furthermore, immunity should be limited if not eliminated for the police and prosecutors; special prosecutors should be hired to investigate police and prosecutorial misconduct; and independent community oversight of police and prosecutors should be mandated, with funding for such oversight boards tied to the funding of police and prosecutors' offices.[120]

There should be a one-time reevaluation of past practices to ensure that innocent people do not remain behind bars only because of poor defenses, lack of experts, or testimony based on junk science or misapplied laws. And in future cases involving "new" crimes or scientific expertise, special federal funds should be made available to conduct one-time assessments of the existence of the crime, the nature of the scientific evidence, and the backgrounds of experts knowledgeable about it. Then, data banks could be created to amass the expertise and experts on the issue (if they are useful, and used at all). Furthermore, all interviews with victims and suspects should be videotaped to guard against coercive or collusive interview techniques.

When wrongful convictions are determined, its victims should be compensated automatically (currently, only California, Wisconsin, Illinois, New York, and Tennessee do so) and all of those, including the mental health and criminal justice professions, who knowingly facilitated false convictions should be prosecuted. Similarly, people who make false allegations of child or spouse abuse in order to obtain custody, gain increased alimony, or sue for battering under VAWA should be denied custody or alimony entirely, and prosecuted as well.

Two policies might improve this situation. One would increase the criminal penalties for making false allegations, and require that anyone making an allegation to the police or to any benefit agency which provides funds based on victim status be read *Miranda*-like warnings about the penalties for making a false report. The second would create a national data bank of false (including delusional) reporters, which could be consulted any time anyone applied for a benefit based on a crime as well as when anyone reported a crime. The first policy would make false allegations less likely, while the second would simplify the investigation of chronic reporters, which would preserve criminal justice resources for more important issues, such as investigating the remaining reports more fully.

Columbia University child psychiatrist Richard A. Gardner has suggested that states that fail to prosecute false accusers or that deprive individuals suspected of child abuse of constitutional due-process protections should be deprived of federal funding. He also believes that all evaluative interviews should be videotaped and that all suggestive interview materials, such as anatomically detailed dolls, body charts, and materials depicting explicit sexual organs should be inadmissible in court. Gardner would also like to see funding provided for treatment programs for the falsely accused and children who have been victimized by being used as vehicles for false accusations.[121] These are not Gardner's only recommendations. Some have already been implemented, and some have been rejected as too extreme, particularly his recommendations to drop the mandated reporter clause.

I fear that dropping mandated reporting, which admittedly forces professionals to report even accusations they suspect are no more than vengeful or hysterical, would be dangerous because many mandated reporters are unqualified to evaluate the veracity of reports. Similarly, I recognize (as does Gardner) that some false accusations are the products of negligence or even delusion. For these reasons I would suggest that mandated reporters should report all accusations, *but* that they should be encouraged—and trained—to offer opinions about the veracity of these claims. One reason that I favor mandated reporting, by the way, is that it documents false as well as true allegations. I would also not favor prosecuting people whose reports are delusional, but, because these are the very people likeliest to make multiple false reports, I would favor documenting their reports and making the fact that they had made past false reports put any future reports in doubt. For this reason I would make a further recommendation: ending anonymous reporting. Anonymity was offered to reporters to protect neighbors and relatives from the wrath of those they reported. However, the law redundantly protects reporters from this possibility by keeping their identities from the people they accused even if their identities are known to authorities. Therefore, anonymous reporting only shields the identities of reporters from the authorities to whom they report, and is, as a result, not only unnecessary, but dangerously undemocratic, because it does not allow those accused to face their accusers. And while I have long been a supporter of increased penalties for violent sex offenders (including civil commitment in mental institutions after completing prison sentences, but *not* expanded community notification, which is poorly implemented, gives community members a false sense of security, and creates an excuse for early release), I now believe that all such efforts should be halted until means of assuring that those targeted for these additional sanctions are really guilty are also implemented.

There must be focus on using and improving objective scientific evidence, so that "expert" mental health opinions become less important to the process. To do so, however, professional standards for scientific-evidence collection, analysis, and court testimony must be improved, and conduct in this area must be monitored and poor conduct punished. As noted, the FBI has found that DNA testing cleared about one-quarter of its sexual assault suspects, or about 2,000 people each year since 1989. In more than half of the cases examined by the Department of Justice, defendants were denied appeals before DNA proved their innocence. However, attorneys and DNA experts Barry Scheck and Peter Neufeld, in an informal telephone survey, learned that the defense contacted DNA experts or asked for retests in fewer than 5% of DNA cases.[122]

One good sign is the expansion of the Innocence Project, originally developed at New York's Cardozo Law School of Yeshiva University by attorneys Peter Neufeld and Barry Scheck. The original project worked only for the exoneration of convicts proven innocent by DNA. The expanded program is working with college law, criminal justice, journalism, and other schools across the country and is no longer limited to cases involving DNA evidence.[123] Already it has made great inroads in the reversals of the Wenatchee, Washington, cases, even winning for one of the formerly accused the right to sue the State Department of Social and Heath Services, the city of Wenatchee, and former police officer Bob Perez.[124]

Surveillance cameras, improved lighting, and other features of environmental design, as well as identification of the likeliest locations of crime, can similarly improve crime detection without compromising civil rights or relying on possibly false or faulty allegations. As a British study, reported by the U.S. Department of Justice, commented:

> To thwart crimes, police must anticipate the place and time of occurrence [of crimes]. . . . Methods that help police focus efforts on where and when crime is likely to occur may be based on knowledge of offender, place, or victim. . . . The same perpetrators seem to be responsible for the bulk of repeated offenses against a victim. . . . Many times crimes remain unreported, with repeat victims often less likely to notify police—frequently for what victims regard as good reasons, including avoidance of revisions or terminations of insurance policies or disillusionment with how police dealt with earlier reports . . . two studies indicated that about 4 percent of surveyed victims suffered approximately 44 percent of the offenses . . . 43 percent of domestic violence incidents occurring over a 25-month period involved only about 7 percent of 1,450 households.[125]

To increase the ethics of the criminal justice system, civil forfeiture should be eliminated, and especially in small communities, prosecutors as well as judges should be rotated to decrease the pressure of "going along" with corrupt practices for the sake of future interactions with the same officials. Similarly, because exclusionary rules and the *Miranda* law are often blamed for the fact that police officers "testi-ly," they should be replaced with sanctions against officers who break rules.[126] Crime prevention would also be improved if some or all of the $3 billion annually granted to assist state and local law enforcement and communities by the Department of Justice to prevent crime were made available to the urban neighborhoods where youth violence is most highly concentrated.[127]

In regard to drugs, instead of focusing on the extent of drug use, harm minimization should be explored.[128] Harm minimization does not entail legalization, but nonenforcement of certain drug crimes under tightly circumscribed rules. For instance, "between 1979 and 1986, a set of guidelines emerged stipulating that coffee shop owners [in the Netherlands who sold *Cannabis*] could avoid prosecution by complying with five rules: no advertising; no hard drug sales on the premises; no sales to minors; no sales transactions exceeding the quantity threshold; and no public disturbances."[129]

Harm reduction, a grassroots movement that began in Amsterdam, now exists to various degrees in Britain, Denmark, Germany, and Switzerland as well as in the Netherlands. It includes needle and syringe exchange, methadone maintenance, safe-use education programs, and the use of treatment as an alternative to incarceration. Harm reduction also entails focusing on helping drug users to take control of their lives and recognize that they have the power to change their relationship to drugs—a concept which is anathema to the "Anonymous" ideologies.[130]

Only needle exchange has been rigorously evaluated. "While it is true that abstinence from drugs (or teenage sex, or drinking among alcoholics) is 100% effective, at reducing harm, this overlooks the contingent nature of abstinence-based programs; the key policy question is whether we are 100% effective at convincing people to *become* abstinent."[131] Harm minimization also calls for treating different drugs and drug uses differently. Some Americans have already taken the step of legalizing the medical use of marijuana. In fact, innovative county supervisors in San Mateo, California, voted to distribute confiscated marijuana to sick people through public health clinics. If approved by the state legislature, this would create the first government-run marijuana dispensary in the nation. Supporters say that dispensing marijuana through county clinics would deliver the drug to seriously ill people whose doctors prescribe it, guarantee quality, and prevent dealers from passing themselves off as humanitarians.[132]

Calls to explore other harm-reduction policies that have proved successful in Europe[133] are also receiving increased interest. In addition, calls for legalization of marijuana for medical purposes are not only forcing a rethinking of marijuana laws; they are engendering state actions in opposition to federal laws as well. Medical marijuana demonstrates that there are different kinds of drugs and different reasons for using them, that drug use and abuse are different, and that the federal government may not have the last word on the subject. In this discussion, doctors' and scientists' voices are heard above those of politicians and moralists. "The passage of Proposition 215 marks the end of 'Just say no'—and the beginning of Americans saying a great many other things about drugs. It is a conversation that the war on drugs may not survive."[134]

This new dialogue is being supported by private foundations such as the Lindesmith Center, which recently published a book exposing common myths about marijuana,[135] and whose founder, George Soros, contributed to the drug-legalization campaigns in California, Arizona, and several other states. This has also prompted increased calls for the National Institutes of Health to fund more studies of the medical uses of marijuana, which it has long avoided.[136]

The educational system can assist in de-sanctification efforts by increasing knowledge of mathematics, statistics, and critical thinking—and by incorporating these more fully into primary and secondary education, so that all American students are exposed to them. In higher education, the standards of all women and minority studies programs should be raised so that they are comparable to other academic departments. Distorted perceptions result largely from the American public's ignorance of science and mathematics. While schools can certainly improve in these areas, we can hardly expect students to comprehend them, or their importance, if they never observe decision making based on mathematics and science practiced by the government, the courts, or the media. Conversely, it can only help students to understand these subjects if they become integrated into daily life, and especially into government action.

None of this will be effected, however, without intense public demand. The public, too, must increase its own skepticism, the demands for accountability that it places on government and the media, and its knowledge of research methods. This will enable people to better assess real risks as well as to de-sanctify snake oil. And when sanctified snake oil perseveres nonetheless, the public must demand sources and definitions, confront disinformation, and sanction its purveyors, whomever they might be. Healthy debate, which requires full explanations of all views on an issue as well as knowledge of the beliefs and facts on which those views are based, will also facilitate the de-sanctification effort. Therefore, forums that do not encourage such debate should be suspect, and should never be publicly funded.

The public must also be mindful of the "industries" that are first created by and later perpetuated by sanctified snake oil, and it must be cautious of misapplied solutions and distorted information. This book has presented many examples of how sanctified snake oil siphons funds from programs with clear goals and more visible results, then uses mandates to require that the public use the less effective programs. Instead, efforts should be made to make basic services, such as education, more attractive to potential users. For instance, since the 1960s, programs like Mobilization for Youth and other legitimate recreational services were justified as "delinquency prevention." Thinking of them this way in turn justified mandating that particular young people make use of them, but such mandates in themselves make the programs unattractive—and make them appear to fail if delinquency does not fall in response to them. Instead, program developers might design educational and recreational programs that attract users, and that are evaluated by skills gained rather than by less relevant (and less controllable) goals.

This skepticism must also be extended to what Dineen calls the Psychology Industry, because although psychologists ask their clients to trust them, they tend to discourage trust and reliance on family and friends. They create the idea, with concepts such as "emotional abuse," "verbal assault," and "codependency," that therapeutic relationships are the only safe relationships. This not only fosters artificial dependency, but interferes with the development of more genuine relationships.[137] Instead, people need to give up belief in quick, total, painless "fixes" and recognize that solutions require work, motivation, and time. In the absence of mandated programs, society must rely on friends and family to encourage (not coerce) loved ones to seek necessary help.

Finally, it is a professional obligation of social workers to bear witness to issues of injustice that are not being adequately addressed in policy arenas. And I consider my *finally* bearing witness to be the realization of a personal obligation to Margaret Kelly Michaels.

But bearing witness is not enough. We must increase oversight of professionals, so that similar damage cannot recur. Legislators and compensation officials must develop case-review mechanisms to thwart compensation abusers and force those identified to reimburse compensation agencies and the "victims" of these methods. The most incompetent and harmful practitioners must be criminally prosecuted as victimizers as well. The horrible injustices that have been permitted to result from therapist incompetence coupled with prosecutorial incompetence and misconduct must be righted by providing mandatory compensation to the falsely accused, and mandatory reviews of every case based on false memories or the coerced testimony of children that resulted in a conviction. Similarly, we must review not only our drug laws, but the cases of the victims of our drug laws.

We can have effective social policy in the United States. But to obtain it, we have to make a concerted, national effort to eradicate sanctified snake oil, by eliminating policies, and industries, that create, support, and perpetuate it.

NOTES

1. J. Valente, "They Steal from the Devastated," *Parade* (June 4, 1995).

2. Robert Pear, "Audit of Medicare Finds $23 Billion in Overpayments," *New York Times* (July 17, 1997).

3. Peter Eisler, "Studies: Home Care Groups Guilty of Billions in Medicare Fraud," *USA Today* (July 28, 1997).

4. Ibid.

5. "City to Pay $9.5 Million to Settle Medicaid Charge," *New York Times* (October 16, 1998).

6. "Fraud and Waste in Medicare," *New York Times* (August 1, 1997).

7. Malcolm K. Sparrow, "Fraud Control in the Health Care Industry: Assessing the State of the Art," *Research in Brief* (Washington, DC: U. S. Department of Justice, December 1998); and Malcolm K. Sparrow, *License to Steal: Why Fraud Plagues America's Health Care System* (Denver: Westview Press, 1995).

8. Quoted in Joe Sharkey, *Bedlam* (New York: St. Martin's Press, 1994).

9. Joe Sharkey, op. cit.

10. Quoted in Joe Sharkey, *Bedlam* (New York: St. Martin's Press, 1994).

11. Joe Sharkey, op. cit.

12. Ibid.

13. Quoted in Joe Sharkey, *Bedlam* (New York: St. Martin's Press, 1994).

14. David S. Hilzenrath, "The Hole in the Medicare Pipeline," *Washington Post National Weekly Edition* (August 18, 1997).

15. Barry Meier, "For-Profit Care's Human Cost," *New York Times* (August 8, 1997).

16. Kurt Eichenwald, "Health Care Company Agrees to Settle Fraud Charges," *New York Times* (May 19, 2000).

17. Ibid.

18. Quoted in Joe Sharkey, op. cit.

19. Joe Sharkey, *Bedlam* (New York: St. Martin's Press, 1994).

20. Tana Dineen, *Manufacturing Victims*, 2d ed. (Montreal: Robert Davies Publishing, 1998).

21. John Erichsen, *On Railway and Other Injuries of the Nervous System* (London: Walton & Maberly, 1866). Also see Allan Young, *The Harmony of Illusions: Inventing Post-Traumatic Stress Disorder* (Princeton, NJ: Princeton University Press, 1995).

22. Herbert W. Page, *Injuries of the Spine and Spinal Cord without Apparent Mechanical Lesion, and Nervous Shock, in Their Surgical and Medico-Legal Aspects* (London: J. and A. Churchill, 1883).

23. Gregg Birnbaum, "Illegal Aliens' New Organs Still Cost Medicaid Arm & Leg," *New York Post* (June 30, 1997).

24. Ken Dornstein, *Accidentally, On Purpose* (New York: St. Martin's Press, 1996).

25. Denis Hamill, "Teenagers Play Wheel of Fortune—and Drivers Pay," *New York Daily News* (July 16, 1997).

26. Ken Dornstein, *Accidentally, On Purpose* (New York: St. Martin's Press, 1996); and Denis Hamill, "Teenagers Play Wheel of Fortune—and Drivers Pay," *New York Daily News* (July 16, 1997).

27. Carl Campanile, "Crash Scams Driving Up Car Insurance," *New York Post* (June 14, 1998).

28. A. Crenshaw, "Covered Against Fire, Theft and Cheaters," *Washington Post National Weekly Edition* (June 21–27, 1993).

29. Susan K. Sarnoff, *A National Survey of State Crime Victim Compensation Programs: Policies and Administrative Methods* (Ann Arbor, MI: University Microfilms International, December 1993); and Susan K. Sarnoff, *Paying for Crime: The Policies and Possibilities of Crime Victim Reimbursement* (Westport, CT: Praeger Publishers, 1996).

30. Alan M. Rubenstein, *Report: Investigation into Breezy Point Day School* (Doylestown, PA: Office of the District Attorney, March 1990).

31. Mark Pendergrast, *Victims of Memory* (Hinesburg, VT: Upper Access, Inc., 1995).

32. Larry McShane, "Bronx Witchhunt Destroyed Lives," *Denver Post* (December 2, 1996).

33. Pamela Freyd and Eleanor Goldstein, *Smiling Through Tears* (Boca Raton, FL: Upton Books, 1997).

34. Cathy Young, "VAWA Perpetuates Stereotypes," *The Women's Freedom Network Newsletter* (summer 1997): 1.

35. "Excerpts from the Supreme Court's Decision on Violence Against Women Act," *New York Times* (May 16, 2000).

36. Martin Kasindorf, "Fraudulent Drivers' Licenses for Sale," *USA Today* (August 19, 1997).

37. Cathy Young, *Ceasefire: Beyond the Gender Wars* (New York: Free Press, 1999).

38. Susan K. Sarnoff, "In Defiance of Justice," *OACLD Vindicator* (summer 1997).

39. Devlin Barrett, "False Rape Claim Sparks Tragedy," *New York Post* (April 5, 1998).

40. Susan Kiss Sarnoff, Telephone interview with Tana Dineen, unpublished, March 1998.

41. Paul Craig Roberts, "False Memories, False Prosecutions," *Washington Times* (January 20, 1998). Also see Rory Carroll, "Report Brands Recovered Memory Techniques as Bogus," *The Guardian* (January 13, 1998).

42. "Expulsion," *Psychiatric News: The Newspaper of the American Psychiatric Association* 35 (May 5, 2000).

43. Michael Jonathan Grinfeld, "Criminal Charges Filed in Recovered Memory Case; Psychiatrists Liable for Millions in Civil Suit," *Psychological Times* (December 1997).

44. Mark Smith, "5 Psychiatric Workers Charged in Scam," *Houston Chronicle* (October 29, 1997).

45. See, for example, Cathy Young, *Ceasefire: Beyond the Gender Wars* (New York: Free Press, 1999).

46. John Wilkens, "Innocent Family Awaits End to Child-Abuse Saga," *San Diego Union-Tribune* (November 14, 1993).

47. John Wilkens and Jim Okerblum, "Rape-Case Therapist Gives Up Licence," *San Diego Union-Tribune* (March 20, 1996).

48. William Glaberson, "Cleared of Child Abuse Five Times, Woman Sues Connecticut for Name of Her Accuser," *New York Times* (January 6, 1997).

49. D. Jones and J. M. MacGraw, "Reliable and Fictitious Accounts of Sexual Abuse in Children," *Journal of Interpersonal Violence* 2 (1987), cited in Stephen J. Ceci and Maggie Bruck, *Jeopardy in the Courtroom* (Washington, DC: American Psychological Association, 1995).

50. William Glaberson, op. cit.

51. Eric Schmitt, "Army Shuts Off Phone Line for Sex-Harassment Reports," *New York Times* (June 4, 1997), 6; and Bradley Graham, "The Army Decides to Cool It on the Hotline," *Washington Post National Weekly* (June 23, 1997).

52. Quoted in Tana Dineen, op. cit.

53. San Diego County Grand Jury, *Child Sexual Abuse, Assault, and Molest Issues, Report No. 8* (San Diego, CA: San Diego County Grand Jury, June 29, 1992).

54. San Diego County Grand Jury 1996–1997, "Victims of Crime Program in San Diego County," *Final Report* (San Diego, CA: San Diego County Grand Jury, June 27, 1997).

55. See, for example, Raymond Hughes, "Protest Path," *New Hampshire News-Leader* (August 15, 1996); Susan Sarnoff, "In Defiance of Justice," *OACDL Vindicator* (summer 1997); and Mitch Weiss, "Citizens Group Casts Doubt on Victims Aid," *Cleveland Plain-Dealer* (September 17, 1995).

56. Joe Cantlupe and David Hasemyer, "Akiki Case Drains Victim Fund. With No Crime, Should Therapy Be Paid?" *San Diego Union-Tribune* (January 31, 1994).

57. Paul Craig Roberts, "Scrambled Justice and Spurious Specialists," *Washington Times* (November 14, 1997).

58. Jack Kresnak, "U-M Cleared in Child Evaluation. Father Loses Lawsuit Over Abuse Inquiry," *Detroit Free Press* (November 26, 1997).

59. D. Jones and J. M. MacGraw, op. cit.

60. Stephen J. Ceci and Maggie Bruck, *Jeopardy in the Courtroom* (Washington, DC: American Psychological Association, 1995).

61. Donna LaFramboise and David Chan, "Sheltered from Reality," *The National Post* (November 23, 1998).

62. Ibid.

63. Larry Sutton, "Dad Cleared of Sex Abuse," *Daily News* (March 7, 1997).

64. Susan Kiss Sarnoff, *A National Survey of State Crime Victim Compensation Programs* (Ann Arbor, MI: University Microfilms International, December 1993).

65. See, for example, Susan K. Sarnoff, "In Defiance of Justice," *OACLD Vindicator* (summer 1997).

66. Cathy Young, *Ceasefire: Beyond the Gender Wars* (New York: Free Press, 1999).

67. Bill Hoffman, "Cops Set to Charge Cowboys' Accuser," *New York Post* (January 12, 1997).

68. Cathy Young, op. cit.

69. Linda Fairstein, *Sexual Violence* (New York: William Morrow and Co., 1993).

70. Alan M. Dershowitz, *The Abuse Excuse* (New York: Little, Brown & Co., 1994).

71. Rita J. Simon and Jean Landis, *The Crimes Women Commit, the Punishments They Receive* (Lexington, MA: Lexington Books, 1991); and Rita J. Simon, *Women and Violent Crime* (Washington, DC: Women's Freedom Network, undated), received August 2, 1997.

72. Michael Janofsky, "Pessimism Retains Grip on Appalachian Poor," *New York Times* (February 9, 1998).

73. Pam Belluck, "Fund-Raiser for Young Victim of Crime Is Sued," *New York Times* (November 27, 1997); and Dahleen Glanton, "Complaints Have State Looking at Girl X Fund," *Chicago Tribune* (November 23, 1997).

74. Art Levine, "The Strange Case of Faked Hate Crimes," *U.S. News and World Reports* (November 3, 1997), 30.

75. Naomi Wolf, *Fire with Fire* (New York: Random House, 1993).

76. James Pinkerton, *What Comes Next?* (New York: Hyperion, 1995). Also see J. Valente, "They Steal from the Devastated," *Parade* (June 4, 1995).

77. Yeheskel Aharoni, *The No-Risk Society* (Chatham, NJ: Chatham House Publishers, 1981).

78. Charles Murray, *What It Means to Be a Libertarian* (New York: Broadway Books, 1997).

79. Yeheskel Aharoni, op. cit.

80. David Shaw, *The Pleasure Police* (New York: Doubleday, 1996).

81. Larry Laudan, *The Book of Risks* (New York: John Wiley & Sons, 1994).

82. Neil Gilbert and Paul Terrell, *Dimensions of Social Welfare Policy*, 4th ed. (Boston: Allyn and Bacon, 1998).

83. Patricia Pearson *When She Was Bad: Violent Women and the Myth of Innocence* (New York: Viking, 1997).

84. John Leo, "Things That Go Bump in the Home," *U.S. News and World Report* (May 13, 1996).

85. Philip W. Cook, *Abused Men* (Westport, CT: Praeger Publishers, 1997).

86. Cathy Spatz-Widom, "Child Abuse, Neglect, and Adult Behavior: Research Design and Findings on Criminality, Violence, and Child Abuse," *American Journal of Orthopsychiatry* 59, no. 3 (1989), 355–367.

87. William Raspberry, "We're Not Bad Guys, Just Doubtful," *Washington Post* (March 17, 1992), quoted in Lisbeth B. Schorr, *Common Purpose* (New York: Anchor, 1997).

88. Richard Morin, "Public Policy Surveys: Lite and Less Filling," *Washington Post National Weekly Edition* (November 10, 1997).

89. Cynthia Crosson, *Tainted Truth* (New York: Touchstone Books, 1994).

90. Mark Gerzon, *A House Divided* (New York: G. P. Putnam's Sons, 1996).

91. Lisbeth B. Schorr, *Common Purpose* (New York: Anchor, 1997).

92. Deborah Tannen, *The Argument Culture* (New York: Random House, 1998).

93. Larry Baron and Murray A. Straus, *Four Theories of Rape in American Society* (New Haven, CT: Yale University Press, 1989).

94. See, for example, Nadine Strossen, *Defending Pornography* (New York: Anchor Books, 1996).

95. Daphne Patai and Noretta Koertge, *Professing Feminism* (New York: Basic Books, 1994).

96. Rene Denfield, *Kill the Body, the Head Will Fall* (New York: Warner Books, 1997).

97. Cathy Spatz-Widom, "The Cycle of Violence," *Research in Brief* (Washington, DC: U.S. Department of Justice, September 1992).

98. David Gelertner, *Drawing a Life* (New York: Free Press, 1997).

99. Elaine S. Povich, "Fenced-In Thinking?" *Newsday* (November 23, 1997).

100. Audrey Kishline, *Moderate Drinking* (New York: Crown, 1994).

101. Andrew C. Revkin, "Unlikely Allies in Fight for Hemp," *New York Times* (June 22, 1997).

102. Lester Grinspoon, Testimony on Marijuana Rescheduling to the U.S. Drug Enforcement Agency, in *Cancer Treatment and Marijuana Therapy*, edited by R. C. Randall (Washington, DC: Galen Press, 1990).

103. For a fuller discussion of this concept, see Richard A. Epstein, *Simple Rules for a Complex World* (Cambridge, MA: Harvard University Press, 1995).

104. Alexis de Tocqueville, *Democracy in America* (New York: Alfred Knopf, 1994).

105. Robert Landauer, "Shape Up or Ship Out," *The Oregonian* (July 11, 1998).

106. Deeann Glamser, "Washington State Testing Therapy for Sex Felons," *USA Today* (January 27, 1997).

107. Lisa Belkin, "How Can We Help the Next Victim?" *New York Times Magazine* (June 15, 1997).

108. Susan K. Sarnoff, *A National Survey of State Crime Victim Compensation Programs: Policies and Administrative Methods* (Ann Arbor, MI: University Microfilms International, December 1993); and *Paying for Crime: The Policies and Possibilities of Crime Victim Reimbursement* (Westport, CT: Praeger Publishers, 1996).

109. Charles Murray, *What It Means to Be a Libertarian* (New York: Broadway Books, 1997).

110. R. Christopher Barden, "Memo to Supporters," National Association for Consumer Protection in Mental Health Practices (December 11, 1994).

111. Reinder Van Til, *Lost Daughters* (Grand Rapids, MI: William B. Eerdmans Publishing Co., 1997).

112. Associated Press, "Malpractice Information Goes Public," *Newsday* (November 5, 1996).

113. Dan Barry, "Now on the Web: Which Professionals Are in Bad Standing, and Why," *New York Times* (February 3, 1997).

114. Richard Willing, "Florida, California Want to Rein in 'Hired Gun' Medical Witnesses," *USA Today* (April 10, 1998).

115. Pamela Freyd, "Editorial," *False Memory Syndrome Newsletter* (September 1997).

116. "Fraud Rules Challenged," *USA Today* (February 10, 1998).

117. Steffi Woolhandler and David Himmelstein, "The Deteriorating Efficiency of the US Health Care System," *The New England Journal of Medicine*, no. 18 (May 2, 1991).

118. Alfred J. Kahn, "Perspectives on Access to Social Service," *Social Work* 15, no. 2 (March 1970), 95–101.

119. Kenneth F. T. Cust, *A Just Minimum of Health Care* (New York: University Press of America, 1997).

120. Many of these concepts emanated from discussions at the Conference on Wrongful Convictions and the Death Penalty, Northwestern University, November 13–15, 1998.

121. Richard A. Gardner, "Revising the Child Abuse Prevention and Treatment Act," *Issues in Child Abuse Accusations* 5, no. 1 (winter 1993), 25–77; and Richard A. Gardner, "Restructuring the Child Abuse Treatment and Prevention Act," *Detroit News* (June 21, 1997).

122. Mark Schoofs, "Genetic Justice," *Village Voice* (November 18, 1997).

123. Cheryl Amitay, *National Association of Criminal Defense Lawyers News Release* (Washington, DC: National Association of Criminal Defense Lawyers, November 27, 1997).

124. Andrew Schneider, "Woman Can File Suit Over State at Mental Hospital, Wenatchee, State May Face Action from Handling of Sex Abuse Case," *Seattle Post-Intelligencer* (June 21, 1999).

125. Ken Pease and Gloria Laycock, *Revictimization: Reducing the Heat on Hot Victims* (Washington, DC: U.S. Department of Justice, November 1996).

126. Burton S. Katz, *Justice Overruled* (New York: Warner Books, 1997).

127. Lawrence W. Sherman, *Preventing Crime: What Works, What Doesn't, What's Promising* (Washington, DC: U.S. Department of Justice, February 1997).

128. P. Reuter, *On the Consequences of Toughness* (Santa Monica, CA: RAND, 1991).

129. Robert J. MacCoun and Peter Reuter, "Interpreting Dutch Cannabis Policy: Reasoning by Analogy in the Legalization Debate," *Science* 278 (October 3, 1997), 47–52.

130. Katherine van Wormer, "Harm Induction vs. Harm Reduction: Comparing American and British Approaches to Drug Use," *Journal of Offender Rehabilitation* 29 (1999), 35–48.

131. Robert J. MacCoun, *The Psychology of Harm Reduction: Comparing Alternative Strategies for Modifying High-Risk Behaviors* (Santa Monica, CA: RAND, 1996).

132. "California Officials Would Give Marijuana to Sick People," *USA Today* (November 19, 1997).

133. See, for example, Elizabeth Olson, "Swiss Weigh Fate of Clinics Offering Legal Heroin," *New York Times* (September 28, 1997).

134. Michael Pollan, "Living With Medical Marijuana," *Sunday New York Times Magazine* (July 20, 1997); Lynn Zimmer and John P. Morgan, *Marijuana Myths, Marijuana Facts* (New York: Lindesmith Center, 1997).

135. William F. Buckley, Jr., "The Fear of Marijuana: A Mythunderstanding?" *New York Post* (October 15, 1997).

136. Associated Press, "Call for Marijuana Study," *Newsday* (August 9, 1997).

137. Tana Dineen, *Manufacturing Victims*, 2d ed. (Montreal: Robert Davies Publishing, 1998).

Bibliography

Accuracy in Media. "The Scandal of News Censorship on TV." *AIM Report*. Washington, DC: Accuracy in Media, September 1997.

Aharoni, Yeheskel. *The No-Risk Society*. Chatham, NJ: Chatham House Publishers, 1981.

Ahrens, Lois. "Battered Women's Refuges: Feminist Cooperatives vs. Social Service Institutions." In *Community Organizers*, 2d ed., edited by Joan Ecklein. New York: John Wiley & Sons, 1984.

American Bar Association Task Force. *The Judicial Response to Lawyer Misconduct*. Chicago: American Bar Association, 1984.

Amitay, Cheryl. *National Association of Criminal Defense Lawyers News Release*. Washington, DC: National Association of Criminal Defense Lawyers, November 27, 1997.

Angell, Marcia. "Trial by Science." *New York Times* (December 9, 1998).

Armstrong, Ken, and Maurice Possley. "The Verdict: Dishonor." *Chicago Tribune* (January 8, 1999).

Associated Press. "Call for Marijuana Study." *Newsday* (August 9, 1997).

———. "ABA Leader Seeks Moratorium on Death Penalty," *Chicago Tribune* (July 10, 2000).

———. "Castrated Molester Given 26 Year Prison Sentence." *USA Today* (March 4, 1998).

———. "Castrated Rapist Tied to 75 New Sex Crimes." *New York Times* (November 28, 1998).

———. "Malpractice Information Goes Public." *Newsday* (November 5, 1996).

Associated Press re: *Pittsburgh Post-Gazette* article (10-part series) (November 21, 1998).

Babcock, Charles. Heard on *Reporters' Roundtable*. C-SPAN, November 9, 1997.

Barden, R. Christopher. "Memo to Supporters." *National Association for Consumer Protection in Mental Health Practices*, December 11, 1994.

Baron, Larry, and Murray A. Straus. *Four Theories of Rape in American Society*. New Haven, CT: Yale University Press, 1989.

Barrett, Devlin. "False Rape Claim Sparks Tragedy." *New York Post* (April 5, 1998).

Barry, Dan. "Now on the Web: Which Professionals Are in Bad Standing, and Why." *New York Times* (February 3, 1997).

Bass, Ellen, and Laura Davis. *The Courage to Heal.* 3d ed. New York: HarperPerennial, 1994.

Baum, Dan. *Smoke and Mirrors.* New York: Little, Brown & Co., 1996.

Beckett, Kathleen. "Culture and the Politics of Signification: The Case of Child Sexual Abuse." *Social Problems* 43, no. 1 (February 1996): 57–76.

Behr, Edward. *Prohibition.* New York: Arcade, 1996.

Belkin, Lisa. "How Can We Help the Next Victim?" *New York Times Magazine* (June 15, 1997).

Belluck, Pam. "Fund-Raiser for Young Victim of Crime Is Sued." *New York Times* (November 27, 1997).

———. " 'Memory' Therapy Leads to a Lawsuit and Big Settlement." *New York Times* (November 6, 1997).

———. "Shelters for Women Disclosing Their Locations, in Spite of Risk." *New York Times* (August 10, 1997).

Benjamin, Daniel K., and Roger Leroy Miller. *Undoing Drugs.* New York: Basic Books, 1991.

Bennett, James T., and Thomas J. Lorenzo. *Destroying Democracy.* Washington, DC: Cato Institute, 1985.

Bennett, Lance. *Public Opinion in American Politics.* New York: Harcourt Brace Jovanovich, 1980.

Berger, Joseph. "Westchester to Limit Revolving-Door Care of Poor Addicts." *New York Times* (June 17, 1997).

Berger v. United States. 295 U. S. 78, 79 L. Ed. 1314, 55 S. Ct. 629, 633 (1935).

Bergin, Allen E., and Sol L. Garfield, eds. *Handbook of Psychotherapy and Behavior Change.* 4th ed. New York: John Wiley & Sons, 1994.

Berlin, Isaiah. *Four Essays on Liberty.* Oxford: Oxford University Press, 1968.

Berman, Richard. "Junk Research Distorts Public Policy." *The Oregonian* (January 4, 1998).

Bernstein, Carl, and Bob Woodward. *All the President's Men.* New York: Simon and Schuster, 1974.

Bernstein, Peter L. *Against the Gods: The Remarkable Story of Risk.* New York: John Wiley & Sons, 1996.

Berry, Kenneth K., and Jason Berry. "The Congressional Censure of a Research Paper: Return of the Inquisition?" *Skeptical Inquirer* (January 1, 2000): 20.

Bertram, Eva, Morris Blachman, Kenneth Sharpe, and Peter Andreas. *Drug War Politics.* Los Angeles: University of California Press, 1996.

Best, Joel. *Random Violence.* Berkeley: University of California Press, 1999.

———. *Threatened Children.* Chicago, IL: University of Chicago Press, 1990.

Beyerstein, Barry L. "Why Bogus Therapies Seem to Work." *Skeptical Inquirer* (September/October 1997): 29–34.

Birnbaum, Gregg. "Illegal Aliens' New Organs Still Cost Medicaid Arm & Leg." *New York Post* (June 30, 1997).

Biscayne, Pierre E. Letter to the *New York Times.* *New York Times* (September 30, 1997).

Bonnie, Richard J., and Charles H. Whitebread II. *The Marihuana Conviction: A History of Marihuana Prohibition in the United States.* Charlottesville, VA: University Press of Virginia, 1974.

Boyatzis, Richard E. "Who Should Drink What, When, and Where If Looking for a Fight." In *Alcohol, Drug Abuse and Aggression,* edited by Edward Gottlieb et al., 314–329. Springfield, IL: Charles C. Thomas, 1983.

Bradshaw, Jonathan, "The Concept of Social Need," In *Planning for Social Welfare: Issues, Tasks and Models*, edited by Neil Gilbert and Harry Sprecht. Englewood Cliffs, NJ: Prentice Hall, 1977, 290–296.

Brandeis, Louis. *Whitney v. California* (1927).

Brennan, Richard P. *Heisenberg Probably Slept Here*. New York: John Wiley & Sons, 1997.

Broder, John M. "Big Social Changes Revive the False God of Numbers." *New York Times* (August 17, 1997).

Brookhiser, Richard. "Why Won't This Nation Go to Pot?" *New York Observer* (November 17, 1997).

Brott, Armin A. "The Facts Take a Battering." *Washington Post National Weekly Edition* (August 8–14, 1994).

Brown, David. Review of *Madness on the Couch*. *Washington Post National Weekly Edition* (November 30, 1998).

Brown, Evelyn. "Social Security Going After Fraud." *Staten Island Advance* (August 19, 1997).

Buckley, William F., Jr. "The Fear of Marijuana: A Mythunderstanding?" *New York Post* (October 15, 1997).

Bufe, C. *Alcoholics Anonymous: Cult or Cure?* San Francisco, CA: See Sharp Press, 1991.

Bureau of Justice Assistance. *DARE Fact Sheet*. Washington, DC: U. S. Department of Justice, September 1995.

Butterfield, Fox. "Death Sentences Being Overturned in 2 of 3 Appeals." *New York Times* (June 12, 2000).

"California Officials Would Give Marijuana to Sick People." *USA Today* (November 19, 1997).

Campanile, Carl. "Crash Scams Driving Up Car Insurance." *New York Post* (June 14, 1998).

Campbell, Terence W. *Beware the Talking Cure*. Boca Raton, FL: Upton Books, 1994.

Cantlupe, Joe, and David Hasemyer. "Akiki Case Drains Victim Fund. With No Crime, Should Therapy Be Paid?" *San Diego Union-Tribune* (January 31, 1994).

Carroll, Rory. "Report Brands Recovered Memory Techniques as Bogus." *The Guardian* (January 13, 1998).

Cauchon, Dennis. "Yet High-Level Supporters Argue, 'It's Better to Have It Than Not to Have It.'" *USA Today* (October 11, 1993).

Ceci, Stephen J., and Maggie Bruck. *Jeopardy in the Courtroom: A Scientific Analysis of Children's Testimony*. Washington, DC: American Psychological Association, 1995.

Chapin, M. "Functional Conflict Theory, the Alcohol Beverage Industry, and the Alcohol Treatment Industry." *Journal of Applied Social Sciences* 18 (1994): 169–182.

Chappell, David. "Providing for the Victims of Crime: Political Placebos or Progressive Programs?" *Adelaide Law Review* 4 (1972): 294.

Chatterjee, Pranab. *Approaches to the Welfare State*. Washington, DC: National Association of Social Workers Press, 1996.

———. "A Market of Human Vulnerability." *Social Development Issues*, 3 (1979): 1–12.

Cheney, Lynne V. *Telling the Truth*. New York: Touchstone, 1995.

Chideya, Farai. *Don't Believe the Hype*. New York: Plume, 1995.

Chin, Jack. Conference on Wrongful Convictions and the Death Penalty. Northwestern University, November 13–15, 1998.

"Chiropractors." *Consumer Reports* (June 1994).

Choi, I., E. Martin, P. Chatterjee, and T. Holland. "Ideology and Social Welfare." *Indian Journal of Social Work* 39, no. 2 (1978): 139–160.

"City to Pay $9.5 Million to Settle Medicaid Charge." *New York Times* (October 16, 1998).

Cockburn, Alexander. "AIDS, Kitsch and Charity." *New York Press* (June 18–24, 1997).

———. "Why the Drug War Works." *New York Press* (June 17–23, 1998).

Cohen, Michael D., James G. March, and John P. Olsen. "The Garbage Can Model of Organizational Change." *Administrative Science Quarterly* 17, no. 6 (March 1972): 1–25.

Coleman, Lee. *The Reign of Error*. Boston: Beacon Press, 1984.

Collins, James J. "Alcohol Use and Expressive Interpersonal Violence." In *Alcohol, Drug Abuse and Aggression*, edited by Edward Gottlieb et al., 5–25. Springfield, IL: Charles C. Thomas, 1983.

Connors, Edward, Thomas Lundregan, Neal Miller, and Tom McEwen. *Convicted by Juries, Exonerated by Science: Case Studies in the Use of DNA Evidence to Establish Innocence After Trial*. Washington, DC: U.S. Department of Justice, June 1996.

Conrad, Chris. *Hemp: Lifeline to the Future*. Los Angeles, CA: Creative Xpressions, 1993.

Contratto, Susan, and M. Janice Gutfreund, eds. *A Feminist Clinician's Guide to the Memory Debate*. New York: Haworth Press, Inc., 1996.

Cook, Philip J., and Michael J. Moore. "Economic Perspectives." In *NIAAA Research Monograph No. 24*, edited by Susan E. Martin, 193–218. Rockville, MD: NIH, 1993.

Cook, Philip W. *Abused Men*. Westport, CT: Praeger Publishers, 1997.

Coontz, Stephanie. *The Way We Really Are*. New York: Basic Books, 1997.

Cooper, Michael. "Police Department Adopts Policy to Protect and Reward Whistle-blowers." *New York Times* (November 26, 1998).

Costin, Lela B., Howard Jacob Karger, and David Stoesz. *The Politics of Child Abuse in America*. New York: Oxford University Press, 1996.

Council on Scientific Affairs. "Scientific Status of Refreshing Recollection by the Use of Hypnosis." *Journal of the American Medical Association* (April 5, 1985).

Crenshaw, A. "Covered Against Fire, Theft and Cheaters." *Washington Post National Weekly Edition* (June 21–27, 1993).

Crosson, Cynthia. *Tainted Truth*. New York: Touchstone Books, 1994.

Currie, Elliott. *Crime and Punishment in America*. New York: Metropolitan Books, 1998.

———. "Crimes without Criminals." *Law and Society Review* 3 (August 7, 1968).

Cust, Kenneth F. T. *A Just Minimum of Health Care*. New York: University Press of American, 1997.

Dao, James. "Albany Is Poised to Require Insurance Coverage of Chiropractic Care." *New York Times* (July 27, 1997).

Davis, Robert C., and Madeline Henley. "Victim Service Programs." In *Victims of Crime: Problems, Policies and Programs*, edited by A. Lurigio, Wesley Skogan, and Robert Davis, 157–171. Beverly Hills, CA: Sage Publications, 1990.

Dawes, Robyn M. *House of Cards: Psychology and Psychotherapy Built on Myth*. New York: Free Press, 1994.

Dawkins, Richard. *The Selfish Gene*. New York: Oxford University Press, 1976.

DeLipsey, Jan Marie, and Sue Kelly James. "Videotaping the Sexually Abused Child: The Texas Experience, 1983–1987." In *Vulnerable Populations: Evaluation and Treatment of Sexually Abused Children and Adult Survivors*, Vol. 1, edited by Suzanne Sgroi. Lexington, MA: Lexington Books, 1988.

Denfield, Rene. *Kill the Body, the Head Will Fall*. New York: Warner Books, 1997.

———. *The New Victorians*. New York: Warner Books, 1995.

Dershowitz, Alan M. *The Abuse Excuse*. New York: Little, Brown & Co., 1994.

Dineen, Tana. Telephone interview by author. March 1998.

———. *Manufacturing Victims*, 2d ed. Montreal: Robert Davies Publishing, 1998.

Ditman, K. S., G. G. Crawford, E. W. Forgy, H. Moskowitz, and C. MacAndrew. "A Controlled Experiment on the Use of Court Probation for Drunk Arrests." *American Journal of Psychiatry* 124 (1967): 64–67.

Dolnick, Edward. *Madness on the Couch*. New York: Simon and Schuster, 1998.

Donziger, Steven R. "Give Kids Straight Dope on Drugs." *Newsday* (February 6, 1998).

———, ed. *The Real War on Crime*. New York: HarperPerennial, 1996.

Dornstein, Ken. *Accidentally, On Purpose*. New York: St. Martin's Press, 1996.

Douglas, William O. *Terminiello v. Chicago*.

Downs, Donald Alexander. *More Than Victims*. Chicago, IL: University of Chicago Press, 1996.

"Do You Get What You Pay For? With Criminal Justice Efforts, Not Necessarily." *Law Enforcement News* (May 15, 1997).

Dreyfuss, Robert. "The Drug War: Where the Money Goes." *Rolling Stone* (December 11, 1997).

"Drug Abuse Resistance Education (DARE)." Washington, DC: U. S. Department of Justice, September 1995.

Duke, Steven B., and Albert C. Gross. *America's Longest War*. New York: Putnam, 1993.

Ecklein, Joan, ed. *Community Organizers*, 2d ed. New York: John Wiley & Sons, 1984.

Edelman, Murray. *Political Language: Words that Succeed and Politics that Fail*. New York: Academic Press, 1977.

Editorial. *Washington Post* (May 24, 1997).

Eichenwald, Kurt. "Health Care Company Agrees to Settle Fraud Charges." *New York Times* (May 19, 2000).

Eisler, Peter. "Studies: Home Care Groups Guilty of Billions in Medicare Fraud." *USA Today* (July 28, 1997).

Elias, Marilyn. "Ritalin Use Up Among Youth." *USA Today* (December 11, 1996).

Elias, Robert. *Victims Still*. Beverly Hills, CA: Sage Publications, 1993.

Ellis, John M. *Literature Lost*. New Haven, CT: Yale University Press, 1997.

Ellis, Richard J. *The Dark Side of the Left*. Topeka: University of Kansas Press, 1998.

Epstein, Richard A. *Simple Rules for a Complex World*. Cambridge, MA: Harvard University Press, 1995.

Erichsen, John. *On Railway and Other Injuries of the Nervous System*. London: Walton & Maberly, 1866.

Erikson, Kai T. *Wayward Puritans*. New York: John Wiley & Sons, 1966.

Etzioni, Amitai. *Capital Corruption*. New Brunswick, NJ: Transaction, 1995.

———. *Modern Organizations*. Englewood Cliffs, NJ: Prentice Hall, 1964.

Ewald, William Bragg, Sr. *Who Killed Joe McCarthy?* New York: Simon and Schuster, 1984.

"Excerpts from the Supreme Court's Decision on the Violence Against Women Act." *New York Times* (May 16, 2000).

Fagan, Jeffrey. "Set and Setting Revisited: Influences of Alcohol and Illicit Drugs on the Social Context of Violent Events." In *Alcohol and Interpersonal Violence*, edited by Susan Martin. Washington, DC: NIAAA, 1993. 161–191.

Fairstein, Linda. *Sexual Violence*. New York: William Morrow and Co., 1993.

"Federal Judge Is Accused of Racism in Civil Trial." *New York Times* (August 3, 1997).

Fonzi, Gaeton. *The Last Investigation*. New York: Thunder's Mouth Press, 1993.

Fowler, Ray (Administrative Director of the APA). Memo Re: "Controversy Regarding APA Journal Article." May 25, 1999.

Fox, James Alan, and Marianne W. Zavitz. "Homicide Trends in the United States." Washington, DC: U. S. Department of Justice, January 1999.

Frankel, Glenn. "The Longest War." *Washington Post National Weekly Edition* (July 7, 1997): 6–8.

Frankfurter, Felix. *The Case of Sacco and Venzetti.* Boston: Little, Brown and Co., 1927.

Frantz, Douglas. "Death of a Scientologist Heightens Suspicions in a Florida Town." *New York Times* (December 1, 1997).

"Fraud and Waste in Medicare." *New York Times* (August 1, 1997).

"Fraud Rules Challenged." *USA Today* (February 10, 1998).

Freyd, Pamela. Editorial. *False Memory Syndrome Newsletter* (September 1997).

Freyd, Pamela, and Eleanor Goldstein. *Smiling Through Tears.* Boca Raton, FL: Upton Books, 1997.

Friedman, Lawrence M. *Crime and Punishment in American History.* New York: Basic Books, 1993.

Friedman, Milton. An Open Letter to Bill Bennett." *Wall Street Journal* (September 7, 1989).

Fumento, Michael. *Science Under Siege.* New York: William Morrow and Co., 1993.

Galaif, Elisha R., and Steve Sussman. "For Whom Does Alcoholics Anonymous Work?" *The International Journal of the Addictions* 30, no. 2 (1995): 161–184.

Galanter, Marc. *Cults: Faith, Healing and Coercion.* New York: Oxford University Press, 1989.

Galper, James. *The Politics of Social Services.* Englewood Cliffs, NJ: Prentice Hall, 1975.

Gardner, Martin. "RMT: Repressed Memory Therapy." In *Weird Water & Fuzzy Logic.* Amherst, NY: Prometheus Books, 1996.

———. "The Tragedies of False Memories." In *Weird Water & Fuzzy Logic.* Amherst, NY: Prometheus Books, 1996.

Gardner, Richard A. "Restructuring the Child Abuse Treatment and Prevention Act." *Detroit News* (June 21, 1997).

———. "Revising the Child Abuse Prevention and Treatment Act." *Issues in Child Abuse Accusations* 5 no. 1 (winter 1993): 25–27.

———. *Sex Abuse Hysteria: Salem Witch Trials Revisited.* Cresskill, NJ: Creative Therapeutics, 1991.

———. "The 'Validators' and Other Examiners." *Issues in Child Abuse Allegations* 3, no. 1 (winter 1991).

Garfield, Bob. "Maladies by the Millions?" *USA Today* (December 16, 1996).

Garfinkel, Lawrence, Catherine C. Boring, and Clark W. Heath, Jr. "Changing Trends: An Overview of Breast Cancer Incidence and Mortality." *Cancer* (July 1, 1994): 222–227.

Gaylin, Willard, and Bruce Jennings. *The Perversion of Autonomy.* New York: Free Press, 1996.

Gelertner, David. *Drawing a Life.* New York: Free Press, 1997.

Gershman, Bennett L. *Prosecutorial Misconduct.* Deerfield, IL: Clark, Boardman, Callaghan, October 1991.

Gerstein, D., and H. Harwood, eds. *Treating Drug Problems.* Vol. 1: *A Study of the Evolution, Effectiveness, and Financing of Public and Private Drug Treatment Systems.* Washington, DC: National Academy Press, 1990.

Gerzon, Mark. *A House Divided*. New York: G. P. Putnam's Sons, 1996.

Gettleman, Marvin E,. Jane Franklin, Marilyn Young, and H. Bruce Franklin, eds. "Editors' Introduction to 'Vietnamization 1969–1975.'" In *Vietnam and America: A Documented History*, edited by Marvin E. Gettleman et al. New York: Grove Press, 1985.

———. "General Introduction." In *Vietnam and America: A Documented History*, edited by Marvin E. Gettleman et al. New York: Grove Press, 1985.

———. *Vietnam and America: A Documented History*. New York: Grove Press, 1985.

Gianelli, Paul C. "The Abuse of Scientific Evidence in Criminal Cases: The Need for Independent Crime Laboratories." *Virginia Journal of Social Policy & the Law* (winter 1997): 439–478.

Gilbert, Neil. *Capitalism and the Welfare State*. New Haven, CT: Yale University Press, 1983.

Gilbert, Neil, and Paul Terrell. *Dimensions of Social Welfare Policy*. 4th ed. Boston: Allyn and Bacon, 1998.

Gilovich, Thomas. *How We Know What Isn't So*. New York: Free Press, 1991.

Glaberson, William. "Cleared of Child Abuse Five Times, Woman Sues Connecticut for Name of Her Accuser." *New York Times* (January 6, 1997).

Glamser, Deeann. "Washington State Testing Therapy for Sex Felons." *USA Today* (January 27, 1997).

Glanton, Dahleen. "Complaints Have State Looking at Girl X Fund." *Chicago Tribune* (November 23, 1997).

Glendon, Maryanne. *A Nation Under Lawyers*. New York: Farrar, Straus and Giroux, 1994.

Godwin, R. Kenneth. "Using Market-Based Incentives to Empower the Poor." In *Public Policy for Democracy*, edited by Helen Ingram and Steven Rathgeb Smith, 163–197. Washington, DC: The Brookings Institution, 1993.

Goldberg, Carey. "Study Casts Doubts on Wisdom of Mandatory Terms for Drugs." *New York Times* (November 25, 1997).

Goleman, Daniel. "A Key to Post-Traumatic Stress Lies in Brain Chemistry, Scientists Find." *New York Times* (June 12, 1990).

———. "More Than 1 in 4 U. S. Adults Suffers a Mental Disorder Each Year." *New York Times* (March 17, 1993).

———. "Severe Trauma May Damage the Brain as Well as the Psyche." *New York Times* (August 1, 1995): C3.

Good, Erica. "How Much Therapy Is Enough? It Depends." *New York Times* (November 24, 1998).

Goodman, Ellen. "Court Program Could Trash Junk Science." *The Statesman Journal* (February 24, 1998).

Gottlieb, Edward et al., eds. *Alcohol, Drug Abuse and Aggression*. Springfield, IL: Charles C. Thomas, 1983, 5–25, 41–58, 314–329.

Graham, Bradley. "The Army Decides to Cool It on the Hotline." *Washington Post National Weekly* (June 23, 1997).

Grant, Tom. "Wenatchee and the Media's Reflexive Acceptance of Hysteria." Paper prepared for "A Day of Contrition Revisited: Contemporary Hysteria Condemns the Innocent." A conference organized by the Justice Committee. Salem, MA: January 14, 1997.

Gremillion, David H. "Domestic Violence as a Professional Commitment." In *From Data to Public Policy*, edited by Rita Simon, 53–59. New York: Women's Freedom Network and University Press of America, 1996.

Grinfeld, Michael Jonathan. "Criminal Charges Filed in Recovered Memory Case; Psychiatrists Liable for Millions in Civil Suit." *Psychological Times* (December 1997).

Grinspoon, Lester. "Testimony on Marijuana Rescheduling to the U. S. Drug Enforcement Administration." In *Cancer Treatment and Marijuana Therapy*, edited by R. C. Randall. Washington, DC: Galen Press, 1990.

Gross, Martin L. *The End of Sanity*. New York: Avon Books, 1997.

Grossmark, Robert. Letter to the *New York Times*. *New York Times* (September 30, 1997).

Gummer, Burton. *The Politics of Social Administration: Managing Organizational Politics in Social Agencies*. Englewood Cliffs, NJ: Prentice Hall, 1990.

Gusfield, Joseph R. *Symbolic Crusade*. Urbana: University of Illinois Press, 1970.

Haack, Susan. "Science, Scientism, and Anti-Science in the Age of Preposterism." *Skeptical Inquirer* (November/December 1997): 37–42, 60.

Haaga, John G., and Elizabeth A. McGlynn. *The Drug Abuse Treatment System*. Santa Monica, CA: RAND, 1993.

Haar, Charles M., and Daniel Fessler. *Fairness and Justice*. New York: Touchstone, 1986.

Hagen, Margaret A. *Whores of the Court*. New York: ReganBooks, 1997.

Hallinan, Joe. "Debate Heats Up—As State Seeks to Stop Paying Therapy Bills." *Seattle News* (January 5, 1997).

Hamill, Denis. "Teenagers Play Wheel of Fortune—and Drivers Pay." *New York Daily News* (July 16, 1997).

Hamowy, Ronald, ed. *Dealing with Drugs*. Lexington, MA: D. C. Heath and Company, 1987.

———. "Introduction: Illicit Drugs and Government Control." In *Dealing with Drugs*, edited by Ronald Hamowy. Lexington, MA: D. C. Heath and Company, 1987, 1–34.

Harer, John B. *Intellectual Freedom*. Santa Barbara, CA: ABC-CLIO, 1992.

Harrell, A. V., B. E. Smith, and R. F. Cook. *The Social Psychological Effects of Victimization*. Final report to the National Institute of Justice, 1985.

Harris, Daniel. *The Rise and Fall of Gay Culture*. New York: Hyperion, 1997.

Hechler, David. *The Battle and the Backlash*. Lexington, MA: Lexington Books, 1988.

Heinl, Colonel Robert D., Jr. "The Collapse of the Armed Forces" (1971). In *Vietnam and America: A Documented History*, edited by Marvin E. Gettleman et al. New York: Grove Press, 1985.

Hentoff, Nat. *Free Speech for Me—But Not for Thee*. New York: HarperPerennial, 1992.

Herer, Jack. *Hemp and the Marijuana Conspiracy: The Emperor Wears No Clothes*. Van Nuys, CA: Hemp Publishing, 1991.

Hershey, Marjorie Randon, and Darryl M. West. "Single-Issue Politics: Prolife Groups and the 1980 Senate Campaign." In *Interest Group Politics*, edited by Allan J. Cigler and Burdett A. Loomis. Washington, DC: CQ Press, 1983, 31–59.

High Times Encyclopedia of Recreational Drugs. New York: Stonehill Publishing, 1978.

Hills, Wes. "Aldridge and Wilcox Molested at Least 2 Children, He Rules." *Dayton Daily News* (September 2, 2000).

Hilzenrath, David S. "The Hole in the Medicare Pipeline." *Washington Post National Weekly Edition* (August 18, 1997).

Hinchliffe, Sara. "Are Satanic Cults Stalking Our Children?" *Living Marxism* 75 (January 1995).

Ho, David. "U.S. Prison Population Exceeds 2 Million." *Chicago Tribune* (August 9, 2000).

Hoffer, Eric. *The True Believer*. New York: Harper & Row, 1951.

Hoffman, Bill. "Cops Set to Charge Cowboys' Accuser." *New York Post* (January 12, 1997).

Hofman, Jan. "Police Tactics Are Chipping Away at Miranda Rights of Suspects." *New York Times* (March 29, 1998).

Hofstadter, Douglas R. "World Views in Collision: The *Skeptical Inquirer* versus the *National Enquirer*." In *Metamagical Themas: Questing for the Essence of Mind and Pattern*. New York: Basic Books, 1985, 91–114.

Hofstadter, Richard. *The Age of Reform*. New York: Vintage, 1955.

Holmes, Steven A. "Even if the Numbers Don't Add Up." *New York Times* (August 14, 1994).

House Ways and Means Committee, April 27–30, 1937. Senate Hearing, July 12, 1937.

Huber, Peter. *Galileo's Revenge*. New York: Basic Books, 1991.

Huff, C. Ronald, Arye Rattner, and Edward Sagarin. *Convicted But Innocent*. Thousand Oaks, CA: Sage Publications, 1996.

Huff, Darrell. *How to Lie with Statistics*. New York: W. W. Norton & Co., 1954.

Huffington, Arianna. "Campaign Dollars Open Doors for Kiddie Prozac." *New York Post* (August 23, 1997).

Hughes, Raymond. "Protest Path." *New Hampshire News-Leader* (August 15, 1996).

Ignatieff, Michael. *The Needs of Strangers*. New York: Viking Penguin, 1985.

Inbau, Fred E., John E. Reid, and Joseph P. Buckley. *Criminal Investigations and Confessions*. 3d ed. Baltimore: Williams & Wilkins, 1986.

Ingram, Helen, and Steven Rathgeb Smith, eds. *Public Policy for Democracy*. Washington, DC: The Brookings Institution, 1993.

Israel, J. *Alienation: From Marx to Modern Sociology*. Boston: Allyn & Bacon, 1971.

Jacobs, Jane. *The Death and Life of Great American Cities*. New York: Random House, 1961.

Jacobsen, Neil. "*The Overselling of Therapy*." *Networker* (March/April 1995).

"Jail Beyond Terms for Sex Predators." *Newsday* (June 24, 1997).

Janis, Irving, and Leon Mann. "Admiral Kimmel at Pearl Harbor: A Victim of Groupthink?" In *Public Administration: Politics and People*, edited by Dean L. Yarrow. New York: Longman, 1987, 251–260.

Janofsky, Michael. "Pessimism Retains Grip on Appalachian Poor." *New York Times* (February 9, 1998).

Johnson, Senator Herman. U. S. Senate Speech. In *Home Book of Quotations*. 10th ed., edited by Burton Stevenson. New York: Dodd, Mead, 1967.

Johnson, Peter. "Crime Wave Sweeps Networks' Newscasts." *USA Today* (August 13, 1997).

Johnson, Ronald C. "Parallels Between Recollections of Repressed Child Sex Abuse, Kidnapping by Space Aliens and the 1692 Salem Witch Hunts." *Issues in Child Abuse Allegations* 6, no. 1 (1994): 41–47.

Johnson, Steve. "Custody Calls Anger Parents." *San Jose Mercury News* (November 26, 1998).

Johnston, David, and Andrew C. Revkin. "Report Finds FBI Lab Slipping from Pinnacle of Crime Fighting." *New York Times* (January 29, 1997).

Jones, D., and J. M. MacGraw. "Reliable and Fictitious Accounts of Sexual Abuse in Children." *Journal of Interpersonal Violence* 2 (1987).

"Judge Orders Prosecutor to Pay." *New York Times* (November 26, 1998).

Kahn, Alfred J. "Perspectives on Access to Social Service." *Social Work* 15, no. 2 (March 1970): 95–101.

Kaminer, Wendy. "Feminism's Identity Crisis." *Atlantic Monthly* (October 1993).

———. *Sleeping with Extraterrestrials.* New York: Pantheon Books, 1999.

Kanin, Eugene. "False Rape Allegations." *Archives of Sexual Behavior* 23, no. 1 (1994): 81–92.

Kanter, Rosabeth Moss. *Commitment and Community.* Cambridge, MA: Harvard University Press, 1972.

Kasindorf, Martin. "Fraudulent Drivers' Licenses for Sale." *USA Today* (August 19, 1997).

Katz, Burton S. *Justice Overruled.* New York: Warner Books, 1997.

Katz, Jon. *Virtuous Reality.* New York: Random House, 1997.

Keithly, L., S. Samples, and H. H. Strupp. "Patient Motivation as a Predictor of Access and Outcome in Psychotherapy." *Psychotherapy and Psychosomatics* 33 (1980).

Kelly, John F., and Phillip K. Wearne. *Tainting Evidence.* New York: Free Press, 1998.

Kelly, Michael. "A Cold, Cruel New Statism." *New York Post* (June 30, 1997).

Kennedy, M., P. Reuter, and K. J. Riley. *A Simple Economic Model of Cocaine Production.* Santa Monica, CA: RAND, 1994.

Kerry, John. "Vietnam Veterans Against the War: Testimony to the U. S. Senate Foreign Relations Committee" (April 22, 1971). In *Vietnam and America: A Documented History*, edited by Marvin E. Gettleman et al. New York: Grove Press, 1985.

Kilpatrick, James J. "Forcing the Faith." *United Press International* (December 27, 1996).

King, Dennis. *Lyndon LaRouche and the New American Fascism.* New York: Doubleday, 1989.

King, Rev. Martin Luther, Jr. "Declaration of Independence from the War in Vietnam" (1967). In *Vietnam and America: A Documented History*, edited by Marvin E. Gettleman et al. New York: Grove Press, 1985.

King, Nick. "Victims Victimized." *Boston Globe* (May 10, 1981): A22.

Kishline, Audrey. *Moderate Drinking.* New York: Crown, 1994.

Kittrie, Nicholas N. *The Right to Be Different: Deviance and Enforced Therapy.* Baltimore, MD: Johns Hopkins University Press, 1971.

———. *The War Against Authority.* Baltimore, MD: Johns Hopkins University Press, 1995.

Klaidman, Stephen, and Tom L. Beauchamp. *The Virtuous Journalist.* New York: Oxford University Press, 1987.

Kleiman, Mark A. R. *Against Excess: Drug Policy for Results.* New York: Basic Books, 1992, 215–216.

Klein, Richard. "Prohibition II . . ." *Wall Street Journal* (June 26, 1997).

Kocieniewski, David. "New York Pays High Price for Police Lies." *New York Times* (January 5, 1997).

Kramer, Michael. "How Cops Go Bad." *Time* (December 15, 1997).

Krauthammer, Charles. "Defining Deviancy Up." *New Republic* (November 22, 1993).

Kresnak, Jack. "U-M Cleared in Child Evaluation. Father Loses Lawsuit Over Abuse Inquiry." *Detroit Free Press* (November 26, 1997).

Kurtz, Howard. "Journalist, Heal Thyself." *Washington Post National Weekly* (June 23, 1997).

Kutchins, Herb, and Stuart A. Kirk. *Making Us Crazy.* New York: Free Press, 1997.

LaFramboise, Donna, and David Chan. "Sheltered from Reality." *The National Post* (November 23, 1998).

Lambert, Michael J., and Clara E. Hill. "The Effectiveness of Psychotherapy." In *Handbook of Psychotherapy and Behavior Change*, 4th ed., edited by S. L. Garfield and Allen E. Bergin. New York: John Wiley & Sons, 1994, 143–189.

Landauer, Robert. "Shape Up or Ship Out." *The Oregonian* (July 11, 1998).

Lang, Alan R. "Alcohol-Related Violence: Psychological Perspectives." In *NIAAA Research Monograph No. 24*, edited by Susan E. Martin, 121–147. Rockville, MD: NIH, 1993.

Lanning, Kenneth. *Investigator's Guide to Allegations of "Ritual" Child Abuse*. Quantico, VA: National Center for the Analysis of Violent Crime, January 1992.

———. "The 'Witch Hunt,' the 'Backlash,' and Professionalism." *The APSAC Advisor*, 9, no. 4 (winter 1996): 8–12.

Lapham, Lewis H. *The Wish for Kings: Democracy at Bay*. New York: Grove Press, 1993.

Laudan, Larry. *The Book of Risks*. New York: John Wiley & Sons, 1994.

Lemanski, Michael J. "The Tenacity of Error in the Treatment of Addiction." *The Humanist* (May/June 1997).

Leo, John. "Boy, Girl, Boy Again." *U.S. News and World Report* (March 31, 1997).

———. "Things That Go Bump in the Home." *U.S. News and World Report* (May 13, 1996).

Leo, Richard A. "False Confessions and Miscarriages of Justice Today." Paper prepared for "A Day of Contrition Revisited: Contemporary Hysteria Condemns the Innocent." A conference organized by the Justice Committee. Salem, MA, January 14, 1997.

Leo, Richard A., and Richard J. Ofshe. "The Consequences of False Confessions: Deprivations of Liberty and Miscarriages of Justice in the Age of Psychological Interrogation." The Journal of Criminal Law and Criminology 88, no. 2 (winter 1988): 426–496.

Levine, Art. "The Strange Case of Faked Hate Crimes." *U.S. News and World Reports* (November 3, 1997).

Levinson, David. "Social Settings, Cultural Factors, and Alcohol-Related Aggression." In *Alcohol, Drug Abuse and Aggression*, edited by Edward Gottlieb et al., 41–58. Springfield, IL: Charles C. Thomas, 1983.

Levinson, Risha. *Information and Referral Networks: Doorways to Services*. New York: Springer Publishing, 1988.

Lewin, Tamar. "Judge Upsets Murder Conviction Focused on 'Repressed Memory.'" *New York Times* (April 5, 1995).

Lewis, Anthony. "Medicine and Politics." *New York Times* (October 13, 1997).

Lewis, Ricki. "Evening Out the Ups and Downs of Manic-Depressive Illness." *FDA Consumer* 30, no. 5 (June 1996).

Lindsay, Lawrence B. "Why Whites Are Never 'Disadvantaged.'" *Wall Street Journal* (October 8, 1997).

Lloyd, David, ed. *A Judicial Response to Child Sexual Abuse*. Huntsville, AL: National Children's Advocacy Center, 1990.

Locke, R. Christopher. "Expert Testimony in the Post-Daubert Era." *CPA Expert* (spring 1996).

Loftus, Elizabeth F., and Katherine Ketcham. *The Myth of Repressed Memory*. New York: St. Martin's Press, 1994.

Ludwig, Arnold M. "Cognitive Processes Associated with 'Spontaneous' Recovery from Alcoholism." *Journal of Studies of Alcohol* 46, no. 1 (1985).

MacCoun, Robert J. *The Psychology of Harm Reduction: Comparing Alternative Strategies for Modifying High-Risk Behaviors*. Santa Monica, CA: RAND, 1996.

MacCoun, Robert J., and Peter Reuter. "Interpreting Dutch Cannabis Policy: Reasoning by Analogy in the Legalization Debate." *Science* 278 (October 3, 1997): 47–52.

Mack, John. *Abductions: Human Encounters with Aliens.* New York: Charles Scribner's Sons, 1994.

Mackay, Charles. *Extraordinary Popular Delusions and the Madness of Crowds.* New York: Harmony Books, 1980. (Originally published London: Richard Bentley, 1841.)

Malan, D. *A Study of Brief Psychotherapy.* London: Tavistock, 1963.

Mann, T. L. "Head Start and the Panacea Standard." *APA Observer* 10 (September 1997): 10, 24.

Martin, Susan E., ed. *NIAAA Research Monograph No. 24.* Rockville, MD: NIH, 1993, 3–36, 37–69, 121–147, 193–218.

Mason, Alpheus. *The Brandeis Way.* Princeton, NJ: Princeton University Press, 1964.

Masson, Jeffrey. *Against Therapy.* New York: Common Courage, 1993.

———. *The Assault on Truth: Freud's Suppression of the Seduction Theory.* Boston: Faber, 1984.

Matsuda, Mari et al. *Words that Wound: Critical Race Theory, Assaultive Speech, and the First Amendment.* Boulder, CO: Westview Press, 1993.

McCord, Joel. "Considerations of Causes in Alcohol-Related Violence." In *Alcohol and Interpersonal Violence,* edited by Susan Martin. Washington, DC: NIAAA, 1993.

McIver, William F., II. "Behind Prison Walls." *Issues in Child Abuse Allegations* 9, nos. 1/2 (1997): 16–24.

McMullen, Marianne. "Cry for Justice." *Dayton Voice* (February 21, 1996).

McNeely, R. L., Philip W. Cook, and Jose B. Torres. "Is Domestic a Human Issue?" *Journal of Human Behavior in the Social Environment* (in press).

McShane, Larry. "Bronx Witchhunt Destroyed Lives." *Denver Post* (December 2, 1996).

Media Monitor. " 'Media Crime Wave' Continues—Crime News Quadrupled in Four Years." Washington, DC: Center for Media and Public Affairs, January–February, 1996.

Meehle, Paul. " 'Psychology' Does Our Heterogeneous Subject Matter Have Any Unity?" *Minnesota Psychologist* (summer 1986): 3–9.

"Megan's Law." *Wall Street Journal* (August 22, 1997).

Meier, Barry. "For-Profit Care's Human Cost." *New York Times* (August 8, 1997).

Merton, Robert. "The Sociology of Social Problems." In *Contemporary Social Problems,* edited by Robert Merton and Robert A. Nisbet, 5–43. New York: Harcourt Brace Jovanovich, 1976.

Merton, Robert, and Robert A. Nisbet, eds. *Contemporary Social Problems.* New York: Harcourt Brace Jovanovich, 1976.

Miczek, Klaus A., Elise M. Weerts, and Joseph F. De Bold. "Alcohol, Aggression and Violence: Biobehavioral Determinants." In *Alcohol and Interpersonal Violence,* edited by Susan Martin, 83–119. Washington, DC: NIAAA, 1993.

Mifflin, Lawrie. "Crime Falls, but Not on TV." *New York Times* (July 6, 1997).

Miller, Ted R., Mark A. Cohen, and Brian Wiersema. *Victim Costs and Consequences: A New Look.* Washington, DC: National Institute of Justice, February 1996.

Mithers, Carol. "Therapists Have a Bad Day in Court." *New York Daily News* (July 11, 1994).

Morin, Richard. "An Airwave of Crime." *Washington Post National Weekly Edition* (August 18, 1997).

———. "Public Policy Surveys: Lite and Less Filling." *Washington Post National Weekly Edition* (November 10, 1997).

———. "Warts and All." *Washington Post National Weekly Edition* (October 13, 1997).

———. "You Figure It Out: The People Can Do the Arithmetic, But They Have a Hard Time Believing the Numbers." *Washington Post National Weekly Edition* (January 6, 1997).

Morrow, David J. "Attention Disorder Is Found in Growing Number of Adults." *New York Times* (September 2, 1997).

Moushey, Bill. "Calculated Abuses." *Pittsburgh Post-Gazette* (December 7, 1998).

———. "The Damage of Lies: Zeal for Convictions Leads Government to Accept Tainted Tips, Testimony." *Pittsburgh Post-Gazette* (November 29, 1998).

———. "Failing to Police Their Own." *Pittsburgh Post-Gazette* (December 13, 1998).

———. "When Safeguards Fail." *Pittsburgh Post-Gazette* (December 6, 1998).

———. "Wrath of Vengeance." *Pittsburgh Post-Gazette* (December 8, 1998).

Moynihan, Daniel Patrick. "What Is Normal? Defining Deviancy Down." *Current* (September 1993): 12–19.

Mulhern, Sherrill. "Satanism and Psychotherapy: A Rumor in Search of an Inquisition." In *The Satanism Scare*, edited by James T. Richardson, David G. Bromley, and Joel Best. Hawthorne, NY: Aldine de Gruyter, 1991.

Murray, Charles. "Americans Remain Wary of Washington." *Wall Street Journal* (December 23, 1997).

———. *What It Means to Be a Libertarian.* New York: Broadway Books, 1997.

Murray, Frank J. "Justices Curb 'Junk Science.'" *Insight* (January 26, 1998).

Musto, David F. "The History of Legislative Control Over Opium, Cocaine, and Their Derivatives." In *Dealing with Drugs*, edited by Ronald Hamowy. Lexington, MA: D. C. Heath and Company, 1987.

Mydans, Seth. "Lawyer for OJ Simpson Case Outs Case." *New York Times* (June 16, 1994).

Naditch, M. P. "Locus of Control in a Sample of Men in Army Basic Training." *Journal of Consulting and Clinical Psychology* 43 (1975).

Nathan, Debbie. "Victim or Victimizer: Was Kelly Michaels Unjustly Convicted?" *Village Voice* (August 2, 1988).

Nathan, Debbie, and Michael Snedeker. *Satan's Silence.* New York: Basic Books, 1995.

National Association of Social Workers Delegate Assembly. *Code of Ethics of the National Association of Social Workers.* Washington, DC: National Association of Social Workers, 1996.

National Association of Social Workers National Council on the Practice of Clinical Social Work. *Evaluation and Treatment of Adults with the Possibility of Recovered Memories of Child Sexual Abuse.* Washington, DC: National Association of Social Workers, June 1996.

National Association of Social Workers, New York State Chapter. "Approved Continuing Education Programs." *NYS NASW Update* 23, no. 5 (November 1998).

National Institute of Justice and the Bureau of Justice Statistics. *Domestic and Sexual Violence Data Collection.* Washington, DC: National Institute of Justice and the Bureau of Justice Statistics, July 1996.

New, Michelle, Lucy Berliner, and Monica Fitzgerald. *Mental Health Utilization by Victims of Crime.* Seattle: University of Washington, January 1998.

New York City Commission on the Status of Women. *Report of the Committee on Domestic Violence.* New York: Office of the Mayor, January 1996.

Novak, Lindsay. "When Domestic Violence Invades the Workplace." *Chicago Tribune* (October 12, 1997).

Office for Victims of Crime. *FY 1998 Concept Paper Solicitation*. Washington, DC: U.S. Department of Justice [undated, obtained by faxback, October 3, 1997].

Office of National Drug Control Policy. *1996 National Drug Control Strategy: Goals and Objectives*. Washington, DC: Executive Office of the President [undated, obtained by faxback, July 10, 1997].

———. *Understanding Drug Treatment*. Washington, DC: The White House, 1990.

Ofshe, Richard. Conference on Wrongful Convictions and the Death Penalty, Northwestern University, November 13–15, 1998. Citing Fred E. Inbau, John E. Reid, and Joseph P. Buckley. *Criminal Investigations and Confessions*, 3d ed. Baltimore: Williams & Wilkins, 1986.

Ofshe, Richard, and Ethan Watters. *Making Monsters: False Memories, Psychotherapy, and Sexual Hysteria*. New York: Charles Scribner's Sons, 1994.

Olson, Elizabeth. "Swiss Weigh Fate of Clinics Offering Legal Heroin." *New York Times* (September 28, 1997).

Osborne, David, and Ted Gaebler. *Reinventing Government*. Reading, MA: Addison-Wesley Publishing Co., 1992.

Packer, Herbert L. *The Limits of the Criminal Sanction*. Stanford, CA: Stanford University Press, 1968.

Page, Herbert W. *Injuries of the Spine and Spinal Cord without Apparent Mechanical Lesion, and Nervous Shock, in Their Surgical and Medico-Legal Aspects*. London: J. and A. Churchill, 1883.

Paquette, Carole. "In Child Abuse Cases, Greater Empathy Espoused." *New York Times* (December 7, 1997).

Patai, Daphne. "The Feminist Turn Against Men." *Partisan Review* (fall 1996): 580–594.

———. *Heterophobia*. New York: Rowman & Littlefield, 1998.

———. "The Making of a Social Problem: Sexual Harassment on Campus." *Sexuality and Culture* 1 (1997): 219–256.

———. "There Ought to Be a Law." *William Mitchell Law Review* 22, no. 2 (1996): 491–516.

Patai, Daphne, and Noretta Koertge. *Professing Feminism*. New York: Basic Books, 1994.

Paulos, John Allen. *Innumeracy: Mathematical Illiteracy and Its Consequences*. New York: Hill and Wang, 1988.

———. *A Mathematician Reads the Newspaper*. New York: Basic Books, 1995.

Pear, Robert. "Audit of Medicare Finds $23 Billion in Overpayments." *New York Times* (July 17, 1997).

———. "Few People Seek to Treat Mental Illnesses, Study Finds." *New York Times* (December 13, 1999).

Pearson, Patricia. *When She Was Bad: Violent Women and the Myth of Innocence*. New York: Viking, 1997.

Pease, Ken, and Gloria Laycock. *Revictimization: Reducing the Heat on Hot Victims*. Washington, DC: U. S. Department of Justice, November 1996.

Peele, Stanton. *The Diseasing of America*. New York: Lexington Books, 1995.

Pendercast, Mark. *Victims of Memory*. Hinesburg, VT: Upper Access, 1995.

Pentagon Papers, The. Boston, MA: Beacon Press, 1971.

Pernanen, Kai. "Alcohol-Related Violence: Conceptual Models." In *NIAAA Research Monograph No. 24*, edited by Susan E. Martin, 37–69. Rockville, MD: NIH, 1993.

Perske, Robert. "The Unusually Vulnerable—Persons with Mental Disabilities." Paper presented at "A Day of Contrition Revisited." Salem, MA: January 14, 1997.

Petersilia, J. R. *Which Inmates Participate in Prison Treatment Programs?* Santa Monica, CA: RAND, December 1978.

Pinkerton, James. *What Comes Next?* New York: Hyperion, 1995.

Piven, Frances Fox, and Richard Cloward. *Regulating the Poor: The Functions of Public Welfare.* New York: Vintage Books, 1993.

"Police Abuse Rare." *New York Times* (November 23, 1997).

Polich, J. Michael, David J. Armor, and Harriet B. Braiker. *The Course of Alcoholism: Four Years after Treatment.* New York: John Wiley & Sons, 1981.

Pollan, Michael. "Living With Medical Marijuana." *Sunday New York Times Magazine* (July 20, 1997).

Popper, Karl. *Conjectures and Refutations: The Growth of Scientific Knowledge.* New York: Basic Books, 1962.

Possley, Maurice, and Christi Parsons. "Lawmaker Goes After Prosecutorial Misconduct." *Chicago Tribune* (June 15, 2000).

Povich, Elaine S. "Fenced-In Thinking?" *Newsday* (November 23, 1997).

Protess, David, and Rob Warden. "Nine Lives." *Chicago Tribune Magazine* (August 10, 1997).

Psychiatric News. "Expulsion." *Psychiatric News: The Newspaper of the American Psychiatric Association* 35 (May 5, 2000).

Purdum, Todd S. "Registry Laws Tar Sex-Crime Convicts with Broad Brush." *New York Times* (July 1, 1997): A1 and A19.

Quirk, Sherry A., and Anne P. DePrince. "Childhood Trauma: Politics and Legislative Concerns for Therapists." In *A Feminist Clinician's Guide to the Memory Debate*, edited by Susan Contratto and M. Janice Gutfreund. New York: Haworth Press, 1996, 19–30.

Rand, Michael R., with Kevin Strom. *Violence-Related Injuries Treated in Hospital Emergency Departments.* Washington, DC: U.S. Department of Justice, August 1997.

Rapping, Elayne. *The Culture of Recovery.* Boston: Beacon Press, 1996.

Rasmussen, David, and Bruce Benson. *The Economic Anatomy of a Drug War.* Lanham, MD: Rowman & Littlefield, 1994.

Raspberry, William. "We're Not Bad Guys, Just Doubtful." *Washington Post*, March 17, 1992. Quoted in Lisbeth B. Schorr, *Common Purpose.* New York: Anchor, 1997.

Ratey, John, and Catherine Johnson. *Shadow Syndromes.* New York: Pantheon Books, 1997.

Rauch, Jonathan. "Washington's Other Sex Scandal." *National Journal* (August 7, 1999).

Reid, P. Nelson, and Philip R. Popple, eds. *The Moral Purposes of Social Work.* Chicago: Nelson-Hall, 1982.

Reiman, Jeffrey. *The Rich Get Rich and the Poor Get Prison.* 2d ed. New York: Macmillan Publishing Co., 1984.

Reuter, P. *On the Consequences of Toughness.* Santa Monica, CA: RAND, 1991.

Revkin, Andrew C. "Unlikely Allies in Fight for Hemp." *New York Times* (June 22, 1997).

Rimlinger, Gaston. *The Welfare State and Industrial Relation in Europe, America and Russia.* New York: John Wiley & Sons, 1971.

Rind, Bruce, Philip Tromovich, and Robert Bauserman. "A Meta-Analytic Examination of Assumed Properties of Child Abuse Using College Samples." *Psychological Bulletin* 124, no. 1 (July 1998): 22–53.

Robbins, Susan P. "Cults." *Social Work Encyclopedia.* Washington, DC: National Association of Social Workers Press, 1995, 667–677.

Robbins, T. *Cults, Converts and Charisma*. Newbury Park, CA: Sage Publications, 1992.

Roberts, Paul Craig. "Benching the Witch Hunters." *Washington Times* (September 13, 1996).

———. "False Memories, False Prosecutions." *Washington Times* (January 20, 1998).

———. "Scrambled Justice and Spurious Specialists." *Washington Times* (November 14, 1997).

Robinson, Kathryn. "The End of Therapy." *Seattle Weekly* (November 13, 1996).

Robinson, Richard. *An Atheist's Values*. Oxford, England: Blackwell, 1975.

Rogowski, Jeanette A. *Insurance Coverage for Drug Abuse*. Santa Monica, CA: RAND, 1992.

Rohsenow, D. J. "The Alcohol Use Inventory as a Predictor of Drinking By Male Heavy Social Drinkers." *Addictive Behaviors* 7 (1982).

Roizen, Judith. "Issues in the Epidemiology of Alcohol and Violence." In *NIAAA Research Monograph No. 24*, edited by Susan E. Martin, 3–36. Rockville, MD: NIH, 1993.

Rosen, Gerald M., Richard J. Nally, Jeffrey M. Lohr, Grant J. Devilly, James D. Herbert, and Scott O. Lillienfield. "A Realistic Appraisal of EMDR." *The California Psychologist* 31 (1998): 25.

Rosenthal, Ed, and Steve Kubby. *Why Marijuana Should Be Legal*. New York: Thunder's Mouth Press, 1996.

Ross, Michael J. *State and Local Politics and Policy: Change and Reform*. Englewood Cliffs, NJ: Prentice Hall, 1987.

Rothman, Sheila M. "There's a Name for What Ails You." *Washington Post National Weekly* (April 21, 1997): 21.

Rotzoll, Brenda Warner. "Settlement Ends Woman's Ordeal." *Chicago Sun-Times* (November 5, 1997).

Royce, James E. *Alcohol Problems and Alcoholism*. New York: Free Press, 1981.

Rubenstein, Alan M. *Report: Investigation into Breezy Point Day School*. Doylestown, PA: Office of the District Attorney, March 1990.

Sackett and Hobbs. *Hemp: A War Crop*. New York: Mason & Hanger Co., 1942.

Sagan, Carl. *The Demon-Haunted World*. New York: Random House, 1995.

Samuelson, Robert. *The Good Life and Its Discontents*. New York: Random House, 1995.

San Diego County Grand Jury. *Analysis of Child Molestation Issues, Report No. 7*. San Diego, CA: San Diego County Grand Jury, June 1, 1994.

———. *Child Sexual Abuse, Assault, and Molest Issues, Report No. 8*. San Diego, CA: San Diego County Grand Jury, June 29, 1992.

———. *Families in Crisis, Report No. 2*. San Diego, CA: San Diego County Grand Jury, February 6, 1992.

———. "Victims of Crime Program in San Diego County." *Final Report, 1996–1997*. San Diego, CA: San Diego County Grand Jury, June 27, 1997.

Sandoz, Charles J. "Locus of Control, Emotional Maturity and Family Dynamics as Components of Recovery in Recovering Alcoholics." *Alcoholism Treatment Quarterly* 8, no. 4 (1991).

Sarnoff, Susan K. "The NIJ/CDC Study on the Incidence and Prevalence of Violence Against Women: A Case Study in Advocacy Research." *Women's Freedom Network Newsletter* 6, no. 1 (January/February 1999).

———. "In Defiance of Justice." *OACDL Vindicator* (summer 1997): 6–7.

———. "The Institutionalization of Misinformation: VAWA II." *Women's Freedom Network Newsletter* (August 1998).

———. *A National Survey of State Crime Victim Compensation Programs: Policies and Administrative Methods*. Ann Arbor, MI: University Microfilms International, December 1993.

———. *Paying for Crime: The Policies and Possibilities of Crime Victim Reimbursement*. Westport, CT: Praeger Publishers, 1996.

———. "Victim Compensation and 'Recovered Memory Syndrome,'" *False Memory Syndrome Newsletter* 6, no. 3 (March 1997).

Satel, Sally L. "Don't Forget the Addict's Role in Addiction." *New York Times* (April 4, 1998).

Scarr, S. "'Head Start and the Panacea Standard.' A Reply to Mann." *APA Observer* 10 (September 1997): 24–25.

Schetky, Diane. "Resolved: Child Sexual Abuse Is Overdiagnosed: Affirmative." *Journal of the American Academy of Child and Adolescent Psychiatry* 28, no. 5 (1989): 789–797.

Schlosser, Eric. "The Prison-Industrial Complex." *Atlantic Monthly* (December 1998).

Schmitt, Eric. "Army Shuts Off Phone Line for Sex-Harassment Reports." *New York Times* (June 4, 1997): 6.

Schmitt, Richard B. "Who Is an Expert? In Some Courtrooms, the Answer Is 'Nobody.'" *Wall Street Journal* (June 17, 1997): A1 and A8.

Schneider, Andrew. "Woman Can File Suit Over State at Mental Hospital, Wenatchee, State May Face Action from Handling of Sex Abuse Case." *Seattle Post-Intelligencer* (June 21, 1999).

Schoofs, Mark. "Genetic Justice." *Village Voice* (November 18, 1997).

Schorr, Lisbeth B. *Common Purpose*. New York: Anchor, 1997.

Sgroi, Suzanne. Letter to Martin Stavis, November 2, 1992.

Shapiro, Bruce. "Victims and Vengeance." *The Nation* (February 10, 1997): 11–19.

Shapiro, Joseph P. *No Pity*. New York: Random House, 1994.

Sharkey, Joe. *Bedlam*. New York: St. Martin's Press, 1994.

Shaw, David. *The Pleasure Police*. New York: Doubleday, 1996.

Sherman, Lawrence W. *Preventing Crime: What Works, What Doesn't, What's Promising*. Washington, DC: U.S. Department of Justice, February 1997.

Shermer, Michael. *Why People Believe Weird Things*. New York: W. H. Freeman and Company, 1997.

Shute, Nancy. "The Drinking Dilemma." *U.S. News and World Report* (September 8, 1997): 54–65.

Siegel, Fred. *The Future Once Happened Here*. New York: Free Press, 1997.

———. "New York: Hooked on Social Spending." *New York Post* (October 5, 1997).

Siegel, Ronald K. *Intoxication*. New York: E. P. Dutton, 1989.

Simon, Rita J. *Women and Violent Crime*. Washington, DC: Women's Freedom Network, undated [received August 2, 1997].

Simon, Rita J., and Jean Landis. *The Crimes Women Commit, the Punishments They Receive*. Lexington, MA: Lexington Books, 1991.

Siporin, Max. "Should Professionals Take Action If Their Colleagues Act Unethically?" In *Controversial Issues in Social Work Ethics, Values and Obligations*, edited by Eileen Gambrill and Robert Pruger. Boston: Allyn and Bacon, 1997, 157–162.

Sloman, Larry. *Reefer Madness: The History of Marijuana in America*. Indianapolis, IN: Bobbs-Merrill, 1979.

Smith, M., and E. Kuchta. "Trends in Violent Crime Against Women, 1973–89." *Social Science Quarterly* 74, no. 1 (March 1993): 28–45.

Smith, Mark. "5 Psychiatric Workers Charged in Scam." *Houston Chronicle* (October 29, 1997).

Smith, Patricia. *Feminist Jurisprudence*. New York: Oxford University Press, 1993.

Smith, Steven, and Susan Freinkel. *Adjusting the Balance: Federal Policy and Victim Services*. Westport, CT: Greenwood Press, 1988.

Smith, Steven K., with Carol J. DeFrancis. *Indigent Defense*. Washington, DC: U.S. Department of Justice, February 1996.

Smith, Susan. *Survivor Psychology: The Dark Side of the Mental Health Mission*. Boca Raton, FL: Upton Books, 1995.

Sniffen, Michael J. "FBI Fired 19 Employees Last Year for Misconduct." *Associated Press* (December 9, 1998).

Solberg, Carl. *Oil Power: The Rise and Imminent Fall of the American Empire*. New York: New American Library, 1976.

Sommers, Christina Hoff. *Who Stole Feminism?* New York: Simon and Schuster, 1994.

Sowell, Thomas. "Victims of the 'Helping Professions.' " *New York Post* (December 27, 1997).

———. *The Vision of the Anointed*. New York: Basic Books, 1995.

Sparrow, Malcolm K. "Fraud Control in the Health Care Industry: Assessing the State of the Art." *Research in Brief.* Washington, DC: U.S. Department of Justice, December 1998.

———. *License to Steal: Why Fraud Plagues America's Health Care System*. Denver: Westview Press, 1995.

Spatz-Widom, Cathy. "Child Abuse, Neglect, and Adult Behaviour: Research Design and Findings on Criminality, Violence, and Child Abuse." *American Journal of Orthopsychiatry* 59, no. 3 (1989): 355–367.

———. "The Cycle of Violence." *Research in Brief.* Washington, DC: U.S. Department of Justice, September 1992.

Specht, Harry, and Mark Courtney. *Unfaithful Angels*. New York: Free Press, 1994.

Stan, Adele M. *Debating Sexual Correctness*. New York: Bantam Doubleday Dell, 1995.

———. "Introduction: Feminism and the Culture of Sexuality." In *Debating Sexual Correctness*. New York: Bantam Doubleday Dell, 1995.

State of NJ v. JQ. 130 NJ 554, 617 A. 2d 1196 (1993).

Stirgus, Eric. "Shabazz Boy Gets 18 Months in Massachusetts Home." *New York Post* (August 9, 1997).

Stone, Deborah A. "Clinical Authority in the Construction of Citizenship." In *Public Policy for Democracy*, edited by Helen Ingram and Steven Rathgeb Smith, 45–67. Washington, DC: The Brookings Institution, 1993.

"Stop Underestimating Us." *Parade* (July 6, 1997).

Strauch, Barbara. "Use of Antidepression Medicine for Young Patients Has Soared." *New York Times* (August 10, 1997).

Straus, Jon C. "College Costs Too Much, Fails Kids." *USA Today* (July 17, 1997).

Stricker, George. "The Relationship of Research to Clinical Practice." *American Psychologist* 47 (1992): 543–549.

Strossen, Nadine. *Defending Pornography*. New York: Anchor Books, 1996.

Summit, Roland. "Abuse of the Child Abuse Accommodation Syndrome." *Journal of Child Sexual Abuse* 1, no. 4 (1992): 153–163.

———. "The Child Abuse Accommodation Syndrome." *Child Abuse and Neglect* 7, no. 2 (1983): 177–193.

Sutton, Larry. "Dad Cleared of Sex Abuse." *Daily News* (March 7, 1997).

Szasz, Thomas. *The Myth of Psychotherapy*. New York: Syracuse University Press, 1988.

———. *Psychiatric Justice*. New York: Macmillan, 1965.

"Taken for a Feminist Ride." *New York Post* (August 3, 1997).

Tannen, Deborah. *The Argument Culture*. New York: Random House, 1998.

Thernstrom, Stephen, and Abigail Thernstrom. *America in Black and White*. New York: Simon and Schuster, 1997.

de Tocqueville, Alexis. *Democracy in America*. New York: Alfred Knopf, 1994.

Tolchin, Susan J. *The Angry American: How Voter Rage Is Changing the Nation*. New York: Westview Press, 1996.

Travis, Jeremy. *Measuring What Matters, Part Two: Developing Measures of What the Police Do*. Washington, DC: U.S. Department of Justice, November 1997.

Treacy, Eileen. Transcripts of *voir dire* by Dominic Barbara, Esq., in re: Ahmed, July 30, October 26, and October 27, 1987.

Trebach, Arnold S., and James A. Inciardi. *Legalize It? Debating American Drug Policy*. Washington, DC: American University Press, 1993.

Trimpey, Jack. *Rational Recovery*. New York: Pocket Books, 1996.

Tuchman, Barbara. *The March of Folly*. Boston: G. K. Hall and Co., 1984.

Tucker, William. "Crime and No Punishment." *New York Press* (March 11–17, 1998).

Tunis, Sandra, James Austin, Mark Morris, Patricia Hardyman, and Melissa Boyard. "Evaluation of Drug Treatment in Local Corrections." *National Institute of Justice Journal* (June 1997).

Underwager, Ralph, and Hollida Wakefield. *The Real World of Child Interrogations*. Springfield, IL: Charles C. Thomas, 1990.

USA Today. October 9, 1997.

USA Today. December 2, 1997.

U. S. Department of Justice. *DEA Briefing Book*. Washington, DC: U.S. Department of Justice, October 1999.

U. S. Department of Justice. *Justice Department Releases Report on Police Integrity*. Washington, DC: U.S. Department of Justice, January 17, 1997.

"U. S. Kids Trailing in Math, Science." *New York Daily News* (February 25, 1998).

Vaillant, George. *The Natural History of Alcoholism*. Cambridge, MA: Harvard University Press, 1983.

Valente, J. "They Steal from the Devastated." *Parade* (June 4, 1995).

Van Til, Reinder. *Lost Daughters*. Grand Rapids, MI: William B. Eerdmans Publishing Co., 1997.

Van Wormer, Katherine. "Harm Induction vs. Harm Reduction: Comparing America and British Approaches to Drug Use." *Journal of Offender Rehabilitation* 29, no. 1/2 (1999): 35–48.

Vasquez, Daniel. "Repressed Memory Under Fire: Franklin Alleges Trial Conspiracy, Seeks Damages." *San Jose Mercury News* (July 1, 1997).

Victor, Jeffrey S. *Satanic Panic*. Chicago, IL: Open Court Press, 1993.

Vinoskis, Maris A. *History of Educational Policymaking*. New Haven, CT: Yale University Press, 1999.

Vobejda, Barbara. "Still Feeling the Pain." *Washington Post National Weekly Edition* (June 9, 1997).

Wakefield, Hollida, and Ralph Underwager. *Return of the Furies*. Chicago, IL: Open Court Publishing Co., 1994.

Wallerstein, Judith B., and S. Blakeslee. *Second Chances: Men, Women and Children a Decade After Divorce*. New York: Ticknor and Fields, 1989.

Wallerstein, Judith S., and J. B. Kelly. *Surviving the Breakup*. New York: Basic Books, 1980.

Wattenberg, Ben. "Kinsey: Kinky But Not Unique." *New York* [*Post* or *Daily News*] (November 22, 1997).

Weisenthier, Vicki Fox, and Michael Allen. "Forced Treatment Doesn't Work." *Washington Post* (August 5, 1999).

Weiss, Michael, and Cathy Young. "Feminist Jurisprudence: Equal Rights or Neo-Paternalism?" *Policy Analysis* (June 19, 1996).

———. Women's Freedom Network. *Brief of Amicus Against the Constitutionality of the Violence Against Women Act*. Houston, TX: Lawson, Weiss & Danziger, 1996.

Weiss, Mitch. "Citizens Group Casts Doubt on Victims Aid." *Cleveland Plain-Dealer* (September 17, 1995).

Wexler, Richard. *Wounded Innocents*. New York: Prometheus, 1995.

Wilkens, John. "Innocent Family Awaits End to Child-Abuse Saga." *San Diego Union-Tribune* (November 14, 1993).

Wilkens, John, and Jim Okerblum. "Rape-Case Therapist Gives Up Licence." *San Diego Union-Tribune* (March 20, 1996).

Will, George F. "Politics Without Ideology?" *New York Post* (January 1, 1998).

Willing, Richard. "FBI's DNA Lab Accused of Bias, Incompetence." *USA Today* (November 26, 1997).

———. "Florida, California Want to Rein in 'Hired Gun' Medical Witnesses." *USA Today* (April 10, 1998).

Wilson, James Q. *Bureaucracy*. New York: Basic Books, 1989.

Wilson, William J. *The Truly Disadvantaged*. Chicago, IL: University of Chicago Press, 1987.

Wolf, Naomi. *Fire with Fire*. New York: Random House, 1993.

Woolhandler, Steffi, and David Himmelstein. "The Deteriorating Efficiency of the US Health Care System." *The New England Journal of Medicine*, no. 18 (May 2, 1991).

Wren, Christopher S. "Maturity Diminishes Drug Use, a Study Finds." *New York Times* (February 2, 1997).

———. "Phantom Numbers Haunt War on Drugs." *New York Times* (April 20, 1997).

Young, Allan. *The Harmony of Illusions: Inventing Post-Traumatic Stress Disorder*. Princeton, NJ: Princeton University Press, 1995.

Young, Bob. "Bewitched." *Williamette Weekly News* (October 22, 1997).

Young, Cathy. *Ceasefire: Beyond the Gender Wars*. New York: Free Press, 1999.

———. "VAWA Perpetuates Stereotypes." *The Women's Freedom Network Newsletter* (summer 1997): 1.

Zinberg, Norman E. "The Use and Misuse of Intoxicants." In *Dealing with Drugs*, edited by Ronald Hamowy. Lexington, MA: D. C. Heath and Company, 1987, 247–279.

Index

Note: "t" indicates a table.

TALK

You're a brave man they tell me.
                                    I'm not.
Courage has never been my quality.
Only I thought it disproportionate
so to degrade myself as others did.
No foundations trembled. My voice
no more than laughed at pompous falsity;
I did no more than write, never denounced,
I left out nothing I had thought about,
defended who deserved it, put a brand
on the untalented, the ersatz writers
(doing what had anyhow to be done).
And now they press to tell me that I'm brave.
How sharply our children will be ashamed
taking at last their vengeance for these horrors
remembering how in so strange a time
common integrity could look like courage.

—Yevgeny Yevtushenko

About the Author

SUSAN KISS SARNOFF is an Assistant Professor of Social Work at Ohio University. She specializes in teaching Social Policy and in analyzing government bureaucracies, public and private benefits, and criminal justice policy. She is the author of *Paying for Crime: The Policies and Possibilities of Crime Victim Reimbursement* (Praeger, 1996), and is currently conducting research on social work regulation and ethics.